John Croaker

John Croaker
CONVICT EMBEZZLER

JOHN BOOKER *and* RUSSELL CRAIG

MELBOURNE UNIVERSITY PRESS

MELBOURNE UNIVERSITY PRESS
PO Box 278, Carlton South, Victoria 3053, Australia
info@mup.unimelb.edu.au
www.mup.com.au

First published 2000

Designed by Pages in Action
Cartography by Chandra Jayasuriya
Typeset by Syarikat Seng Teik Sdn. Bhd., Malaysia, in 10.5 point Giovanni Book
Printed in Australia by Australian Print Group

National Library of Australia Cataloguing-in-Publication entry

Booker, John, 1941– .
    John Croaker: convict embezzler

    Bibliography.
    Includes index.
    ISBN 0 522 84894 X.

    1. Croaker, John, 1788–1824. 2. Convicts—New South Wales—Biography.
    3. Convicts—Employment—New South Wales. 4. Brewing industry—New
    South Wales—History. 5. Bookkeeping—Australia—History. 6. New South
    Wales—Social life and customs—1788–1851. 7. Great Britain—Social life
    and customs—18th century. 8. New South Wales—Social conditions—
    1788–1851. 9. Great Britain—Social conditions—18th century. 10. New
    South Wales—Economic conditions—1788–1851. 11. Great Britain—
    Economic conditions—18th century. I. Craig, Russell James. II. Title.

305.5609944

Contents

Illustrations

Acknowledgements

This book has emerged from the belief of Russell Craig, based on research over several years, that the significance of John Croaker is under-represented in the commercial history of New South Wales. Although collaboration with John Booker was largely fortuitous, it has proved a most successful fusion of ideas and interests. Each author has brought to the task the benefit of his specialised knowledge. Russell Craig is well versed in the accounting history of New South Wales, while John Booker has a deep understanding of early English banking, in which Croaker was professionally trained.

Despite these complementary strengths, a book on this scale is necessarily the product of much new research, enhanced by the advice and assistance of friends, colleagues, and especially those whose knowledge of the wider aspects of colonial history is more extensive than ours. At the Australian National University (ANU) in Canberra, Russell Craig gratefully recognises the enthusiasm of fellow academics, and practical assistance. The project could not have been completed without support from the ANU's Faculty Research Grants Scheme. Also at ANU the encouragement and assistance of Simon Ville and Mac Boot of the Department of Economic History, and Joan Rabey and Marian Young of the Department of Commerce, is very much appreciated. John Booker acknowledges the interest of Lloyds TSB Group in this book, although the bank has no corporate role in its production. The relevance of the book to the company's archivist lies in the devolution to Lloyds Bank of most of the early banking business in Canterbury, Margate, and other towns in East Kent.

The excellent endeavours of several research assistants, both paid and informal, merit our warmest thanks. We acknowledge the sterling work in Australia of Christine Broad, Kal Stening and Cora Num, and in England of Phil Davies, Sally Thompson and Libby Gabbett. Particular gratitude is due to Lisa Gwaltney, our enthusiastic Spanish-speaking emissary who researched centres of information in Chile and Spain with tireless persistence and great good humour. Our gratitude extends also to descendants of John Croaker in Australia, especially Judy Lindsay, June Maitland, Marilyn Milford, Charles Croaker and Beverley Smith, always supportive and willing to impart information. Also providing valuable assistance were Kevin Baker, Edgar Penzig, Alan Kay, the Kent Family History Society, the Faversham Society, and Paul Pollak, archivist to The King's School, Canterbury.

Staff in many public repositories in England and Australia have been very generous with their time and advice, and without them the jigsaw would have so many missing pieces as to spoil the picture. We thank Margate Library; Public Record Office, Kew; British Newspaper Library, Colindale; British Library, Bloomsbury; London Library, St James's Square; Guildhall Library, City of London; Centre for Kentish Studies, Maidstone; Canterbury Cathedral Archives, Canterbury; Maritime Information Centre, Greenwich; County Record Office, Lincoln; Bank of Ireland Archives, Dublin; National Library of Australia, Canberra; State Library of New South Wales, Sydney; Campbelltown City Library, New South Wales; Archives Office of New South Wales, Sydney; and Westpac Archives, Sydney. We are particularly grateful to the Mitchell Library, Sydney, for permission to reproduce John Haslam's narrative account of his voyage to New South Wales in 1816.

We wish to record our special thanks to Margaret Steven of the Research School of Social Sciences, ANU, a renowned colonial historian. Dr Steven has been generous in her encouragement and has proved a patient sounding board for opinion and advice. Similarly we have had the benefit of the experience and wisdom of Ted Burke (who also commented in detail on the draft manuscript), and of the specialised knowledge of Professor John Ritchie. We should stress, however, that all statements and conclusions, and any mistakes, are the responsibility of the authors alone.

Finally we are most grateful to our wives, Pam Booker and Annette Craig. They have each tolerated a husband welded to his computer, as e-mail has made practicable a collaboration between hemispheres which, a few years ago, would have taken twice as long and been half as worth-while.

John Booker
Lloyds TSB Group Archives
London

Russell Craig
Department of Commerce, ANU
Canberra

Introduction

John Croaker (1788–1824) was an English-born bank clerk, whose life spans two cultures, three continents, and both sides of the law. As he was only 36 when he died, there is a special need to justify his importance. This introduction explains what he did, why it matters, and the wider benefits of studying his career.

Croaker was born in Canterbury, Kent, in humble circumstances, the second oldest of seven children. His father, who was illiterate all his life, worked for John Abbott, a gentleman brewer in the parish of St Dunstan's. No details are known of Croaker's education, but he was apprenticed to a banker at Ramsgate in 1808. Three years later he married Susannah Kidder Kemp, the orphaned daughter of a Canterbury corn chandler. In the same year (1811), Croaker became principal clerk to John Sackett, who ran the Isle of Thanet Bank in Margate. Soon afterwards Abbott was embroiled in a scandal over adulterated beer and Croaker saw the reputation of his father and his patron suddenly ruined. It is possible that Croaker himself was involved in the brewery's creative book-keeping and the episode unhinged him: soon, he was cheating in the bank's ledgers. After detection, he absconded on his own to Calais, early in 1815, with some stolen assets. Against a promise from Sackett that all would be quietly arranged if the money were surrendered, he returned to Margate. To Croaker's chagrin, the agreement was dishonoured. Having forfeited his wife's property as well as his own to repay the deficit, he was arrested and imprisoned. In a poorly-conducted trial at Dover Sessions in October 1815, he was convicted of embezzling the proceeds of a bill of exchange. Croaker was sent to a hulk at Sheerness, awaiting transportation for fourteen years. His appeal to the Prince Regent via the Secretary of State, on the grounds of Sackett's reneged agreement, was rejected. Susannah was given leave to join him in the colony with their two young children, but it is uncertain who paid their fare.

In October 1816 the Croakers arrived in New South Wales in different ships. Granted an immediate ticket of leave by Governor Macquarie, Croaker was employed as a clerk in the justiciary, perhaps as a result of Susannah's negotiations with the new judge advocate with whom, by good chance, she had travelled out from England. Croaker also established himself as a dealer in commodities. His arrival coincided with the foundation of the Bank of New South Wales and Croaker set up their book-keeping procedures according to the system of double entry. There are good reasons for believing that he introduced this system to the colony as a whole. He went on to help the directors with their book-keeping difficulties in later years, but never held an official post in the bank, nor had an account there. Late in 1817 Croaker applied for a conditional pardon, which the governor granted.

Collaborating with brewers, Croaker probably established one of the colony's first malthouses. He began to incur minor debts which were settled by distraint on his goods, following a court order. When his position in the judge advocate's office became untenable, as a result of the law-suits, Croaker moved to the police office as principal clerk. Susannah, meanwhile, had established a small private school, and Croaker himself was initially successful in dealing. Domestic circumstances reflected their joint achievements: Croaker had a government servant, Susannah employed a maid, and the family lived in pleasant surroundings. Three more children were born in the space of five years. From 1820, however, Croaker's fortunes declined rapidly. An inquiry into the colony's affairs, a change of governor and regulatory moves favouring spirits rather than beer, left him deprived of a salaried job, backing the wrong product and irretrievably in debt. He tried to move into the spirits trade, but was unsuccessful.

Granted a free pardon by Macquarie (one of the governor's last indulgences), Croaker left New South Wales for England in 1823. He was probably accompanied by his eldest son and, it seems, intended to re-establish his business and solvency by renewing old acquaintances in East Kent. What happened thereafter is largely a matter for speculation, but he was never seen again in England or New South Wales. His son survived him, and Croaker's widow went on to even greater respectability in the colony, marrying the man who succeeded her husband as clerk in the police office.

From this brief calendar of events emerges Croaker's chief importance: he introduced double-entry book-keeping to the Bank of New South Wales, the prime mover of economic growth in the colony. But history does not erect statues to heroes of accounting procedures, and some wider values must be found in Croaker's life and times. They are not difficult to discover. Throughout his career he generates a succession of interesting issues which test and probe the parameters of knowledge and challenge perceived views. Most episodes in Croaker's life offer the opportunity to use him as a window on the economic, judicial and social conditions of his age, both in England and New South Wales.

Book-keeping aside, there are four main areas in which Croaker is historically useful.

Banking

As Croaker's father was uneducated, the normal perception, based on Victorian commentators, that bank clerks were recruited from the middle classes, is immediately challenged. Croaker's advancement is testimony to the powers of patronage, in this instance of his father's employer, and to the unique circumstances in East Kent where small banks proliferated. With one eye on London and the other on the continent, these firms formed a cabal. It will be seen that bankers were not so much rivals as inter-dependent, linking arms to drag back on his feet any member who stumbled. If Croaker is believed—and his argument is strong—the behaviour of his employer did not meet an acceptable standard for the principal of a bank. But the cabal stayed strong and although Sackett suspended payment on his notes, neither his personal estate nor his customers were seriously embarrassed.

Once he was in New South Wales, Croaker's familiarity with banking was put to good use. The charter of the Bank of New South Wales is examined in this book as if through his eyes, and its provisions compared with banking in England. As the only man in the colony who had ever been entrusted with the day-to-day running of an English banking-house, Croaker was able to influence procedures as well as book-keeping. He had no first-hand knowledge of joint-stock companies, but the bank's promoters had little knowledge of local banking, and the Bank of New South Wales was a hybrid of the two. We argue that he was a vital, albeit small, component in the bank's conception. There is a suggestion, based on new evidence introduced here, that the banking experience of J. T. Campbell, traditionally credited with expertise in the bank's accounting systems, has been over-rated—in which case the reliance on Croaker would have been so much greater. Thereafter, the bittersweet relationship between Croaker and the bank is a key to his downfall. The Bank of New South Wales apparently did not do enough to help him.

The book attempts to break new ground with an analysis of documentary credit, again with Croaker's activities as the focus. His trial gives an opportunity to review procedures relating to the bill of exchange in England. Having arrived in the colony, Croaker found himself at an advantage. He was able to understand better than most people the potential for the use (and abuse) not only of bills of exchange but of promissory notes, the colony's main medium of credit. He was the first man with a ticket of leave to test the directors' attitude towards discounting. Through his activities it can be seen to what extent the economy of New South Wales was *sui generis*. The colony floated like a leaking vessel, its sides patched with paper credit. As dealers and merchants drew, assigned, re-assigned, and discounted their bills and promissory notes, the balance of debt between any two parties was impossible to control. Croaker's career is a measure of the immaturity of the economy, exposing its worst practices and explaining how, why, and to what extent, credit was at the centre of commercial activity. This is an economic analysis of the colony from a new angle.

Brewing

The scandal which overtook the Canterbury brewery shaped Croaker's career as deeply as his experience in banking. There was nothing new in the practice of adulterating beer, by the introduction of chemicals and narcotics, but for Abbott the timing was dreadful. It was bad enough that he was a magistrate, but the accusation coincided with a power struggle between the Excise Office and the Lords of the Treasury. In the House of Commons, it was alleged that Abbott (who had been fined £500) was dealt with too leniently because of the influence of those, including the Dean of Canterbury Cathedral, who wrote letters in his support. Croaker's father was named in the House as the employee who handled the base ingredients, and the incident spawned a vindictive pamphlet against Abbott himself. The case for Croaker's own involvement, as accountant, is found arguable, although he was never openly accused of complicity. We discuss the effects of the case on Croaker's parents, who continued to live and work in the parish of St Dunstan's.

In New South Wales Croaker's theoretical knowledge of brewing, and more especially of malting (his brother-in-law was a Canterbury maltster) encouraged him to join with two of the colony's brewers to produce a more palatable product, based on Kentish hops and perhaps a better strain of barley. There is little doubt that the enterprise he established at Upper Pitt Street, Sydney, advanced the art of malting. Indeed, it seems that he, in conjunction with Nathaniel Lawrence and Thomas Middleton, built the colony's first malthouse on a commercial scale. The brewers' losing fight against the lawful introduction of distilleries is seen against the thrust and despair of Croaker's endeavours, as he tried and failed to stay abreast of the changes. There is also an insight into the colony's agricultural practices, in relation to the growing of hops and barley, and into the unscrupulous acquisition of land.

Law

Croaker's trial was no show-piece for British justice, although widely reported. The alleged offence (embezzlement under the Act of 1799) appears to have been a specimen charge, but no evidence was brought before the court to substantiate other previous indictments. The case against him rested, in essence, on whether or not Sackett had authorised him to have two accommodation bills discounted to strengthen the bank's account with its London agents. There can be no doubt that Croaker misappropriated some of the proceeds, but there is a ring of truth about his defence—that Sackett was an absentee principal, obsessed with speculation in the national debt, and had promised that misdemeanours would be forgiven as long as the money was returned. The trial judge, Kenrick, appeared to accept Croaker's argument that an oral undertaking had been broken, notwithstanding Croaker's guilt under the criminal law and the impropriety of such an agreement (on the part of Sackett) in the first place.

When the verdict was announced, there was confusion. Kenrick's initial sentence on Croaker was only seven years transportation, but he appears to have corrected it to fourteen after at least one reporter had left the court-room. This embarrassment had an unfortunate consequence at the appeal stage. When Kenrick was asked by Lord Sidmouth, the Home Secretary, for his views, he had no wish to be reminded of this mishandled case. In a rambling, barely-legible letter to Lord Sidmouth, Kenrick dismissed Croaker's argument out of hand, referring to a conviction under 'the Bankers Act', 'specific robbery', and similar puzzling assertions. By happy contrast, the decision to allow Susannah and her children to join her husband in New South Wales, although shrouded in mystery, points to British justice being ultimately fairer in equity than in law.

While a clerk to the judge advocate in New South Wales, Croaker experienced the colony's unique brand of civil justice. He was increasingly sued by his debtors, at first with a clinical detachment from any concern for his own liquidity. The social disgrace attaching to debt in England was absent. The owed and the owing continued to do business with each other, and litigation was no barrier to good relations. With ready money being scarce, it was normal for a debtor to ignore a court order for payment and let the provost marshal distrain on personal goods for whatever he could find. This is a new perception of the colony's legal procedures. Croaker's case also demonstrates that there was one rule for the educated and worldly, and another for the illiterate and inept. While the latter could end up in a debtor's gaol, a man of Croaker's ability was too useful in the colony to be locked away. Once his creditors had realised all they could reasonably expect, they did not press him to penury. In short, the fate of the debtor seemed to depend not on the basic distinction between a free settler and a convict, but on his potential to destabilise an economy likened in this book to a house of cards.

Social values

In England the system of patronage allowed Croaker to break out from his humble beginnings and aspire to a middle-class profession. The up-bringing of Susannah is equally of interest, illustrating a commercial hierarchy in the closely-regulated city of Canterbury and the importance of family connections when young children were left without parents. In the context of New South Wales, aspects of status become especially interesting. Croaker was to benefit from the colony's unique system which allowed, and indeed expected, literate convicts to play a part in the civil administration. He is also a prime example, in his work for the bank, of a prisoner being picked for his expertise in the profession which had led to his downfall. In this way Croaker illustrates the far-sighted, if controversial, confidence of Macquarie in individuals whose careers might have been wrecked by misfortune, rather than by innate wicked-ness. The wholly contrary opinion of free settlers—'once a thief, always a thief'—can be seen coming into play. It is interesting to contrast Croaker's status with that of his wife. She arrived in the colony with no stain on her character (although, according to one report circulating in England, she had intended to join her husband in Calais), and was entitled to pursue a career which added to, rather than relied upon, her husband's prestige.

A backdrop to all these events is provided by the inquiry of Com-missioner Bigge, ordered by the Secretary of State to investigate and report upon the colony's way of life and the success, or otherwise, of Macquarie's liberal stance. Although no animosity is recorded between Bigge and Croaker, the commissioner contributed to the latter's downfall. Croaker was at the heart of Bigge's rejection of a system which allowed officials of the colonial administration to have commercial pursuits which impinged on their proper duties with a possible clash of interests.

While 'convict biography' is a well-established medium, arising automatically from the study of most figures of importance in the early history of New South Wales, the present work seeks to approach the genre from a new angle. It develops a middle ground between, on the one hand, strictly autobiographical works (of which *The Memoirs of James Hardy Vaux* is the classic example) and, on the other hand, the relatively recent assessments of the lives of colonial figure-heads. This middle ground is peopled by clerks and artisans without whose commitment and expertise the infrastructure of colonial administration, fragile and corrupt as it was, could simply not have existed. It is time to examine the men and women on whom the limelight only flickered. Looking through their eyes, the interpretation of history can be enriched and explained.

Analysis and adventure need not be at loggerheads. The reader will discover a fast-moving drama ending in mysterious death. Croaker was not a boring man, and if this book can be a lively read, it will be doing him no disservice.

1   Birth, Beer and Banking

Kent, in the commentaries of Caesar writ,
Is termed the civillest place of all this isle.[1]

These lines of Shakespeare suggest that Julius Caesar would have been very disappointed with the leading character of the story about to unfold. John Croaker can be cast in more than one light, and the shadier side of his character has produced most of the documentation. Yet his erratic career helped introduce reliable book-keeping methods to an infant Australia. Sir Walter Scott also produced a couplet about men of Kent, in which he acknowledged their attraction to women.[2] Perhaps Croaker conforms better with this last appraisal, although not for Scott's reasons. But if he fails, in sum, to meet the ideals and standards of classical literature, the far-flung adventures of his brief career suggest a story-line worthy of popular fiction.

There are still unresolved episodes in Croaker's life—not least how he came to lose it—and the difficulties begin with his name. Most English surnames lend themselves to a variable form, but the problem is rarely so convoluted. Historically, there is no difference between Croaker, Croker, Crocker and Craker.[3] These are variants of one habitation name deriving from Calvados in Normandy, whence the French Crèvecoeur (i.e. heart-breaker) became anglicised initially as Crawcour. Some analysts see an alternative origin in an occupation name deriving from the Old English word *crocca*, meaning an earthenware pot; hence a Crocker was a potter. Although the names Crocker and Croker are the commonest variants, the *International Genealogical Index*, which has some authority in these matters, muddies the waters still further by treating Croker and Crocker as main surnames, but Croaker as a variant of Crocher.

As Croaker's father, also called John, was illiterate, it is impossible to establish which of these names was usually associated with his more distant forebears. The spelling of the name is known only from the handwriting of others, notably the local parson whose phonetic interpretation of the spoken word, more often than not, was Croker. But other sources, like rates and tax records, are a catalogue of inconsistency, and what was Croaker to one assessor was Croker to the next. This book, for the sake of uniformity, treats the name as Croaker once the discussion of variants has been completed, and it was probably John Croaker himself who established that spelling. As for the family's origins, there is little evidence of any substantial Kentish colony of Crokers or Croakers, other than the one being discussed, although the name occurs fitfully in the west of the county.

A glimpse of earlier roots is often suggested by the middle forenames of children. John Croaker junior's eldest son was baptised John Wilkinson, and the second Thomas Lawrence Pennel. As one John Wilkinson was a witness at Croaker's wedding, it seems reasonable to assume that the Wilkinsons were family.[4] As there is no evidence of the name in the fairly-well documented pedigree of Croaker's wife, it seems likely that his mother, whose name is cast as both Ellenor and Eleanor (perhaps evidence of illiteracy on her part as well), was born Wilkinson. But no marriage of an Eleanor Wilkinson to a John Croker or Croaker has been traced. More problematical are the names Thomas Lawrence Pennel, and it will be better to discuss them at a later stage; suffice it to say at the moment that none of these names appears to mark evidence of kinship.

The earliest documentary reference to our Croaker family is the baptism of John Croaker's brother, Henry Croaker, in the parish of St Dunstan's, Canterbury, on 30 July 1786.[5] There, over the next fourteen years, another six children of John and Eleanor were born, and John Croaker, the subject of this book, was the second child and son, baptised on 9 March 1788. His parents were to spend the rest of their working lives in the parish. At that time St Dunstan's was, as it remains today, a vibrant and handsome suburb.[6] Because it lay outside the walls it was not, administratively, a part of Canterbury, but was a focus of development as the city outgrew its perimeter. The hub of the parish was St Dunstan's Street, now bisected by a railway line, stretching a quarter of a mile from the bastion of Westgate to the division of roads to London and Whitstable. Both these routes were of strategic importance to Canterbury. They were lifelines to London and navigable water. With a population of 10 000, Canterbury was still a fair-sized city, foremost in Britain in religious importance, and fulfilling administrative and military roles. But its commerce was in decline. The textile and silk trades had lost out to other parts of England, although Canterbury muslins, a mixture of cotton and silk, were still popular, and the city had busy markets every Wednesday and Saturday.[7] London was 56 miles away by turnpike road,

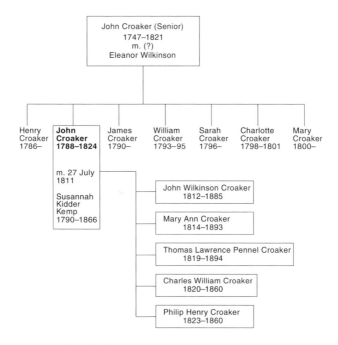

John Croaker's immediate family

but the most cost-effective communication with the capital was via the port of Whitstable, six miles to the north.

At his parents' home in St Dunstan's Street the young John Croaker would often have been woken, at four in the morning, by the stumbling rattle of the Dover mail, making its way to the Fountain inn after the nine-hour sprint from London. Perhaps he stayed up some nights to watch the colourful return coach, bustling westward with fresh horses. On Saturdays, no doubt, he marvelled at the heavy wagons lurching to Whitstable, where sailing boats known as hoys exchanged London hardware for Kentish cloth and produce, and waited for the turn of the tide. At 2s 6d for the voyage, against 18 shillings by land,[8] there were many foot passengers prepared to brave the fogs and storms of the Thames estuary, squashed and soaked on the shelterless deck. And all day, every day, the carts, the diligences, the carriers' wagons, the soldiers, the pedlars, and the penniless, passed his door to and from Faversham, Sittingbourne, and the Medway towns.

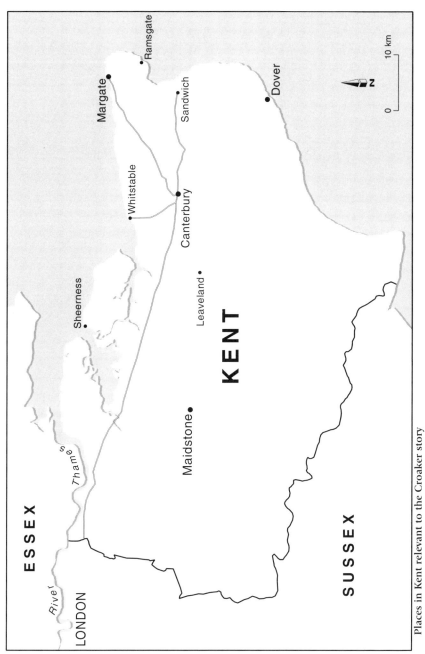

Places in Kent relevant to the Croaker story

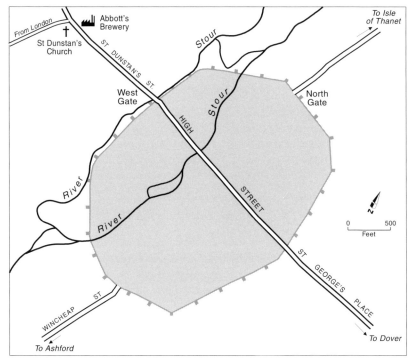

St Dunstan's parish in relation to the walled city of Canterbury

Elsewhere in St Dunstan's Street, Croaker must have seen things which turned many another child into a wiser adult. The street contained the gaol for the eastern division of the county, and the Westgate itself was the city prison for both debtors and criminals. A few years earlier, prisoners had been allowed out to a grille, to 'discourse with passengers, receive their alms, and warn them . . . to manage their liberty . . . to the best advantage'.[9] At the other end of the street was a more subtle salutary influence in the form of the parish church, famous for the tombs of William and Margaret Roper. William had been the biographer of Sir Thomas More, the famous Lord Chancellor (converted from knight to saint in 1935) who had the temerity to stand up to King Henry VIII and paid the ultimate penalty in 1535. Margaret Roper had been More's daughter. She caught her father's rotting head, tossed to her by its guardian on London Bridge where it had been impaled for a month, and preserved the remains in spices until her death. The skull was then buried in St Dunstan's church.[10]

Across the road, a few yards towards Westgate, still stands the Tudor gateway, one of the many and venerated attractions of this historic city, which led to what was once the Ropers' mansion. The site of the house became occupied by a large brewery. There survives to this day, alongside the gateway, the remains of its business, which ceased in 1929.[11] The main relic is a tall, red-brick block, dated 1866 on a keystone, and made slightly less bleak by some blind arcading at the highest level. Just beside it, hard against the old gateway, is an equally tall building with 1776 and several initials incised in the brickwork at eye level. Here, or very near here, worked John Croaker, senior, whose son of the same forename was to be influenced for life by the brewery's heady mélange of sounds and smells. Established by John Abbott, it was not the first commercial brewery in Canterbury, nor was it the largest.[12] But soon it was to have a notoriety.

Abbott was born on the Isle of Thanet about 1745.[13] He came from a landed family but had only a 'confined' education—certainly not at the King's School, Canterbury, where most of the established or aspiring middle classes sent their sons. In the early 1780s he decided that farming was not in his line and moved with a large and growing family to St Dunstan's, to set up as a brewer. At roughly, or even exactly, the same time, he took John Croaker senior into his brewery: Croaker's death notice in 1821 stated he had been 36 years in Abbott's service.[14] How the two men came to know each other has proved impossible to establish, but it was no half-hearted arrangement. As Croaker was not, apparently, a St Dunstan's man, and he was illiterate, he would have needed a settlement certificate to live there. No such certificate can be traced.[15] The presumption is that Abbott gave an undertaking that his servant, and his servant's family, would not become a charge on the parish.

Abbott became very well connected socially, which was to make his ultimate disgrace the more wretched. He was a magistrate, a friend of the Dean of Canterbury and of members of parliament. He made himself a freeman of the city by redemption (in other words, purchase) in 1789, and at one point his contribution to the poor rate of St Dunstan's was a third of the total levy.[16] The brewery house was large, and needed to be, as the Abbotts had five sons and four daughters. Some of the sons were educated at the King's School, and the second eldest, also called John, joined his father in the business.[17] The Abbotts had two public houses in St Dunstan's and paid land tax on several other properties which were residential, and presumably occupied by their employees.[18] One of these, in 1798, changed hands from 'Brenchley' to 'Croaker'. As it was rated at 8 shillings, and most small dwelling-houses in the parish (including

Abbott's other ones) were rated at 4 shillings, it was either a cottage of moderate size, or one not divided into two tenements. The fact that the Croakers had escaped mention in assessments over the previous thirteen years can be attributed to one of two reasons: either they lived in the brewery house proper, perhaps in the attics, or they were not the main tenants in a divided cottage. The second alternative seems more likely.

The growth of the Croaker family group had been marred by deaths. By 1798 four sons and two daughters had been born, but one son (William) and one daughter (Charlotte) had not survived infancy. Another daughter was born in 1800, so the Croaker parents entered the 19th century with boys of 14 (Henry), 12 (John), and 10 (James), a girl of 4 (Sarah) and a newly-born baby girl (Mary). They must have been falling over each other in the cottage, although such conditions were by no means unusual for the period. Where the young Croakers were educated is unknown, as their childhood lay in the obscure period before the National Society, founded in 1811, established a school for poor children in most populous parishes. Canterbury was certainly well endowed with charity schools, of which the Blue Coat School and the Eastbridge Hospital were the best known.[19] It is possible that the Croaker children could have been 'poor' enough for admission to one of these schools, but as St Dunstan's was outside the city walls, they would have found it difficult to qualify. The educational system within St Dunstan's was no doubt run also on a charitable basis, but without the formalised structure of a landed endowment, created by a benefactor's will, such as existed within the city. There was an elementary school in St Dunstan's Street at some stage after the move of the county gaol to another part of the city, but John Croaker is unlikely to have attended.[20] There was also a central school in the city, run by 'The Society for the Education of the Poor, throughout the Diocese of Canterbury', but this was established after Croaker's primary education would have finished.[21]

The Croaker children, other than John, seem to have achieved no academic distinction. For Henry and Sarah, there is no historical trail; Mary was later to compound the family ignominy by giving birth to an illegitimate son;[22] James was apprenticed in 1803 to a Canterbury tinsmith and brazier called John Fisher, which opened one doorway to being a freeman of the city.[23] Fisher remains in focus throughout the 1820s, but his apprentice fades from view. As for John Croaker, however, wherever he received his elementary schooling, he must have developed as a literate and numerate young man or his career would never have begun. In 1808, at the age of about 20, he gained employment as a clerk in a new banking-house at Ramsgate run by John Garrett.[24] This was a monumental achievement for a young man with his background, and prompts questions about recruitment into banking in East Kent, and about the training or patronage which Croaker needed to gain admission. He fell well short of the criteria mentioned by J. W. Gilbart, the patriarch of Victorian banking: 'Candidates for the office of bank clerks are usually the sons of the middle class of tradesmen, or of professional men, as clergymen, officers in the army or navy, or persons in the service of Government'.[25] Gilbart noted that during the Napoleonic wars, when sons of gentlemen were recruited to national duties, sons of tradesmen were rather more in evidence. He recognised advantages and disadvantages in each class. Sons of gentlemen were more literate and courteous, but their minds were often elsewhere, in country pursuits, and the dull routine of banking was rather beneath them. Tradesmen's sons, on the other hand, were better acquainted with the world of business and knew the importance of earning a living. Croaker's father was not even a tradesman, and his son seems further distanced from the prospect of a job in banking by Gilbart's concern for the 'religious and virtuous' qualities required in an applicant's parents.[26] He wrote about 'moral principle' and the need for 'excellence at home'. Future events were to prove that John Croaker senior was not the paragon of propriety whom Gilbart demanded.

The age at which a bank clerk was recruited was identified by Gilbart as 'usually about nineteen', at least in London, although younger in country areas.[27] He thought 'two or three years in a merchant's counting-house' was the best preparation for a banking career, as a boy just out of school was unproven and unworldly. Curiously, he made no reference to the wider aspects of recruitment, which often entailed articles of apprenticeship, and invariably a surety for good conduct. Enough deeds survive from Croaker's period to indicate that a bank clerk was in much the same relationship to his employer as was an apprentice to a manual trade, and was bound for between four and seven years.[28] The typical declaration— 'his master faithfully to serve, his secrets to keep, his lawful commands everywhere gladly to do'—transcended all county boundaries and most lines of business. An abstemious life style, sleeping on the premises, avoiding such stated diversions as marriage, fornication and gambling, and the frequenting of inns and playhouses, was invariably demanded. How far the average apprentice obeyed these requirements is a moot point, as the words of 'The Lincolnshire Poacher' bear melodious testimony.[29] But bankers were at the strict end of the spectrum of tolerance. Sir William Forbes, an eminent Scottish banker of the late 18th century, lamented that he had slept only one night out of the Edinburgh banking-house of his masters in over six years of apprenticeship.[30]

As Croaker's job with Garrett lasted some three years, less than the minimum period of apprenticeship, it can be concluded that he had already served a period of more or less formal training elsewhere, say from the age of sixteen. The fact that he is omitted (in contrast to his brother James) from recorded lists of apprentices in Kent and London, does not by itself mean he had no formal apprenticeship, as lists are not comprehensive.[31] But it is perhaps more likely that his preliminary training was of a less formal nature, either in another bank or in the counting-house of a brewer or merchant, where he would have assisted with the book-keeping. In all this period the altruistic hand of John Abbott, the brewer, can be pictured guiding the young Croaker towards a brighter, richer future in the life style of the middle classes. He might even have trained Croaker himself. Without him the gulf between a cottage in St Dunstan's and the banking-house in Ramsgate was simply unbridgeable. Social considerations aside, a patron was needed to find the inevitable surety necessary for Croaker's good conduct. Sums between £250 and £1000 were normal, usually in the form of a bond entered into by the clerk's father, sometimes in combination with other relatives. The illiteracy of Croaker's father did not necessarily mean he was penniless, nor did it disbar him from such a bond, validated by a witnessed cross, but Garrett would have sought comfort in the legible signature of Abbott.

The assumption of an understanding between Abbott and Garrett rests partly on the belief that the two men were well known to each other. Both hailed from St Lawrence-in-Thanet (now Ramsgate), and their landed families would have been acquainted over several generations. The Garretts were more elevated in social circles,[32] but Abbott's stock was rising among the Establishment in Canterbury, especially the clergy. However, other relationships and combinations can be suggested, and Garrett may have accepted Croaker following a specifically banker-to-banker understanding. But even if he did, it must have been Abbott who first introduced Croaker, by one means or another, to the private side of the counter.

There were two main banking firms in Canterbury at this time:[33] the earlier and main one, with origins in the hop trade, was The Canterbury Bank of Gipps, Simmons & Gipps, founded in 1788, which became Payler, Hammond, Simmons & Gipps in 1800. For most of the 19th century it was known simply as Hammond's Bank, as other partners faded from prominence. Ledgers have survived, revealing that Abbott was not a customer, so there is no reason to suppose young Croaker was taken on there, even if Abbott had thought it worth while to approach the partners. Established very soon afterwards, however, was The Canterbury Union Bank, of which the principals were Baker, Denne, Kingsford, Wigsell and Kingsford. Both these banks had connections with brewing. The former had the main account of the largest Canterbury brewery, that of Flint & Co. in Sturry Street, to whom they lent £7100; but Flints also held £1000 advanced by John Baker of the rival bank, and the Kingsfords were soon to join them in the brewing business.[34] As John Baker also had substantial interests in St Dunstan's, a banking link with Abbott is a very strong possibility. It is therefore arguable that, about 1804, Abbott introduced Croaker to Baker, who taught him the rudiments of banking (or got him accounting experience in Flint's brewery), and that Baker and Abbott together were able to persuade Garrett, four years later, to give Croaker a clerkship. Abbott remains the best source for the inevitable surety.

Croaker's disastrous career was to highlight the fragility of a country banking system which was under-capitalised, often incautious, and frequently over-exposed to its own paper money.[35] A person could become a banker almost by accident, and by many routes. Perhaps he had an established commercial business which had generated surplus capital which might be lent out at interest. Or, conversely, he sought to attract capital for his business by accepting deposits, on which he paid interest; or maybe he allowed credit to his customers, even beyond the limits normally extended by the bill of exchange. There was also a route into banking by the professions: solicitors often organised mortgages and gave financial advice, and those who remitted money to some central repository might use it on their own account in the interval between transfers to London. The unifying characteristic of these country banks— by a restriction which was to last until 1826—was that the number of partners could be no more than six.[36] The only joint-stock bank which could lawfully operate before then, south of the Scottish border, was the Bank of England. There thus arose, across the length and breadth of England and Wales, a plethora of small banking firms seeking to finance and service the Industrial Revolution in its manifold aspects, as well as meeting the needs of corporations, institutions, and the rich.

While sharing the broad characteristics of the system at large, the bankers in East Kent were also, in a sense, in a world of their own. The geography of Kent robbed them of steady intercourse with professionals in other counties, a phenomenon only shared by bankers in West Cornwall. But Kent was on the doorstep of London, and through its fertile fields, hop grounds, and laden orchards passed most of the travellers to

France and the rest of Europe. Such international activity, coupled with the natural fecundity of the county traditionally called 'the Garden of England', led to a cluster of banks disproportionately dense for the size of the area. In 1797 there were 253 private banking firms in all the country, including Scotland (but excluding London), and in England and Wales alone there were some fifty counties.[37] Yet in East Kent there were no fewer than ten banks: The Canterbury, and Canterbury Union, Banks, which have already been mentioned; Jemmet & Co. at Ashford; Fector & Minet, and Latham & Co. at Dover; Oakley at Deal; Harvey & Co. at Sandwich; Austin & Co. at Ramsgate; Cobb & Co. at Margate; and Bennett & Co. at Faversham. Furthermore, the whole scene was in constant flux, with partners changing, banks closing, and new banks beginning.

The leading bank of this group was Cobbs at Margate. Founded by Francis Cobb in 1785, the firm is an example of the classic connection between banking and brewing, the former evolving naturally from the profits of the latter, and from the powerful reputation of its proprietors.[38] Because Margate was part of Dover Cinque Port, the Cobbs held the post of Deputy to the Mayor of Dover, and a succession of civic responsibilities, passing from father to son, led to nothing less than a dynasty. Distinction led to business, and the Cobbs were soon supplementing their banking and brewing by running agencies in shipping, salvage and insurance, while acting as vice-consuls for many European countries.[39] Without one strong firm at its centre, the whole network of East Kent banks was in danger of progressive collapse from a 'run', like a line of tottering dominoes. The art of prudential banking was to keep enough funds liquid to meet a panic, while ensuring that the rest of the capital was earning money.

The day-to-day business of the East Kent banks included the acceptance of money on deposit, the granting of loans and mortgages, the issue of banknotes, and the discounting of bills of exchange. It was the banknotes and bills which were to bring Croaker to grief. A bill of exchange worked something like a modern cheque, but with an in-built facility for credit. Let us suppose a corn chandler was selling grain to a miller. While this was being delivered, the chandler sent his bill to the miller, payable in, say, three months. The miller accepted the bill by signing it, and passed it back to the chandler, who then had three options: he could keep it in his bill box for three months and then claim the money; he could endorse it and pass it on elsewhere, perhaps to one of his own creditors, who would regard it as 'money' if he knew and trusted the acceptor (that is, the miller); or he could take it to a banker who would discount it for a fee. In other words, the banker would pay the chandler rather less than the face value of the bill, and he himself (or anyone else who acquired the bill) would claim the full amount from the miller when the bill matured. The economy of the Industrial Revolution was geared to the drawing, acceptance, discounting and honouring of bills of exchange. It was a handy short-term, self-liquidating instrument of credit, with the potential to make the holder some fast money.[40] A variant of this document, known as the accommodation bill, will be shown later to have caused Croaker's conviction.

As for banknotes, these were technically promissory notes, because the issuer promised the bearer that the stated sum would be redeemed as money of real value—that is to say, gold or silver. Banknotes gave a ready form of remittance within an area coterminous with trust in the issuer. One of the interesting aspects of East Kent, where travellers often wanted gold to take to the Continent, is that the banks all agreed to honour each other's paper; couriers went to and fro between the towns carrying redeemed banknotes, fastened to little messages like: 'We shall esteem ourselves much obliged by your doing the needful with the enclosed . . . '.[41] The 'needful' was the cancellation of the notes, as they had been redeemed in another town, and the posting of an entry in the issuing bank's ledger to the credit of the bank which had paid out. It was hoped that discrepancies in payments between the banks would, over the year, even out, or an exchange of gold would be needed to square the books. Each bank was affiliated to a London banking-house, where the agent could pay against its correspondent's banknotes, receive and arrange credits, and buy stock for the country bank's partners and customers.

To understand the background to Croaker's trial, the reader must be aware of how easily an imprudent banker could be ruined. The classic danger for a bank was to issue notes beyond its ability to honour them. Every rumour of insecurity in a public house or market place could degenerate into panic: holders of banknotes could demand real money, and the Bank of England was no more immune to these scares than the country banks. Hence the Suspension of Cash Payments in 1797 when the Bank, instructed by a Government under pressure in the French Wars, refused to honour its printed promise.[42] If a run got out of control, a banker stood to lose not only his business but his house and estate, as there was no principle of limited liability in English country banking in those formative years.[43] In the folklore of banking, stories abound of ingenious deceptions to restore calm, like sacks of—to all appearances— gold sovereigns which held nothing beneath but meal.[44] Or men were 'planted' in the bank queue who withdrew some gold, raced round to the back of the bank to give it in again, and then rejoined the throng, clogging up the process until others lost patience and went away. It was the mass banking failures of 1825, in which some ninety firms collapsed, which led to a change in the law to allow joint-stock banks to be founded locally, subject to various restraints in favour of the Bank of England.[45]

When Croaker joined Garrett's bank in 1808, certain assumptions can be made about his duties. He was not the managing clerk, and land tax returns for Ramsgate, under Garrett's heading, suggest that Croaker's immediate superiors were John Constable and Richard Blaxland.[46] In other words, Croaker was the junior, and much of his time would have been spent posting up the ledgers and cash-books. Day-to-day trans-actions of banking were recorded roughly in waste books, and it was for Croaker to fair-copy the details to the satisfaction of his bosses. At inter-vals, the books were 'called-over', which meant that the two senior clerks would have checked and ticked entries in one book against correspond-ing entries in another. It is important, in view of Croaker's subsequent career, to state that his book-keeping was double-entry. This method, sometimes known as the Italian system, will be discussed more fully in chapter 6. The acceptance of this principle in English banking is of such antiquity that the textbooks of the 19th century simply took it for granted. Perhaps the first banking theorist was Thomas Joplin, writing in 1827, who merely referred to 'the common mode of book-keeping by double entry', with no attempt to argue its case—as he did for other banking procedures.[47] The prevalence of the system can be proved, quite simply, by an examination of surviving ledgers from banking-houses which traded in the late 18th century. Typical of these firms were The Canterbury Bank, and Cobb & Co. of Margate, whose double-entry ledgers have survived from 1788 in the first case, and 1802 in the second.[48] In view of the interwoven relationship between the East Kent banks, there can be no reason to doubt that their book-keeping methods were compatible.

As Croaker entered service at Ramsgate beyond the age of a raw apprentice, it is probable that his previous training had included instruc-tion in double-entry. This has some slight bearing on the speculation as to where this training might have been, a point discussed above. Perhaps the balance is tilted slightly in favour of another bank, rather than a merchant's counting-house, as it must be doubtful whether a merchant, in a relatively small way of business, would have bothered with double-entry accounting. If that thought is translated to the context of brewing, then Flint & Co., with their twelve tied houses, probably found it worth while, whereas Abbott, with perhaps only two, did not. Another possibility altogether is that Croaker was taught to keep accounts at wherever he was educated. It was by no means uncommon for charity schools to teach accounting methods, and the Eastbridge Hospital at Canterbury was one of them.[49] Also, a nearby private school, Elham Academy, took boys between 13 and 15 years old to qualify 'them for most respectable commercial pursuits' within two years.[50] There was no shortage in bookshops generally of manuals for the amateur enthusiast.[51]

While Croaker settles in at Ramsgate, tots up his balances, and widens his experience, it is time to head back to Canterbury and trace the early years of Susannah Kidder Kemp, whom he was destined to marry.

2   Leaveland, Love and Illegality

The family background of Susannah Kidder Kemp offers a wider view of the trade and prosperity of Canterbury than was glimpsed in the discussion of St Dunstan's. It also paints a scene of privilege, such as the infant John Croaker never knew. Within the city walls, commerce was still under the control, although to a declining extent, of freemen, whose powers were rooted in municipal charters. These people, at times, served also as members of the Common Council, and some rose to become aldermen (and therefore magistrates), and even mayor. As Canterbury was one of the few English cities which was also a county in its own right, the Common Council controlled justice and litigation, and formed a unifying tier of local government over and above the urban parishes, which were too small to be effective in secular matters. The freemen were thus doubly favoured, protecting not only their business but also the environment in which it was done.[1]

There were five ways of becoming a freeman—by birthright, on the father's side ('patrimony'); by purchase ('redemption'); by marrying a freeman's daughter; by gift; and by apprenticeship.[2] It is, therefore, possible to trace the privilege descending through several generations of a family. One freeman by marriage was Henry Kemp, born about 1761, who was Susannah's father. The business activities of Kemp are rather elusive: when he married in 1786 he was a haberdasher of the parish of St Alphage, later moving to The Precincts. Within four years, however, he was a corn chandler in St Margaret's, and when he died in 1803, aged only 42, he was a yeoman of Bridge Street in St George's.[3] Haberdashery appears to have gone by the board, but farming and chandlery were compatible, as the former activity produced crops to be disposed of by the latter. Even when seriously ill, Kemp still owned the freehold of the business in St Margaret's Street, run by tenants, and he held a lease of

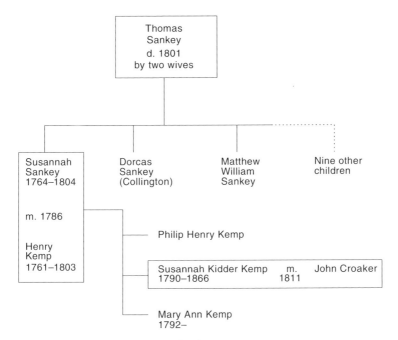

Susannah Kidder Kemp's immediate family

Donjon farm, several cottages, and hop-grounds in St Mary Bredin and St Mildred's.[4]

Kemp's wife was born Susannah Sankey. Her father was Thomas Sankey, grocer and chandler, a freeman of substance and influence, and an active member of Common Council.[5] Another distinction for Sankey was the size of his family: by his first wife he had seven children, and by his second another five.[6] It was Sankey's wish, as a testator, that his affairs should be continued by his widow and offspring. Two of his sons, Matthew William and Thomas, were already in his line of business, although not in partnership with their father. The family also had a connection with malting and brewing (assuming that another freeman, William Webster Sankey, was a relation), and it was to brewing that Matthew William Sankey turned his hand, none too successfully, after the turn of the century.[7] Of Thomas Sankey's twelve children, only the first four by his first wife are at all relevant to the Croaker story. These were three daughters, Dorcas, Susannah, and Sarah, and Matthew

William, mentioned already. Susannah married Henry Kemp, discussed above; Sarah is only of passing interest as she married another haber-dasher, one Richard Gowland; Dorcas married Richard Collington, and they will feature below.

Henry and Susannah Kemp had one son, Philip Henry, and two daughters, Susannah Kidder (who was to marry John Croaker), baptised 4 July 1790, and Mary Ann, some nineteen months her junior.[8] It can be deduced that the Kidder element in Susannah's name derives from her maternal grandmother—Thomas Sankey's first wife of whom nothing definite is known. Marriage licences indicate that Kidder was fairly common as a local surname, not just in Canterbury but in certain out-lying parishes such as Hastingleigh, where they were yeomen farmers. Thomas Sankey refers in his will to a 'much respected relation', Richard Sankey, who was also a farmer at Hastingleigh,[9] and it might not be co-incidence that the name Dorcas was represented in both the Sankey and Kidder families at much the same time. Thus, if there was no blood relationship between Sankeys and Kidders, there were other reasons to suggest the families were close. As for Kemps and Sankeys, the great-est proof of affinity is the fact that Henry and Susannah Kemp were both buried in the Sankey family vault in Harbledown churchyard.[10]

This genealogical sketch has been necessary, firstly to indicate that Susannah Kidder Kemp was 'better born' than her future husband and, secondly, to suggest areas from which the support soon to be vital for herself and her sister, as orphans, might have come. As regards the first point, it was no difficult matter for a freeman trader of humble origins to acquire the trappings and title of a gentleman, simply by being success-ful over many years and thereby well-off. Whether this achievement moved him and his family above the level of the lower middle classes—which was reached automatically—depended on the friends he chose to cultivate, the education he gave his children, and the more altruistic interests which he pursued in his spare time. In the case of Henry Kemp, a premature death robbed him of these opportunities for advancement; Thomas Sankey, who died in 1801 aged 63, was 'universally respected'[11] but had not quite reached the social acceptability of, for instance, John Abbott, the St Dunstan's brewer. But what both Kemp and Sankey had certainly achieved, by wisdom and application, was a sizeable bank account.[12]

Susannah Kemp survived her husband by just over a year. She died in July 1804, aged 39, leaving her son and two daughters in the guardian-ship of her brother, Matthew William Sankey, and her brother-in-law, Augustine Kemp.[13] The latter lived at Ospringe near Faversham, but with three sons and four daughters of his own,[14] his assistance could not have been very material. Nevertheless, he and his children were clearly intimate with their orphaned relatives, as Philip Henry Kemp, who had inherited his father's real estate, went on to marry a cousin before joining the Customs and Excise service in London.[15]

The problem of finding a new home for Susannah Kidder Kemp, then aged 14, and her younger sister, Mary Ann, was solved not by Matthew William Sankey, the other guardian, but by Dorcas Collington, their aunt. The children's plight was the more wretched as their grandfather, Thomas Sankey, had died before their parents; there were thus a dozen young people of varying ages to test the charity of kinship and drain family resources. The young Kemp girls were fortunate, however; their mother's will bequeathed them her personal estate, up to a total value of £1600, beyond which the proceeds were to augment the inheritance of Philip Henry, their brother.[16] It was, therefore, to the affectionate arms of close family, and with knowledge of money for their own upkeep, that Susannah and Mary Ann took the diligence to Faversham in the late summer of 1804, heading for the little village of Leaveland.[17]

The Collington family whom the girls joined had, some fifty years earlier, teetered through one of the most hideous scandals in the history of East Kent. To understand this disaster, it is helpful to have in mind the lie of the land. Leaveland was an ancient parish on the road from Faversham to Ashford. The country was rolling, fertile and wooded, with a gentle downward slope to the north. The small acreage of Leaveland was matched by its low population—a mere 57 in the first national census of 1801. What passed for the centre of the village was actually in the parish of Badlesmere, while Throwley (or Throwleigh) abutted on the north-west. The chief landowners, and hereditary lords of the manor, were the Watson family, formerly surnamed Monson.[18] As well as Rockingham Castle in Northamptonshire, from which they had once derived an earldom, the Watson family held Lees Court, a grand 17th-century mansion in Sheldwich, Kent, a parish which adjoins both Throwley and Badlesmere. In 1760 Lewis Watson of Lees Court was created Baron Sondes, and it happened that the descent of the estate from his son to his grandson in 1806 took place within two years of the Kemp girls arriving at Leaveland.

In this countryside, whose beauty belied a sub-current of lawlessness more or less connected with contraband, the Rev. Nathaniel Collington bought a small estate of some 55 acres in 1701.[19] This land was copyhold of the manor of Leaveland, which means that the title to the estate was based on the court rolls of the manor, of which the tenant had an extract

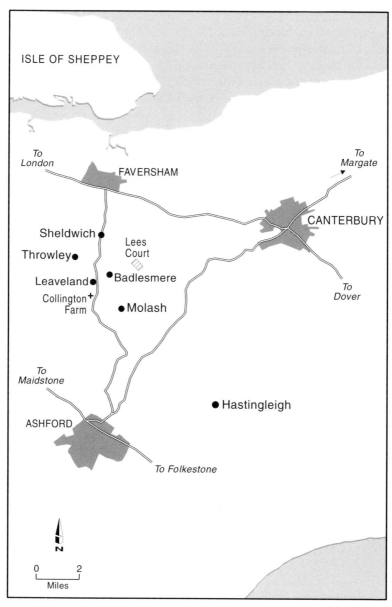

Leaveland and environs

or copy. Every so often—and not at all often in the case of Leaveland—there was held a meeting of all the tenants of the estate, known as a court baron. It was the proceedings of this court, ratifying changes of tenure that had occurred since the last one, which constituted the 'rolls', although by 1801 it was more normal for such records to be in the form of a book. It was, then, within this manor that Collington bought land, and it was situated in the parishes of Throwley and Leaveland, and comprised at least two houses. Collington was the well-respected rector of Pluckley (about ten miles to the south-west) for 59 years, and lived to be 93.[20] On his death in 1735, his son John inherited the estate and set up as a farmer in the main house, then apparently in Throwley, but these days in Leaveland.[21] If John Collington's career to that date had been a catalogue of broken apprenticeships and failed business ventures, it was now to veer from irresponsibility to sadistic villainy.

His first wife, who was beaten, humiliated, and sometimes imprisoned in a saw-pit for days on end, bore ten children before her premature death. These were ragged, battered, illiterate and unbaptised; when six of them died young they were buried in the orchard. By a second wife, Collington had another six children who received no better treatment than the rest. Meanwhile, Collington was convicted of 'owling' (the smuggling of wool) and was an inveterate poacher—'the terror of six parishes round him'. The Dowager Countess of Rockingham had a cottage built specifically to house a gamekeeper to keep Collington off the Lees Court estate. Collington's solution was to burn it down. Events came to a head when his second son, starved and bruised, was taken in by John Clarke, a local churchwarden. Clarke applied to Collington, who was quite well-off, for maintenance, and when this was refused he acquired a distrainment order from a magistrate. Collington's answer was characteristic. He had Clarke beaten up by ruffians, who also set fire to his barn and hay. But this time there was retribution. Collington was arrested, charged, and tried at Maidstone Assizes, where one of his accomplices turned King's evidence. Collington, aged only 53 and still by title a gentleman farmer, was hanged with one of his thugs, at Penenden Heath, Maidstone, on 7 April 1750.

In the aftermath of such an anti-social man, it is difficult to imagine how any individual named Collington could ever again raise his or her head in the parishes of Throwley and Leaveland. But the economics of existence came first, and John Collington, son of the hanged, continued to live in the farmhouse.[22] He had two sons who were less happy to stay around. These were John Wheler Collington, whose middle name touchingly recalled the surname of his grandfather's first wife, bullied to extinction, and Richard. The former son was commissioned into the 33rd Foot, and travelled to India where he acquired a chronic illness which was to end his career.[23] He died near Halifax, Yorkshire, in 1808, where he had bought a farm, but legacies to his brother's children, and the choice of Matthew William Sankey as an executor, show he stayed well in touch with his roots.[24]

Richard Collington, when a young man, moved away to Sholden, near Deal, but clearly had links with Canterbury, where he met Dorcas Sankey.[25] They married in 1786, and Collington thereby became a free-man of the city. By trade, Collington was a victualler, so it can be assumed that his business was connected to some extent with that of his father-in-law, the grocer. Two other Collingtons made it to the ranks of Canterbury freemen: some 25 years earlier, a Nathaniel and a Samuel Collington had both won apprenticeships in the city,[26] and as the name is so unusual in Kent, it can be assumed they were of the Leaveland stock. Thus the Collingtons were able to re-integrate into local society with a speed, and to an extent, which indicates that they were regarded as the victims of their forebear and in no way tainted by the blood of kinship. During all those years the fateful farm passed from father to son, with the name of each new copyholder enrolled in the court records of the manor of Leaveland. Eventually, Captain John Wheler Collington and his brother Richard held the property in their joint names, with Richard and his family in residence.[27] In 1798 Richard Collington died, only in his late thirties, leaving his widow Dorcas at the farm with three children, John Wheler junior, Grace and Frances. As Dorcas was left only an annuity of £20 a year from her husband's estate,[28] she was probably glad to offer a home to the orphaned Kemp girls, with their comfortable trust fund.

Despite the passage of fifty-odd years since the scandal, it can be imagined that the Kemp girls spent a nervous first night in the mellowed-brick farmhouse which had become their home. The Collington children, except Frances, were significantly older and Grace, at least, was growing rapidly out of childhood. Within two years, while still a minor, she married Daniel Amos of the adjacent parish of Molash, a liaison which followed on the heels of an earlier Amos–Collington marriage of 1788.[29] Several branches of the Amos family, yeomen farmers, seedsmen, and limeburners, were well represented in Molash, so no doubt there were young children with whom the Kemp girls and Frances could play.[30] This was just as well, because Leaveland itself offered few distractions and no other society from the lower middle class.[31] The only other house in the village of any substance was Leaveland Court—much larger than the Collington farm—where William Dodd lived until his death in 1802.

Dodd was a rich man, originally perhaps a miller or a farmer, whose prosperity had earned him not only a nice property but the title of gentleman—a designation which the Kentish descendants of John Collington, the hanged, appear to have lost. A clear idea of this wealth can be had from his will.[32] He left one daughter £2300; the other one was in business with her husband, William Smart, and they were in debt to Dodd, who waived £1000 of the capital. Smart had already sold Halstow mill, near Sittingbourne, to Dodd, who bequeathed it to a son, also called William, together with over £2000 and, again, a reduction in debt. Leaveland Court (which had been called Leaveland Farm until Dodd renamed it)[33] passed to the other son, Thomas, but his father's housekeeper was allowed to keep her chamber and effects there until she could take full occupation of another house which Dodd owned near by. Both sons also inherited, jointly, large tracts of marsh and arable land near Faversham.

Whether or not Thomas Dodd had offspring, he was well into middle age when the Kemp girls arrived in the village; thus any children were likely to have left home before their father took possession of Leaveland Court. The point is significant, because some way must be found to explain the excellent education which apparently came the way of Susannah Kidder Kemp, enabling her in later life to set up as a teacher. As there was no school within Leaveland, and the Collingtons were not of the status to employ a tutor, it would be convenient to find another local family with whom the Collington and Kemp children might have taken lessons. Given the wealth of the Dodds, their proximity, and the streak of generosity which was certainly evident in William senior, it is particularly disappointing that no connection can be made.

Alternative and intriguing possibilities arise. The first is that Susannah was taught by Edward Francis Kidder, a freeman of St Margaret's, Canterbury, described both as a writing master and later a schoolmaster, who was conceivably a relative.[34] This man, the son of a Canterbury barber, fell on hard times, and by 1796 had received poor relief in the parish workhouse.[35] Given these circumstances and the lack of evidence of his existence into the 19th century, it seems likely that any instruction he gave Susannah was in the earlier years of her childhood, perhaps before the age of ten. The second possibility is that there was some arrangement by the owners of Lees Court, little more than a mile away from Leaveland across footpaths, whereby children from certain local families were educated at the expense of the estate. As there was no National School for Sheldwich, Badlesmere and Leaveland until 1814,[36] the idea of some kind of informal, charitable arrangement for children resident within the manors of Baron Sondes gains a certain credibility.

Such a free school had certainly existed at one time in Throwley, founded by Sir Thomas Sondes in 1592.[37] An enquiry into local charities published in 1837 mentioned only that proceeds from Bellhorn farm in Throwley, owned by Lord Sondes, were distributed in winter to the poor of Sheldwich.[38] It is interesting that the marginal summary referred to 'Lady Sondes' School', implying that education was still at the heart of the charity, but this role had been abandoned in favour of poor relief. It is therefore possible that Susannah, from 1804, was educated either at Throwley or in the estate office at Lees Court, or even in part of the mansion, thanks to the patronage of Baron or Lady Sondes. The further thought then arises that she was taught by the Rev. Philip Parsons (1729–1812), domestic chaplain to Lord Sondes, a respected scholar and a dedicated schoolmaster.[39] The aristocratic links, however tenuous, which Susannah might have acquired in her education, would help to explain the clarity and confidence of her later correspondence, and perhaps suggest a source for the influence which she apparently exerted, some ten years later, in securing a passage to New South Wales.

As for John Croaker, there is no reason to believe he had any personal links with the Leaveland area, so it must be wondered how he and Susannah met. The likelihood is that they knew each other from childhood. Although Canterbury was small in area, they lived at diametrically opposite ends of the city; thus a reason other than neighbourship must be found to account for their initial meeting. It is possible that the brewery of John Abbott was a factor. Among the raw materials it needed—assuming certain malpractices soon to be discussed had not yet arisen—were hops, and it can be speculated that the Hastingleigh hop-grounds of Kidder or Sankey, or both, were a source which Abbott used. It is easy to imagine that carts which carried hops to Abbott might also have carried corn to Henry Kemp, the chandler, and that his daughters sometimes went along for the ride from one drop-off to the next. Indeed, as Henry Kemp also owned hop-grounds,[40] he might have supplied Abbott himself. At the brewery, Susannah would have met the young son of the man who paddled the mash tun, and the two youngsters can be pictured getting on well, giggling at the slurp and splash of the liquor, and poking a sly finger into the swelling yeast.

It took seven years, from her arrival at Leaveland in 1804, for Susannah's friendship with John Croaker to develop into love. How they maintained the momentum of their relationship is problematical, and suggests that Croaker's training or employment, before arriving at Ramsgate in 1808, gave him an opportunity to maintain the link. For instance, it would be nice to think that Croaker was apprenticed at the bank which held Susannah's trust fund; the nearest bank to Leaveland was at Faversham, and Augustine Kemp, one of her trustees, lived near by. A Canterbury bank is a more likely proposition for the Kemp trust fund, given the wider family connections. However, the idea of a raw young Croaker working for Tappenden & Co. of Faversham, bankers (established 1790), fits not only his liaison with Susannah but maybe the inherent instability of Tappendens, who crashed in the country-wide 'runs' of 1815.[41] For the years after 1808, when Croaker was definitely at Ramsgate in a job which allowed him little freedom, it is easier to picture Susannah, aged 18 and more, making the 30-mile journey to him, rather than vice versa. There are Kemps recorded as freeholders at Ramsgate,[42] and the ramifications of Susannah's family, although Canterbury-based, allow at least the possibility that she had access to hospitality from relatives there. Sitting on the harbour wall, watching the ships sail for Flanders and the Baltic, the lovers had the tang of salt air to sharpen their affection. Perhaps they dreamed of travel and adventure in the wider world. Unhappily, the voyages which lay in store for them were less than romantic.

On 27 July 1811 John Croaker and Susannah Kidder Kemp were married in the tiny parish church at Leaveland.[43] The bride was barely twenty-one, but at last she was in control of her own destiny and inheritance. She can be pictured as vivacious and self-possessed; the groom, a rather short young man with a florid face, also carried himself well.[44] For the last three years he had been dealing with moneyed people, and had leanings towards a life-style which his parents had never known. Any unease once harboured by Collingtons, Sankeys, or Kemps about a possible mismatch, in terms of social inequality, would have been long forgotten. John Wheler Collington gave Susannah away and Mary Ann Kemp was a bridesmaid. The two other witnesses, Sarah Winter and John Wilkinson, are more obscure, but the latter at least is likely to have been family on the Croaker side; the absence of John Croaker senior and Eleanor from the register was no doubt due to their illiteracy rather than their non-attendance.

The home for the newly-weds was Margate, not Ramsgate. It so happened that Susannah's majority coincided with the end of the banking-house of John Garrett. There was nothing untoward about Garrett stepping down: there had been another bank at Ramsgate, also from 1808, run by Burgess & Canham, and in 1811 Garrett sold out to them.[45] He had also been trading out of Margate, where he disposed of his interest to one John Sackett. Either because he did not fit the new arrangements at Ramsgate, or because he was offered a better deal under Sackett, Croaker decided his future lay in Margate. With his new bride, he took possession of the rooms behind the banking-house in Cecil Square, and settled into a new career of trust and responsibility as the managing clerk to a solitary principal, who lived in grand style next door. Croaker was to receive half the profits of the firm if they exceeded £400, and a guaranteed £200 if the profits were less.[46]

Sackett was not new to banking but in deciding to trade alone he might have wished for better auspices. His own introduction to the profession appears to have taken place in 1808, when a partnership of Garrett, Boys, Garrett, Sackett and Burgess succeeded to the business of the Isle of Thanet Bank (founded in 1793) which had run into difficulty.[47] With the Garretts pulling out, Burgess now focusing on Ramsgate, and Boys reverting to his original business as an attorney-at-law, John Sackett's brave decision to continue the Isle of Thanet Bank in his own name merited a colleague more reliable than Croaker. But at the same time, Sackett's own sense of responsibility, and his integrity as a gentleman banker, are not without question.

Sackett's background was not untypical of the small-time country banker. He came from landed, farming stock in East Kent who were widely distributed across Thanet. The family was so extensive that the exact identity of the John Sackett in question, as opposed to others of the same name, is difficult to confirm.[48] The family were boat owners and their hoys brought raw materials for the construction of Margate waterfront.[49] The loss of one of their corn hoys in 1802 was a cause for public subscription to support bereaved families of the crew.[50] It appears Henry Sackett had the most influence in Margate, and he died in 1815, aged 70. His son, John Henry Sackett, could possibly be the banker under discussion.[51] In any event, Croaker's boss can probably be identified with the John Sackett of Margate, gentleman, who died in 1834;[52] if this is correct, then the defence claim in Croaker's trial, that 'Mr. Sackett's memory was so very frail',[53] was more a biting allegation of incompetence than a statement of old age. The other noteworthy aspect of the Sacketts was their strong connections with London. When Henry Sackett died, he was described as of Kennington Green in St Mary, Lambeth, and directories show that one Thomas Sackett was a shipwright in nearby Bermondsey.[54]

There is nothing to suggest that Croaker went off the rails while working at Ramsgate. Indeed, Garrett testified at the trial that Croaker 'had universally born [*sic*] a very good character'.[55] Whether that was by inclination or constraint is open to doubt, as Croaker's junior position under two scrutinising clerks left him no room for deceitful manoeuvre. At Margate, however, he virtually ran the business—or rather what business there was, because with Cobbs such a strong and established force, and the population of Margate only 6000, such accounts as came their way were likely to have been opened by people who had their reasons for avoiding Cobbs. The nature of that business was therefore concerned largely with aspects of the liquor trade, wholesale and retail, maintained by individuals who were in competition with Cobbs in their capacity as brewers and wine and spirits merchants.[56] It should not be inferred, however, that business rivalry led to any element of animosity between Cobbs and Sackett, or that Sackett's customers were necessarily at odds with Cobbs. Local banking left no room for grudges. Bills of exchange were discounted by Cobbs for Sackett, and for customers of Sackett, and money raised through rates and banked by Cobbs was given to Sackett in large helpings for the relief of the poor.[57] Cobbs also received from Sackett his property tax and, as treasurers to the Pier and Harbour Company, they paid him for goods, including the herb sainfoin, used as animal feed and imported by his hoys.[58]

This cohesion between local bankers was soon to be tested by Croaker's trial. The evidence of Croaker's personal contact with the Cobbs is slight, although their bill ledgers include the discount of a bill for £16, under the name of Croaker, as early as 1808.[59] As Croaker was then barely 21, and the junior clerk at Garrett's bank, this transaction probably has little significance. It would certainly be unsafe to regard it as a sign of independent trading. The absence of Croaker's name from Cobbs' later books does not mean he was uninvolved with them, as business was usually entered under the name of the bank or its principal. However much the names Sackett or Sackett & Co. occur in Cobbs' ledgers, more or often than not it was Croaker's job to handle the transaction. Sums of mesmerising size, like the £700 over three months which Cobbs paid over from the overseers of the poor account in 1812,[60] might well have instilled in Croaker the first stirrings of dishonesty. If so, then an incident later that same year would have done nothing to dissuade him from criminal activities.

This incident centred on a plausible young man, passing himself off as a naval officer, who attempted to gain money from several country bankers by various illegal means.[61] Having arrived at Margate, he took a letter of credit to Cobbs who, experienced as they were, would have nothing to do with it. The same ploy was then tried on the other bank in town, with another letter of credit drawn on a different London banking-house; this time it worked, and he gained £20. It can be assumed that Croaker, as the first point of contact, was the person who was duped. The forgery was soon spotted, possibly by John Sackett, and the man was arrested as he boarded a London mail coach. An offence of this gravity, together with other incriminating property on the young man's person, merited the death penalty, but as the felon was under 20 years old, Sackett did not press for the full rigour of the law. This interesting episode is doubly instructive: the naivety of paying against a letter drawn on a bank which was not the London agent of Sackett & Co., and for which no corroborating signature had been received, calls Croaker's common sense and professionalism into question; and the fact that John Sackett had shown leniency in this instance could have persuaded Croaker that his boss was a soft touch. If that was really what he thought, he got it very wrong.

The number of embezzlements made by Croaker, over three years from 1811, can only be glimpsed from allegations and indictments, some of which were never brought to court. He is thought to have gone seriously wrong about six months before his committal to Dover Gaol,[62] that is to say from the summer of 1814, but the exact details and dates of all indictments brought against him were never stated. It might have been that his initial deceits were too small to be noticed, or that he covered his tracks very skilfully. In any event, he descended very suddenly into reckless behaviour, and is said to have incited a brother clerk (presumably his own junior in the firm) to 'improper conduct'.[63] Croaker seemed to know what he was doing, yet was powerless to control himself. The 'J.C.' who advertised his services 'as Clerk or Writer, or to keep a Tradesman's Accounts' in the *Kentish Gazette* of 16 August 1814, was surely John Croaker, trying desperately to get out. He might also have been the 'X.Y.Z.' who inserted a rather more ambitious advertisement in the same newspaper in the preceding June.[64] Reasons must be found to explain the complete disintegration of his character and loss of direction.

Croaker's own excuse, in a letter to Sackett, was that 'imprudent speculations' had got the better of him.[65] This was interpreted by the press as dabbling in the public funds, by which was meant the buying and selling of interest-bearing securities issued by Government to finance the national debt. These securities, referred to collectively by the strange name of omnium, were also to be revealed by the trial as an obsession of

John Sackett. It was common for local bankers across the country to speculate in omnium both for their clients and on their own account. It will be seen shortly that Sackett's exposure to what amounted to an addiction to gambling was only a little less dangerous than Croaker's. But a further question then arises—were there reasons for Croaker's sudden obsession? The answers to this seem to lie more in his private life than in his job at the bank, and there is more than one explanation to be considered.

The young Croaker household had been enlarged by the birth of a son, John Wilkinson, in 1812, and then in September 1814 by the birth of a daughter, Mary Ann.[66] The second pregnancy would have deprived Susannah of an independent livelihood as a school teacher, the designation under which she was later to blossom in New South Wales. Despite his high salary, Croaker could have been living beyond his means, and if Susannah owned a school, rather than taught in one—a point to be discussed later—he would have needed to pay another teacher to keep the enterprise alive. But a more fundamental reason presents itself, harking farther back into Croaker's origins. There can be no doubt that he was deeply affected by certain contemporary events in Canterbury, which besmirched the names of his father and his patron, John Abbott. The strong possibility of his own implication in the scandal must also be examined. The disreputable doings in Canterbury stirred even the somnolent back-benches of the House of Commons. The reader's curiosity in this matter, having been aroused, must now be satisfied by a change of scene: the curtain falls temporarily on Margate and rises again over the brewery of John Abbott in St Dunstan's Street, Canterbury, where serenity was coming to an end.

3   A Distasteful Business

For reasons which were never officially disclosed, the St Dunstan's Brewery, owned by John Abbott and managed by John Croaker senior, was raided by officers of Customs & Excise in the early summer of 1814. There was fumbling panic in the brewhouse. The excisemen drew off some liquor for analysis and searched the premises, outbuildings, and gardens for illegal ingredients. Chemicals, poisons, medicines and drugs were discovered in use, in storage, or hastily hidden. Others were retrieved from a broken cask, flung to the ground so as to scatter the contents. In a few grim minutes, one of Canterbury's most respected citizens was embroiled in a scandal as distasteful as the poisoned porter he had marketed through his public houses.[1]

Abbott stood specifically accused of making 200 gallons of liquor composed of beer grounds, stale beer, sugar-water, distillers' spent wash, sugar, molasses, vitriol, quashia, *cocculus indicus*, grains of paradise, guinea-pepper, liquorice, opium, cow-powder, and other material such as to gladden the heart of a sorcerer. Another ten counts of adulterating beer were soon added. The normal and lawful ingredients of hops and malt, which attracted excise duty, were singularly absent. In a defence which was to earn him ridicule, he accepted that malpractice had taken place, but denied it had been conducted with his knowledge, and far less with his approval. He claimed that his education had been limited and non-mercantile; he had only become a brewer to escape from farming; and he knew nothing of the technicalities of producing porter, which he left to Croaker. But the Excise Office would have none of it. Abbott was definitely aware of the drugs, because he lied about the quantities which were held. And was he not ultimately responsible in any case? And did he not make payments for whatever ingredients were used?[2]

Apart from his social disgrace and lost magistracy, Abbott faced a fine of £9000. This would undoubtedly have made him bankrupt. In a move of questionable wisdom, the middle class of Canterbury agreed to rally round. There was one avenue open—not an escape route, but a possibility of damage limitation. The Excise Office was accountable to the Treasury, whose Lords held an appellate jurisdiction, recently granted, tailor-made for the defence of offending in ignorance. Gerrard Andrewes, who was the Dean of Canterbury (although living in London), Sir William Curtis of Ramsgate, John Baker, Member of Parliament for Canterbury, and at least one other dignitary,[3] wrote to the Lords of the Treasury in support of Abbott's memorial for leniency. Clearly there was collusion between the letter-writers, as references were made to a sacked employee called George Blake, alleged to have informed on Abbott out of 'insanity and revengeful malice'[4]—a man whom the Excise Office dismissed as irrelevant to its investigation.

It so happened that this was one of the first cases where the Lords of the Treasury were asked to exercise their new powers, and it was to bring into focus all the tensions and jealousies which the privilege created. In January 1815 the Commissioners of Excise were asked to stay proceedings in the Abbott affair and reconsider their decision.[5] They replied to the Treasury with a tough letter justifying their unshakeable belief in his guilt, and requesting the freedom to continue the prosecution without further delay. The Lords were unimpressed and found in Abbott's favour, restricting his penalty to a nominal £500, plus the costs of the Crown. But to the gratification of the Commissioners, it was to prove a Pyrrhic victory. Dissatisfaction with many decisions being made at the Treasury moved Henry Brougham, in April 1816, to propose a motion in the House of Commons questioning the remission of excise prosecutions, among which the Abbott case was central to his point. Brougham, later to become Lord Chancellor,[6] was already a parliamentary force, and the Lords of the Treasury anxiously reviewed their position. Two weeks before the debate, they instructed the Commissioners of Excise to send them the original papers on two cases, one of which was Abbott's.[7] The Commissioners, with only token tact, declined to send original papers as that was not the custom; they offered copies instead, which would take some time to produce. Rankling at this insubordinate response, which arrived on a Saturday, the Lords of the Treasury tartly ordered the Commissioners' chairman to appear before them on Monday, bearing the originals. But it was the Commissioners, thanks to Parliament, who were to have the final satisfaction.

The Commons debate was a triumph for Brougham, who was passionate in his cause and meticulously briefed. Full facts of the Abbott case, delivered in Ciceronian rhetoric, stunned and amused the House.[8] Abbott was exposed as naive and pathetic—if not a potential murderer, then certainly a poisoner. As for his supporters, Curtis was too old a friend of Abbott to be significant; Baker was accused of soliciting Abbott's support for electoral gain; and the unfortunate Dean was put through the verbal mincer. His letter had included the suggestion that Abbott's case was of limited seriousness as it concerned only ale-drinkers. Such infelicity was a politician's godsend. Was the very reverend gentleman not saying that the extermination of ale-drinkers was less important than Abbott's reputation? What a spiritual disaster! Presumably if Abbott were poisoning the drinkers of port and claret, it would be a different matter. As for the surname Croaker (by whatever spelling), it was all too good to be true. Croak was a slang verb for to kill as well as to die; and then there was John Wilson Croker,[9] secretary of the Admiralty, a parliamentarian with a sharp tongue and a career route already mapped to higher office. With what relish did Brougham tell the House that Abbott's man who distributed the cow-powder 'as need required, to the cow or the porter', went by the name of Croaker.

In themselves, these parliamentary proceedings, a full year after his fine, would not have worried Abbott to any degree. True, *The Times* picked up the parliamentary debate,[10] but in a sense it was yesterday's news, and the real ignominy he suffered in St Dunstan's would have run its course in 1815. The story, however, held yet another twist. John Fairburn, a London bookseller, published an extract from Abbott's memorial to the Treasury, the full text of the letters from Andrewes, Curtis and Baker, and a report of Brougham's speech (paraphrasing the Hansard account with intriguing variations).[11] Luridly entitled *POISONOUS BEER!!*, and making no bones about Abbott's guilt, the pamphlet was clearly intended for circulation in Canterbury, where it has survived,[12] rather than in London, where it was printed. From the use of original sources and the general tenor, it is difficult to see the real authorship as lying anywhere but in the Excise Office—a vicious last word from a moral victor.

For Abbott, this must have been deeply wounding and he became ill enough to make his will in February 1817.[13] As for his brewery, it seems to have continued but on a much reduced scale. The evidence for this lies in the land tax and parish rates, where Abbott's contribution dropped sharply, although his assessment remained high enough to indicate some commercial activity.[14] In April 1821 Flint & Kingsford, the main Canterbury brewers, took over his payments and the brewery returned to normal capacity. Abbott himself got over his illness and survived to at least 1825, when he was about 80 years old and still well-off.[15] The circumstances of

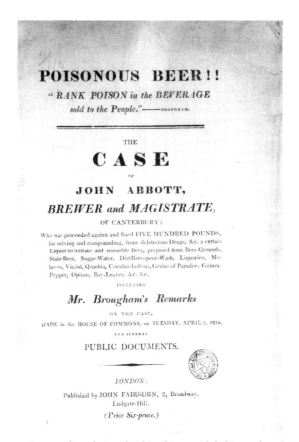

POISONOUS BEER!!

" RANK POISON in the BEVERAGE
sold to the People."——BROUGHAM.

THE

CASE

OF

JOHN ABBOTT,

BREWER and MAGISTRATE,

OF CANTERBURY:

Who was proceeded against and fined FIVE HUNDRED POUNDS,
for mixing and compounding, from deleterious Drugs, &c. a certain
Liquor to imitate and resemble Beer, prepared from Beer-Grounds,
Stale-Beer, Sugar-Water, Distillers-spent-Wash, Liquorice, Mo-
lasses, Vitriol, Quashia, Coculus-Indicus, Grains of Paradise, Guinea
Pepper, Opium, Bay-Leaves, &c. &c.

INCLUDING

Mr. Brougham's Remarks

ON THE CASE,

MADE in the HOUSE OF COMMONS, on TUESDAY, APRIL 2, 1816,

AND SEVERAL

PUBLIC DOCUMENTS.

LONDON:

Published by JOHN FAIRBURN, 2, Broadway,
Ludgate-Hill.

(Price Six-pence.)

John Croaker senior was directly involved in this scandal. (Reproduced with the permission of the Dean and Chapter of Canterbury)

his death are obscure, and his testamentary wish to be buried in the family vault at St Lawrence-in-Thanet appears not to have been honoured.

Even at low output, the St Dunstan's Brewery could only have continued through 1815, and beyond, with a change in management. That is to say John Abbott junior, who appears to have been in no way implicated in the scandal, must have taken charge.[16] As for ale-drinkers, it seems possible that certain die-hards (an ironically appropriate description) continued to trust his brew. After all, adulteration was widespread,[17] and it was never suggested that the poisonous qualities in Abbott's liquor would have a deleterious effect in anything but the long term; if the ale tasted reasonable to unfussy palates, the drinkers might not have borne a grudge. The whole question of Abbott's offence should be seen in the context of a widespread, national malpractice in brewing which had been developing since the 17th century with the ready availability of imported drugs, and the unfortunate ability of hop sellers and maltsters to price themselves out of the market. In November 1812 John Abbott himself had called an urgent meeting of brewers in East Kent, when it was learnt that a steep rise in the cost of hops and malt had forced the London Porter Brewery to re-price its ale at five shillings a barrel.[18]

Although it is tempting to see the rising cost of raw materials as a main reason for Abbott's brewery to debase its product, the discussion should be widened. The year 1814, when Abbott was raided, saw a cessation of hostilities with France, and therefore a slackening in the military market for beer, which the Kentish brewers had been exploiting for so long.[19] Yet the ensuing drop in retail prices was alleviated by no diminution in the price of raw materials or excise duty.[20] The source of Abbott's hops was the subject of speculation in chapter 2; the source of his malt can be attributed with greater confidence. Behind the brewery were the maltings of May Inge, of which remnants are still visible. Inge came from Littlebourne, to the east of Canterbury, but owned property in St Dunstan's besides the malthouse.[21] He is of interest in the Croaker story for several reasons, not least as the future husband of Mary Ann Kemp, whom he married in 1816 while her sister, Susannah, was sailing out to Australia to join her transported husband. The Inge–Kemp link strengthens the scenario for the Croaker–Kemp introduction, discussed in the previous chapter. The possibility of May Inge being somehow involved in the adulteration seems very real. With the brewery and the malthouse lying cheek by jowl, Abbott's supply of malt, in his 'legal' years, could scarcely have come from anywhere else. When the brewery decided to use unlawful ingredients, Inge would surely have wanted compensation, and perhaps the price of his silence. And perhaps Inge was more directly connected with the fraud: in 1834 one Mary Inge, a drug addict recently out of gaol, was found dead in a stack of hop-poles in St Dunstan's from an overdose of laudanum.[22] This might have been a coincidence of names, but she came from Sturry (very near Littlebourne), and it can be shown from rating assessments that May Inge's involvement in St Dunstan's, where she died, continued into the 1830s.

The availability of drugs was growing so fast that, by 1814, men were earning a living by travelling out from London, peddling illegal ingredients to country brewers, and giving instructions for their use and future supply.[23] Within London itself the position was rather better. A parliamentary inquiry in 1818 found that over the previous six years only one of the eleven metropolitan breweries had used deleterious ingredients. That one had employed its own chemist and was fined £100 and had to forfeit its dray and horses. The normal penalty was stated to be £500, with half the money going to the informer. As this was exactly the fine levied on Abbott, it must be questioned whether the zeal of the Excise Office in his case was not especially vindictive. If it can be conceded that his guilt in the offence was satisfactorily proven, it is nevertheless possible that he was set up by both sides for their own ends—the victim of a nasty power struggle between the Treasury and the Excise Office. Had this struggle not erupted at that precise time, his case would have been dealt with by far less public means. If this argument is not accepted, there seems no reason why Abbott's case should stand head and shoulders above the myriad other prosecutions for adulteration which were happening all over England.[24]

In terms of the Croaker story, the Abbott scandal raises many issues, but it will be helpful now to follow to their natural conclusion the lives of John Croaker senior, and his wife Eleanor. Croaker senior was as much a victim of the proceedings as his master. He had been named in Parliament, he was named again in the pamphlet—with a spelling reflecting how he had become known in Canterbury—and he had not the least defence for his actions, as Abbott had laid the blame at his door. Undoubtedly it was Croaker who scattered the incriminating drugs when the raid began, and he was clearly Abbott's *de facto* brewer, in charge of each stage of production. In one respect only was he fortunate, in that the legal blame lay not with him but with his employer. This was not enough to keep him his job, and Croaker found a new livelihood, while continuing to enjoy the cottage which Abbott had provided.[25] Having made him the scapegoat, Abbott and his son had the decency to stand by him.

In August 1814, and at regular intervals thereafter until his death in 1821, John Croaker senior received payments from the churchwardens' rates as a supplier of brushes for St Dunstan's church.[26] His bills were generally around 7 shillings a time, sometimes twice a year, and it can be assumed that Croaker took up the retailing of brushes (and, conceivably, their manufacture at the level of a cottage industry) when he lost his position as a brewer. This little affair, however, remains rather mysterious. Several questions present themselves. Was there a living in it? What kind of brushes were they, and why did the church need so many, so often? And how did an illiterate man draw up a bill? The answer to some of these points can be deduced from the decision of the vicar, in Croaker's day, to remove systematically the whitewash which had been disfiguring the church interior.[27] A job on that scale would have worn out many scrubbing brushes. As for the accountancy side, it might be an indication of Eleanor Croaker's literacy and numeracy that bills were composed and presented, although the continuing lack of consistency in the spelling of Croaker throughout her lifetime seems to argue otherwise. Another possibility is that John Croaker junior did the paperwork. It certainly appears that an independent living was possible, from this business or some other, as the Croakers paid their own rates to the churchwardens and the overseers of the poor.

John Croaker senior died on 12 August 1821, aged 74, at his cottage in St Dunstan's. The *Kentish Chronicle*, in recording this fact, noted that for thirty-six years he had been 'a faithful and honest servant' of John Abbott.[28] There is an implication here that he was regarded locally as a victim of Abbott's prosecution rather than a cause. Six days before he died, in a will of touching simplicity, he left everything to Eleanor. He could barely make a smudged cross on the paper.[29] His description in the will as a 'labourer' does nothing to solve the mystery of his brushes; on the other hand, the fact that he left a personal estate worth nearly £100 suggests there was more to his activities than labouring. The widowed life of Eleanor Croaker is no help in resolving the mystery. Only two elements are known: one is that she continued to live in the cottage in St Dunstan's, and pay her rates, although the landlord became May Inge, rather than the Abbotts, in 1821; the other is that she supplied brushes to the church on her own account until November 1825.[30] After that, Eleanor disappears from record and the only certainty is negative—she was not buried in St Dunstan's churchyard with her husband. The assumption must be that she had moved out of the area.

As far as John Croaker junior is concerned, the events in Canterbury are highly relevant to his life story, but it is difficult to be certain in what way. That there was some connection between the downfall of the brewery, which had dominated his childhood, and his misdemeanours in Margate, cannot reasonably be doubted. The coincidence of timing between the excisemen's raid and his own known offences could hardly be more exact. In chapter 2, there was brief discussion of how Croaker, till then a blameless bank clerk as far as is known, suddenly became disorientated and recklessly criminal. Certainly his immediate family circumstances might have played a part in this, but the overwhelming probability is that the St Dunstan's brewery scandal had for some reason shaken him to the core. The problem can be analysed at two levels: one of these argues a simple position of stunned consternation, arising from ignorance of the facts or only a vague awareness of what was going on; the other argues quite the opposite—a devious implication in the book-keeping aspects of the fraud.

3 A Distasteful Business / 43

As a prelude to both discussions, it can be agreed that Croaker owed the brewery and its environment something more than nostalgic affection. He was born and raised in its shadow, and maybe met his future wife there. But, more importantly, he owed its owner his escape route from the menial life of his parents. Abbott had been his mentor and his patron, a man whose middle-class credentials opened doors of opportunity on which Croaker, unaided, would have knocked in vain. Against this background, if Croaker had known nothing of the adulteration scandal, it can be well understood that the sudden public exposure—involving, as it did, his own father—would have disturbed his equilibrium. Whether it would have so unbalanced his intellect as to send him speculating wildly in the public funds, or misappropriating money, is another matter. But there is a second possibility here: it can be foreseen that, in his panic reaction, he envisaged Abbott ruined for life, and his parents out on the street, and heading for the workhouse. With a growing family of his own, he could hardly have supported them, despite his fine salary. Were, then, his illegal deeds aimed at acquiring money quickly for the altruistic reason of saving his parents' dignity?

Sadly, the honourable if misguided attitude which this motive implies is difficult to argue. It would have been naive to expect it to work: other residents of St Dunstan's would have questioned the Croakers' source of continuing money, and the couple could scarcely have concealed it. From that point on, it was only a matter of time before the public realised that Croaker was embezzling for his parents' support. Furthermore, it was particularly noted at Croaker's trial that he conducted himself 'in a very collected manner'.[31] This sits uncomfortably with the notion that he defrauded irrationally for the sake of his parents. Moreover, if that story had been true, it would surely have been a major plank in his defence. What better way to win over a jury than plead that wrongs had been committed for the most respectable of reasons? Few people blame Robin Hood because he stole from the rich to give to the poor.

As regards the suggestion that Croaker was personally involved in the fraud, it is, unfortunately for Croaker's memory, easier to sustain his guilt. Given his upbringing in the brewery's shadow, and at least a possibility that he was trained as a clerk in its counting-house before moving into banking, he was in a position to know much about the administrative side of the business, such as the purchase and control of materials and the associated book-keeping. It can be accepted from the evidence of Abbott's supporters, as set out in their published letters, that their beleaguered friend had not the least business acumen. He had been brought up as a farmer, and was well able to accept the social and judicial responsibilities which matched his status within the minor gentry, but he had neither training nor interest in the finer points of running a commercial venture. If he left the brewing to John Croaker senior, might he not also have left the creative accounting to Croaker's son?[32]

The only surviving reference to accounting in the documentation of the Abbott case is a remark by the Excise Office, in their submission to the Lords of the Treasury, that Abbott must have known of the illegal ingredients in his brewery 'by the payments made for the large quantities procured'.[33] Abbott argued that the day-to-day business of the brewery was delegated to others and that he was unaware of what went on. The Excise Office chose not to believe him, and this is hardly surprising. It seems compatible with Abbott's character that he was as lax with his accounting as he was with his brewing: the procedures and returns could well have been handled by someone on his behalf, and the chances of that someone being John Croaker junior look very good. The ploy was gradually to reduce the quantities of hops and malt passing through the books, thereby reducing the duty, while using the profits of sales from liquor of deteriorating quality to purchase an increasing amount of drugs. Clearly, some hops and malt had always to be on the books, but if the maltster, for instance, would accept money for a nominal supply of malt which he never delivered, and if there were no public outcry at the quality of the brew, the defrauding could last indefinitely and with great profit to the brewery and its suppliers.

An explanation can now be hazarded for Croaker's behaviour. When word reached him, at Margate, that the brewery had been raided, he was seized by a guilty panic. It was too late to save his father's name, because the man in charge of the brew could not have escaped an immediate responsibility for its contents. But would the excisemen at some stage conclude that someone other than Abbott was responsible for the accounts? And if so (or indeed if not), would a distressed and bewildered Abbott reveal the name of his book-keeper? Young Croaker began, at every opportunity, to embezzle his way to a solution. He would make enough money, quickly and by whatever means, to leave the country, expecting at any day that the representatives of justice would come to arrest him. He might even have been the victim of blackmailing threats, from the brewery's erstwhile suppliers of malt and hops. But the knock at the door never came; Abbott, for whatever selfless reason, did not reveal that the young man whom he had championed and groomed to a life of middle-class respectability was no more than a cheat. When it dawned on Croaker, after several weeks, that he had not been betrayed, he realised that he had over-reacted. It was then that he placed the advertisements to begin a new career. If he could get out of banking, quickly and with some dignity, it might just be that his embezzlements against Sackett and his customers would not come to light. Perhaps he still had time to make an honest man of himself, and give the disgraced John Abbott the satisfaction of knowing that the faith he placed in his protégé had not been entirely in vain. The advertisements, however, came to nothing, and Croaker soon realised he was too deeply in trouble to escape detection. His position was irretrievable and he decided to make for the Continent.[34]

At the end of 1814 John Sackett, who was in London, received the startling news that his managing clerk had absconded and that there was a run on his bank.[35] The run was quickly dealt with, thanks no doubt to the support of the other banking firm in Margate, the Cobbs, but Sackett was left with his books in disarray and no one to run his business. It is quite possible to believe he had not the least idea that anything was going wrong. A few weeks later Sackett received a letter dated 17 January 1815, at Dover, from Croaker, who was clearly in a miserable state, but unwilling to mention the affair of the brewery. If Abbott had not 'shopped' him, then he in turn owed it to Abbott to keep quiet; by so doing, he also diminished the possible charges to be laid against himself. He therefore explained his behaviour as the result of impetuous speculation in the national debt. He knew that Sackett himself speculated in this way, and therefore his boss might have had some sympathy. If this sympathy were not forthcoming, it would have occurred to Croaker that Sackett's addiction to the purchase of interest-bearing securities, which he could ill afford, might provide a defence for himself against accusations of reckless conduct, if not embezzlement.

Croaker's letter went on to deprecate his own 'folly', and admit he was 'rendering miserable the "best of women" and two sweet cherubs'.[36] On this point, it is very possible to believe him, although the fact that Susannah was miserable does not clear her of knowledge or even involvement in Croaker's activities—a point which will be discussed below. From this stage, events moved very quickly. At Margate, on receipt of Croaker's letter on 18 January, Sackett went straight to John Boys, his solicitor, and a plan was hatched to make Croaker return of his own volition.[37] Because he had written from Dover, it was a near-certainty that he was heading for Calais, and two men were dispatched immediately to track him down. One was a local merchant, Robert Brooke, and the other was John Baker, managing clerk to John Boys. Croaker would have known and trusted them both, Brooke at roughly the level of Sackett, and Baker as an equal, and probably a close friend. Brooke and Baker duly made for Dover, where they made contact with the local banking firm of Fector and Minet.[38] The main reason for this was to gain credibility in the eyes of the French police, in case Croaker resisted. As a matter of law, the authorities in Calais had no power to expel Croaker over an alleged breach of trust in England, and they had to be persuaded to take an interest in him simply as a foreigner without a passport. Such a transgression was only of notional importance, as passports could be granted on arrival. Nobody in Dover knew Calais better than Fector and Minet, and their application to the French authorities ensured that the police intervened. It was no doubt also through these bankers that Brooke and Baker, while still at Dover, acquired the services of a French-speaking mariner called William Keys.

On 19 January 1815 the three men arrived in Calais and toured the lodging houses. Late at night, they traced Croaker to the Kingston Hotel, and Brooke explained his credentials as a disinterested mediator: he was empowered to state that if Croaker would surrender the money and papers in his possession, and return to England, the whole affair 'should be quietly settled'. The involvement of the French police was barely needed. Croaker accepted Brooke's word, gave him money from about his person amounting to £1092, and the little group, in as relaxed a frame of mind as the circumstances allowed, set off immediately for Margate. Croaker undoubtedly trusted that a deal could be struck, and there are strong reasons for supposing that Brooke and Baker believed in the sincerity of their own mission. According to a later affidavit of William Keys, the interpreter, Brooke had also urged Croaker to return 'for the sake of his wife and two infants'.[39] Although this does not necessarily imply the innocence of Susannah, it speaks more loudly in her favour than a report in the *Kentish Chronicle* that: 'His [Croaker's] wife was arrested in England as she was about to set out to join her husband'.[40]

This last quotation was actually reported speech, as the Kent newspaper was translating, on 31 January, an account of Croaker's apprehension in Calais, which had appeared in *Le Journal de Paris* three days earlier.[41] The French story was itself dated at Calais on 22 January—three full days after the event—and does nothing but blur the perception of Croaker's true position. It seems the reporter at Calais obtained a police document, after it was filed, and copied its mistakes or introduced them himself. The broad substance of the French report—that 'Crowkar' was an absconding banker's clerk from Margate, traced to the Kingston Hotel, where he gave up his property—was correct. It may not have been correct, however, that this money was surrendered to the police, and it was definitely incorrect that the amount of money recovered amounted to '36,000 pounds sterling'.[42] The interesting point about the French report is that it includes little pieces of information, some of which are found nowhere else, and are unverifiable.[43] These tidbits state that Croaker was carrying unissued banknotes, which seems entirely possible; that his breach of trust was attributed to speculation in the public funds, which was, of course, his own story; that one hundred guineas had been offered for his arrest in England, which is new information; and that his wife was arrested on the way out to join him.

It is appropriate now to arrive at some judgement as to Susannah's position. The testimony of William Keys, and Croaker's letter to Sackett, seems to imply that she was innocent. The French account that she was arrested must be wrong, otherwise there seems no reason for her not to be charged. It is therefore unlikely that she was setting out for Calais, presumably with two infants, unless she was guiltless, in straitened circumstances, and simply planning to talk her husband into returning to England to accept his responsibilities as a father and an employee. One other point must be borne in mind: when Croaker absconded from Margate it was still 1814, so he was on the run for at least two or three weeks before he wrote to Sackett. It seems impossible to conclude that he had simply walked out on Susannah and his family, and made no contact with her over that period. She probably knew he was going to Calais; she might have known he was at the Kingston Hotel; she might indeed have planned to join him; but none of this is sufficient to convict her of any implication in criminal activities, at Canterbury or Margate, which her husband is known or believed to have perpetrated.

As Croaker retraces his steps, perhaps almost with a sense of relief, to settle his score at Margate, it remains to speculate briefly on why he fled abroad. It was certainly not a move which makes immediate sense. The only smart element was the timing: the Continent, so long closed because of the French Wars to all but the most intrepid Grand Tourists, was now being eagerly rediscovered, and Dover–Calais was by far the shortest and most practicable route. But if Croaker wished to get lost in the crowd, then it was ridiculous to write to Sackett from Dover, which as good as signalled his destination to be Calais; and once there, it was pointless to stay overnight as the risk of detection would be that much stronger. He presumably had some gold about him, but his main money consisted of Isle of Thanet banknotes, bearing Sackett's signature or not even issued. It is most unlikely that these would have been accepted anywhere on the Continent, with the possible exception of Ostende, which had a packet boat connection with Margate,[44] and there were probably agency arrangements between the banks in the respective towns. But if Croaker had been making for Ostende, why mark time in Calais, and with what bewilderment would an Ostende banker have greeted the sudden appearance of an English bank clerk wishing to get rid of his master's paper?

If account is also taken of the lack of any obvious way for Susannah and two infants discreetly to join Croaker abroad, then the flight to Calais simply reinforces the inept and illogical offences which he had committed earlier, and points once again to his total disorientation so soon after the scandal of the Canterbury brewery. There is, of course, one last possibility: that history is concealing a wider and murkier depth to the Croaker story, and that one day a gamut of answers and a gallery of new names will add a flavour of international intrigue to Croaker's Kentish misdemeanours. But for the time being he must remain a feckless, shell-shocked bank clerk with a subliminal wish to bring himself to justice.

4   The Trial, and Tribulations

Croaker, with his escort, arrived back in Margate on 22 January 1815.[1] He was presumably allowed to see his wife and children, albeit briefly, before appearing in front of a local magistrate, the Rev. W. F. Bayley, vicar of St John's. Ironically, it was Bayley who had baptised Croaker's children, but now the face was unsmiling. The solicitor John Boys, who was acting for Sackett, was also clerk to the magistrates and he accepted Croaker into his house overnight. This was a compromise arrangement; Croaker had not yet been charged or even arrested, but was a hostage to his own fortune at the home of an officer of the court. There was felt to be no great risk of his absconding again. Over the next two days Croaker and Sackett each put their version of events to the magistrates, and Brooke produced the money taken from Croaker at Calais. Sackett was formally asked whether he could identify the banknotes as his personal property, and he had to reply in the negative. They might well bear his signature, but so did all the other notes of the Isle of Thanet Bank in circulation. Unless he kept a record of the serial numbers of notes in his own possession, it was impossible to claim ownership.

What followed then was a little act of theatre, probably made with the tacit support of the magistrates. The money was formally returned to Croaker, 'who immediately and spontaneously' surrendered it to Sackett as the first repayment of the money he had, by implication, misappropriated. But then, from Croaker's point of view, matters took a turn for the worse. He was further remanded, to give John and Thomas Garrett, as friends of Sackett (John Garrett being presumably the former banker at Ramsgate), the opportunity to persuade him to surrender his real estate, including property of his wife.[2] This, they said, would be held by them as trustees for Sackett, who would thereby acquire an indemnity against further discrepancies found in the books of his bank, and would enjoy the product of the leasehold rents. Croaker was told not to worry: he had only to sign the deed of assignment, and if Sackett decided to press for Croaker's prosecution, 'it should be so managed as to do [him] no harm'. Croaker was clearly suspicious, because it took him two days to agree. Personal effects and real estate, both freehold and leasehold and valued between £3000 and £4000, were duly assigned to the Garretts. Thus, in one scribbled signature, Croaker deprived his wife of the inheritance that had come her way following the death of her brother (who had been her father's heir). Sackett was asked by the Garretts if he agreed to the assignment and the arrangement; and he formally replied that anything the Garretts did, he 'accepted as his own act'.

Already giving concern, events for Croaker now went downhill even faster. What he was being promised and what was happening around him were two different things. No sooner had he signed the deed than he was formally charged with having embezzled upwards of £1000. He was committed overnight to the London Hotel, in the charge of a constable, and the next day he and John Garrett went over Sackett's books to discover the irregularities. At the end of the day Croaker suffered another shock. No longer was he sent to the familiar surroundings of a Margate hotel; it was now the squalid cells of Dover gaol, set within the fastness of an impregnable castle. He was shackled into irons and committed for trial at the next General Sessions of the Cinque Ports. Sackett, meanwhile, lost no time in broadcasting his clerk's guilt. John Boys placed a notice dated 26 January 1815 in the local newspapers, requesting creditors of John Croaker to surrender all realisable assets to make up the deficiency in Sackett's books.[3] For Croaker and his family the humiliation was now public and events were gathering a momentum which denied all prospect of the discreet settlement which had enticed him back to England.

If the strict application of law had so far been acting in favour of Sackett, it was now Croaker's turn to benefit, albeit briefly, from its more compassionate face. He still had friends, perhaps orchestrated by Susannah, although their identity is not revealed in surviving court papers.[4] John Abbott, a year earlier, would have been top of the list, but now he was in the thick of his own problems at St Dunstan's Brewery, and if the speculations made above about Croaker's own involvement there are anything like correct, it was in both men's interests to avoid each other. The names of only two of Croaker's 'friends' can be guessed with confidence, on the grounds that they both testified for him as character witnesses in the later trial: one was John Garrett, who was evidently more dismayed by Sackett's tactics than he was shocked by Croaker's fraud, and the other was Benjamin Kidman, a new figure in this story. Kidman was a Margate wine merchant, who traded out of Hawley Square.[5] He also had many dealings with the Cobbs, and was widely respected in the town as a philanthropist, establishing a charity to apprentice boys for a seafaring career.[6] He had announced his intention to give up the wine business in 1811, but he appears to have retained it until 1815.[7] As Kidman was also a religious man, it seems well within his character that he would have worked behind the scenes for his errant young friend, even at the risk of offending Sackett.

It was Susannah and these men, therefore, with or without others, who probably obtained a writ of habeas corpus on 13 February 1815, or within three weeks of Croaker's committal.[8] The aim of this commonly-used instrument was to test the validity of a prisoner's conviction and secure his release on bail before the case came to trial. But the law was defeatingly slow. The writ was not returned until 25 April, along with the 'body' of the prisoner, to judges sitting in chambers in London, who had earlier sent the magistrates at Margate a writ of *certiorari* to establish the facts of the committal. The judges, led by the eminent Lord Ellenborough, reviewed the evidence, listened to the depositions of John Sackett, Robert Brooke, John Baker, and also one Robert Baker, and heard representations of counsel from both sides.[9] Sackett was now alleging that the fraud amounted to £3000, while Brooke's version of events in Calais was that Croaker had offered to return Sackett all his money, and reveal the whereabouts of the rest of it, if he (Sackett) would not press charges.[10] This was a new twist, and differed significantly from the versions of Baker and Keys who deposed that the idea of clemency had been a carrot-on-a-stick proffered by Sackett's side, to which Croaker had responded. Another new element introduced at this stage was the unfortunate fact, revealed when the bank's books were scrutinised by Garrett, that Sackett's account with Robarts & Co., his London agents, was carrying an unauthorised credit of £600.

The defence pressed for a total discharge on the grounds that the money recovered from Croaker in Calais could not be proven as the property of Sackett; but the more realistic aim was bail, for the technical reason that the warrant of detainer had omitted the adverb 'feloniously' in connection with the word embezzled. The prosecutor, on the other hand, argued that the word which had been used instead, 'fraudulently', came to the same thing, and on this point the judges agreed with him; and, anyway, the gravity of the case suggested that bail was inappropriate.

Croaker, therefore, was returned to his miserable conditions in Dover gaol, where he would have several more months to consider the vicissitudes of life and his diminishing chance of ever enjoying it again.

Counsel for the defence at this hearing, and also later, was John Gurney, who in time became a judge, a baron of the Exchequer, and a knight of the realm.[11] He gained a notoriety for dispensing 'the strictest justice', which the occasional lenient sentence did nothing but bring into sharper relief.[12] In 1815 he was still a barrister on the home circuit, well into middle age, with a reputation for skilful pleading at several trials of national importance. Ironically, it was in 1816, after he failed to get Croaker discharged, that he was elevated to the status of King's Counsel. The choice of Gurney for the Croaker trial was not fortuitous. According to one press report, he 'was specially retained',[13] which raises the interesting question—by whom? Croaker's solicitor is not known, and the choice of Gurney suggests further the influence and resources of Kidman and Garrett and even Abbott, all of whom had London connections.

Throughout the hot, flag-waving summer of 1815, when Englishmen drank themselves dizzy in celebration of Napoleon's defeat, Croaker rotted and roasted in his prison cell. In May he had been given a brief glimpse of the wider world, when he was taken unexpectedly to Dover Sessions: the intention was to try him for embezzling a cheque for £10 13s paid into Sackett's bank by a Margate brewer called Hunter, the charge having been agreed by the grand jury.[14] It was a slapdash indictment, and Gurney had no difficulty in getting the charge postponed. Later it was dropped altogether. The prosecution had not given the prisoner the necessary two days notice of the trial, and was forced into an admission of Croaker's good character before the alleged offence had taken place. But there was a warning of 'several other indictments' still to be made, and if Croaker had harboured any lingering hope that Sackett would consider him sufficiently punished, then the short trial in May undeceived him.

It is difficult to know how Susannah, with a baby and child of three, coped during these long months. Her husband was in gaol, her own inheritance was signed away, she was presumably ousted by Sackett from the bank flat,[15] and whatever teaching job she held in Margate would not have survived the social disgrace of her position. That she had worked as a teacher, before and between her confinements, is a reasonable assumption, given her experience in this field before she emigrated.[16] If she had run a school on her own account, then, social disgrace aside, she would have lost it in the assignment of her real estate to Sackett's trustees. It can be assumed that such near family as Susannah possessed would have rallied round her, but they were hardly in a position to help. Her husband's parents had worries of their own, and her sister, Mary Ann, was living in St Mary Bredin, within Canterbury, and planning her marriage to May Inge, the maltster.[17] It also seems unlikely that Dorcas Collington, in advancing old age, would have welcomed the little family back to Leaveland, although they might have stayed there in the short term. The only certain fact is that by early 1816 Susannah was writing from 'London', and the best guess is that she was staying with her brother's widow in Clerkenwell.[18]

On 18 October 1815 Croaker stood trial at Dover Sessions before Mr Recorder Kenrick accused of embezzling £3000 in Exchequer bills, the property of his employer.[19] This was undoubtedly the same £3000 as had been mentioned in the habeas corpus hearing, and the range of other allegations against him were, for one reason or another, not proceeded with. It had been intended to try Croaker, at the same time, on a charge of forgery (under which, if convicted, he risked the death penalty), but the grand jury did not accept the indictment. As for the other allegations—the misappropriation of Hunter's cheque and the bank's agency account—it was felt either that the main charge was so strong that they were not needed, or that the quality of the evidence on the lesser charges risked an acquittal. Thus, with only one charge against Croaker on the indictment sheet, the prosecution set about its case. Counsel on that side was now John Adolphus, taking over from Mr Marryat (or Marryot) and Mr Knapp, who had acted in April and May respectively, while Croaker was still represented by John Gurney. Adolphus was also an authoritative writer on contemporary English and French history. His most famous case as a barrister, five years after the Croaker trial, involved the unsuccessful defence of the Cato Street conspirators, convicted of plotting the death of Lord Castlereagh, the unpopular foreign secretary.[20]

Adolphus rehearsed the story of Croaker's flight, his letter to Sackett (which 'abounded with falsehoods'), and the apprehension in Calais. It appears that the machinations in Margate, which would have done little to further the prosecution cause, were not dwelt upon. Instead, Sackett was called to the stand, and he explained the details of the alleged embezzlement. According to his story, he had held two bills of exchange at his bank, one for £2000, the other for £1000, both issuing from 'Messrs. Rayner and Co. as a payment of a deposit on some advances made'.[21] When he returned to Margate from London, after Croaker had absconded, the bills were missing; Croaker had taken them to London for discounting by one Phillip Griffith, who was probably the wine merchant then trading at 53, Pall Mall,[22] and who had been forewarned of the transaction by a letter from Croaker dated 18 June 1814. Griffith duly discounted the bills of exchange for three £1000 Exchequer bills.[23] It might appear that he was simply swapping two pieces of paper for three worth exactly the same, but he was in effect discounting (that is to say, buying at less than face value) because Exchequer bills at that time were worth less than their denomination.[24] Armed with these new bills—a more liquid form of money—Croaker went to Robarts & Co., Sackett's correspondent bank in Lombard Street, and paid in the money to Sackett & Co.'s account. The allegations at this point become sketchy, but it seems that one of these three bills was later paid to Messrs Rayner, in part settlement of their debt, and Croaker misappropriated the other two, despite claiming 'that a friend had lent him the money'.

Croaker's defence saw the story in a different light. The law only allowed Gurney to plead the case to a certain point, and it was a matter for Croaker himself to address the jury, which he did 'in a very collected manner, and at some length'.[25] He claimed that Sackett needed the money from Rayners to finance a purchase of omnium then being arranged on his behalf by Messrs Robarts, and that he had written to Rayners for bills of exchange on Sackett's instructions, as ready money was in short supply. Croaker regarded himself as authorised to get the bills discounted by Griffith privately, because Sackett was owed a favour by Griffith and, in any case, it was 'disreputable' for a banker to seek a discount of bills for his own ends. Croaker was undoubtedly right on that point, as the inference would be drawn that Sackett's liquid assets were below the sum which he was seeking—an alarming revelation about a man who could be called upon at any time to honour in gold several thousand pounds worth of his own paper money. Croaker's story also makes sense in respect of Robarts & Co., as Sackett would have forfeited their confidence by asking them to accept Rayner's bills in payment for the securities. But if the money were, in a sense, laundered by Griffith, then all they saw was Exchequer bills and Sackett saved his dignity.

There are several technicalities to be explained at this stage. First, the bills of exchange which Sackett received from Rayners would probably have been accommodation bills.[26] These were widely used, often none too creditably, as little more than a contrivance to secure a loan. Sacketts would have been the drawer—the party who made out the bills—and Rayners the acceptor. The text of the bills would have stated that, in sixty days, Rayners undertook to pay Sackett £2000 in one bill, and £1000 in the other. (There were probably two bills, rather than one, in case Sackett did not need or expect to get both discounted.) The normal procedure was then for the drawer (in this case Sackett) to take the bill or bills, which carried the signature of the acceptor (Rayners), to a discount house (Griffith), which would then encash them at just below nominal value. The discounter, at the end of sixty days, then went to the acceptor and asked for the full sum. But because this was a trumped-up exercise between knowing parties, the drawer would repay the money to the acceptor before the discounter came knocking on the acceptor's door. In other words, the accommodation bill, if it worked, gave the drawer a loan of up to sixty days, interest free, to provide short-term liquidity.

In this instance, there is no evidence of how the affair turned out, but it can be presumed that Griffith went to Rayners for his money, when the bills matured, but Rayners had only received from Sacketts one-third of the debt. Thus, one way or another, there was a shortfall, which precipitated Croaker's disorganised flight to Calais. These matters were of little consequence in the trial itself, because the judge felt that the case was 'laid on a narrow compass'.[27] Indeed, the only point of issue, according to Recorder Kenrick, revolved around the transaction at Messrs Robarts' counter, and whether Croaker intended the Exchequer bills to be for his own use. Within this limited argument, there were two distinct but connected elements: whether Sackett needed the money to finance his purchase of securities (Sackett's evidence, after all, had not even raised the subject of omnium); and whether there was enough money in the agent's account all the time, in which case Sackett had no need to ask Croaker to act as he (Croaker) said he did. In addressing the jury, Kenrick spoke generally of Croaker's 'vilest and most detestable enormities', a phrase which seems too strong for the context. He pointed out that Croaker's defence had failed to show there was insufficient money in the agency account to pay for the stock. It was also not in Croaker's favour that his letter to Messrs Robarts, accompanying the paying-in of the Exchequer bills, made no mention of this imminent payment, which he was supposed to be making on Sackett's behalf. Furthermore, John Southan, Robarts' clerk, testified that he had no knowledge of when the instalment was due. In a nutshell, said Kenrick: 'If there was plenty of money at Robart's [*sic*] no remittance would be required, but if there was no money Mr. Sackett would have given the necessary directions [to Croaker to pay in the bills]'. Depending on which of these stories the jury believed, Croaker was guilty or innocent.

Benjamin Kidman and two members of the Garrett family, one being Croaker's former employer, were among witnesses who testified to his previous good character. With Kenrick's final instruction, that if doubt subsisted such testimonies should 'have their weight', the jury retired. It was but a token discussion and, fifteen minutes later, they returned with a verdict of guilty. Croaker can be imagined with his confidence wavering, his florid face drained of colour, and his voice beginning to falter. He now had a last chance to address the court, before Kenrick passed sentence, and could only repeat the points in which he passionately felt the injustice lay. What about the agreement reached in Calais? Did it count for nothing? Had he not fulfilled his part of the bargain? The money on his person had been surrendered, and in this trial he had not denied that the bills of exchange which he had discounted were the property of Sackett.

Kenrick was uncomfortable. The case, if proven, was nevertheless distasteful. It was not his business to be critical of Sackett, but he clearly had no difficulty in believing that Croaker's story of the 'arrangement' was the true one. It made not the least difference in law that certain assurances had been given, but it was quite wrong, on the part of Sackett, to have made them. In an unequivocal, if inelegant, piece of prose, no doubt with one frosty eye on the prosecution benches, Kenrick summed up the position: 'However disreputable the promises made might be, it was the duty of the parties to prosecute; it was a duty they owed to their country, and most likely if they had not prosecuted, they would have been prosecuted in their turn, for not prosecuting.' Yet Kenrick felt he could not overlook Croaker's co-operation, and the way he had been bluffed, and his instinct was to reflect these matters in the sentence. He acknowledged that 14 years transportation was the norm for such an offence, 'and he conceived that the extent of the crime in this case, as well as its intricacy, proved that artfulness was not wanting in the prisoner'. But in view of the wider circumstances of the case, Kenrick delivered Croaker the following sentence: *'That you be transported beyond the Sea to New South Wales, or as the Privy Council will direct, for the term of seven years'.*[28]

Unfortunately for Croaker, what followed in the next two minutes was an extraordinary change of mind on the part of Kenrick. It is best glimpsed through the press. There were three accounts of the Croaker trial published, the fullest being in the *Kentish Gazette* of 20 October 1815, which differed significantly from that of the same date in the *Kentish Chronicle*. The London *Times*, on 23 October, printed a report strongly resembling that in the *Kentish Gazette*, but with several omissions. It is possible, therefore, that there were three different reporters at the trial, although the likelihood is of only two, and that the man from the *Kentish Gazette* sold on his story in an abridged form. Be that as it may, the *Kentish Gazette* and *The Times* both reported Croaker's sentence to be seven years (the quotation above coming verbatim from the former), whereas the *Kentish Chronicle* made it fourteen, which is what it turned out to be. On 24 October the *Kentish Gazette* printed an apology, stating that its reporter had made an error and that the sentence was fourteen years and not seven.

For the reputation of British justice, this episode is troublesome and bizarre. Given the degree of detail in the report of the *Kentish Gazette*, and the extent to which its reporter used exact text, there seems only one explanation of events. Kenrick did indeed pass a seven-year sentence, but the mistake was rectified before the court rose, but after at least one reporter had left the room. It would have taken just a couple of tense minutes for a flustered clerk of the court to intimate respectfully to his lordship that the mitigation of a sentence for which the legislature, in his own words, 'directed' a sentence, was most unwise. Kenrick, in a discom- fiture only marginally less than Croaker's, but for a wholly different reason, would have hastily corrected his decision. Thus when the court rose, Croaker, according to the record, was sentenced to fourteen years, and the earlier sentence of seven was to be ignored as a slip of the tongue. Fortuitously, history has been more even-handed. At the time, the reporter was the scapegoat for having made an 'error'; but his only mistake was to leave a fraction early, perhaps to meet his editor's dead- line. Indeed, in making possible the above deduction as to Kenrick's indecision, his premature departure was wholly constructive.

As Croaker returned to his manacled misery in Dover gaol, it is easy to picture the despair of Susannah, and the embarrassed sense of remorse felt by those who, like the prisoner, had believed that Sackett would be as good as his word. There were clear grounds for an appeal and, three days after the sentence, Croaker set about it. In a petition to Lord Sidmouth, the Home Secretary, he reiterated the promises which had been made to him, the fact that his real and personal estate had been assigned to the Garretts in trust for Sackett, and the assurance which Sackett had given that prosecution would not result.[29] This petition was sent to Susannah who would have badgered all involved to be true to their conscience. The actual submission of the appeal was handled not by a solicitor, but by one John Sivewright, writing from Tavistock Square in London.[30] Sivewright, who also had an office at 37 Cornhill, in the City, is typical of the intriguing characters who flit in and out of the Croaker story, and whose relationship with him is tantalising and imponderable.

To the Right Hon.ble Lord Viscount Sidmouth
Secretary of State for the Home Department &c &c &c

The Petition of John Croaker a convict in Dover Gaol.
Humbly Sheweth

That your petitioner was tried
at the Sessions held for the Town &port of Dover on the
18th of this October last past and convicted of Embezzling
from his late employer John Sackett Banker Margate
two bills of exchange value together 3000£ — and
received the severe sentence of fourteen years transportation

That your petitioner previous to
his committal was solicited by the friends of the
prosecutor — at the prosecutors earnest request — to
endeavour to settle this unfortunate affair — solemnly
pledging himself to respect any arrangement they
might be enabled to make.

That according to such wishes and
relying on the honor of the parties. Your petitioner was
induced to make an assignment of his real &personal
Estate to Thomas & John Garrett Esquires in trust
for the benefit of the prosecutor — at the same time
receiving an assurance from them, and the prosecutor
in their presence, that no prosecution should in
consequence take place, — yet in open violation of
this pledged faith, your petitioner was indicted and
convicted as aforesaid. he therefore under the
peculiar circumstances of the prosecution — humbly
prays your Lordships permission to transport
himself and family for the given time:

And your Petitioner as in duty bound
will ever pray —
Dover Town Gaol October 21st 1815.   J Croaker

Petition of John Croaker and his wife Susannah (part only) against his conviction
(Public Record Office HO 47/55)

Sir,

I respectfully submit to you the
Inclosed papers in the case of my husband
John Croaker, convicted of Embezzlement and
now on board the Retribution Hulk.

His petition states, as the fact is, a great breach
of faith made by the Prosecutor & his Agents
whereby he was not only induced to return
from France, but to give into the hands of the
Prosecutor, after such return, a sum of One
Thousand & Ninety Two Pounds which had, by
the Magistrate, been restored to I Croaker as
his own—and also to assign a property belonging
to myself as the affidavits more particularly
set forth—which but for the pledge made
him, would have been an ultimate support
for myself & children instead of being left
to misery & want—these facts are fully
confirmed by the affidavits Inclosed.

1st of John Baher, managing Clerk to John
Boys Atty to the Prosecutor, who went to Calais
to request the said John Croaker to return

By profession, at the time of the trial, Sivewright was a merchant, but by 1817 he was described as a stockbroker, and he later became the keeper of the lottery office at 141 Oxford Street.[31]

Again, the law took agonisingly long to react. Not until February 1816, when Croaker was already on the hulk *Retribution* at Sheerness, was Lord Sidmouth in a position to look into the matter and Sivewright, hoping for an exercise of the royal mercy, despatched him the papers. These consisted of Croaker's letter from the previous October, a strikingly poignant plea from Susannah, urging the return of 'my birthright and my children's hope',[32] and the affidavits of John Baker and William Keys, discussed above. There can be little doubt as to the accuracy of these testimonies, as Keys was a disinterested party and neither man had anything to gain from lying. Baker, indeed, whose affidavit was particularly long and detailed, had something to lose from telling the truth. He had evidently resigned, or been sacked, for acting against the interests of his master's client, and it was as the 'late' managing clerk to Boys that he signed his deposition.

Lord Sidmouth felt the case had some merit, as the file was duly presented to the Prince Regent. An instruction then followed to Recorder Kenrick to review the appeal papers, state his own opinion of the propriety of the indictment, and make a recommendation, if justified, for the exercise of the royal prerogative.[33] Kenrick at that time was on holiday in North Wales; he was caught on the hop without trial notes, and, more significantly, not the least inclination to support natural justice in a case which he had nearly bungled, and which would fade mercifully from attention once Croaker was overseas. Any sympathy which he had once felt for Croaker was now utterly dissipated, and in a rambling, irrational, and questionably accurate response,[34] he raised not the least excuse for the prisoner's pardon. The question of Sackett's promises was handled as an incidental, if not an irrelevant, consideration in a trial which had been conducted fairly and squarely by the dictate of law. As for Croaker, he had been cheating Sackett 'daily' by altering the accounts; he was a dyed-in-the-wool reprobate, and if ever there was a case when the law should take its proper course, this was it. Lord Sidmouth might not have been convinced by this, but the Prince Regent, in his fickle state of mind and with distractions of the flesh, was not the ideal man to sense an injustice. Croaker's appeal was rejected.

In many ways the Croaker trial was remarkable. Although most of the points to be discussed below are apparent only from a modern perspective, the court proceedings were sufficiently interesting, or maybe controversial, at the time, to encourage a Margate publisher to recount the story in a booklet, advertised in December 1815.[35] It is unfortunate that no copy has been traced,[36] because an understanding of the local feeling towards Sackett might have emerged. Even before the trial, his position in Margate as a banker, if not as a citizen, was becoming increasingly untenable. Confidence in his paper money would have been low, the support of the Cobbs could not last indefinitely, and it is very probable that Croaker's expertise, during his honest years, was genuinely missed. On 6 August 1815 Sackett was forced to announce that he could no longer honour his notes, but he wished to assure his customers that his personal estate was equal to all the demands of his creditors.[37] This confidence was put to the test when his house in Church Fields (Margate), the bank, and other properties comprising eleven lots in all, were auctioned on 17 August 1815.[38]

The Isle of Thanet Bank was thus wound up even before Croaker went to court, and Sackett's description, in all the press reports of the trial, was accurately termed 'late banker' or 'late Proprietor'. For the other banking-houses of the region this failure threatened to be calamitous in the short term, as a run could start and spread with a speed which defeated the most conscientious attempts of solvent bankers to match their liabilities with gold. Sackett's wording had been reassuring, so as not to provoke panic, but later in August the clearly worried firm of Burgess & Co. wrote to Cobbs, asking what they were to do with the useless Isle of Thanet notes in their possession.[39] Cobbs could do nothing but exercise, with something less than enthusiasm, their role as linchpins of the East Kent economy. They agreed to honour Sackett's notes,[40] or at least those presented to them by other bankers, so when the Isle of Thanet Bank passed out of existence, it did so with few repercussions.

In a sense, Sackett got his just deserts, because if he had kept his agreement with Croaker, the losses to the firm had been so small, and the assets surrendered by Croaker so considerable, that confidence could have been restored quickly with minimal damage. Croaker could simply have been sacked and told to leave the area. As Kenrick stated, a deal should never have been made; but, once it had, it was dishonourable for Sackett to renege. In the eyes of his customers and creditors, better a banker who stood by his word, than one who not only broke it, but denied having given it in the first place. The arrangement would have been seen for what it was—a ruse to get Croaker back into custody, which deceived not only its victim but those who executed Sackett's commission. It is interesting that Kenrick, while he was prepared to go a little way in condemning Sackett's position, had instructed the jury 'that the conduct of the Master in this case, was not to be enquired into'.[41] This had the effect of removing from their arena all consideration of whether or not an agreement had been reached, and it appears to have hampered the defence from calling witnesses to support the same point—until the appeal stage. There is also no sign that Southan, the clerk from Robarts & Co., was asked to state whether or not there was sufficient money in the agency account to meet Sackett's payment for stock, which was allegedly then due. Yet virtually on this point alone Croaker's fate was determined.

Another troublesome aspect of the Croaker case, to modern eyes, is the legal basis of the charges against him. The trial was a criminal matter, as the prosecution was in the name of the King, but in another sense the prosecutor was Sackett. Confusion between the words 'feloniously' and 'fraudulently', discussed above, merely reinforces the grey area which stood between civil and criminal actions. As the trial opened, prosecuting counsel asserted that the 'case was fully within the act to prevent embezzlement of property by servants from their masters';[42] thus the banking element had no bearing, and a grocer's assistant or a merchant's clerk were indictable by their employer to the same extent. Counsel's reference was to the Embezzlement Act, 1799.[43] But his statement was in total contrast to Kenrick's view of the case, when the latter was replying to Lord Sidmouth. What he wrote then was that the conviction was 'under the Act commonly called the Bankers Act', an assertion which could not possibly be right, as no such act existed.[44] Kenrick's letter even went on to refer to a 'specific robbery' (underlined in the original), which is no more understandable.

The Croaker trial seemed to produce nothing but losers. A bank failed, reputations were lost, and the legal process was shambolic in concept and flawed in execution. Admittedly, a guilty man was eventually punished, but retribution owed less to logic and due procedure than to a succession of deteriorating circumstances, reminiscent of the awful inevitability of a Greek tragedy. Perhaps if one person was ultimately responsible for Croaker's conviction, then it was not the man himself, nor was it Sackett, Gurney, Kenrick, or even (by his absence) John Abbott. Arguably, it was Garrett the banker, as he was uniquely in a position to help. True, he acted as a character witness for Croaker, but he could have done a lot more. He knew all the parties well and was clearly respected. Croaker trusted him with property, after a heart-to-heart discussion, and Sackett said publicly that anything Garrett decided in this matter was all right by him. Baker's deposition implies that Garrett was neutral, therefore he could only have been shocked by Sackett's duplicity.

Once Croaker was convicted, and the appeal was afoot, Garrett had to choose between divided loyalties. If he did nothing, Sackett had won the day. But if he made a deposition about the truth of events, as did Baker and Keys, then Sackett would have been shown up by one of his own collaborators. The deposition of a senior banker coupled with that of the managing clerk to Sackett's solicitor, might well have had Croaker released. Garrett must have been approached by Susannah, but he declined to become involved. Perhaps if Croaker had been heading for capital punishment he would have intervened, but the Isle of Thanet was a small place and its principal families had to live together. Thus Garrett stayed silent, and perhaps spent the rest of his life making peace with his conscience.

The postscript on the trial belongs to Messrs Cobb, as they alone saw any benefit. They took over Sackett's business, thereby enjoying a monopoly of banking in Margate for many years to come, and purchased for £15 the very counter behind which an ambitious John Croaker had once demonstrated his pride in a new responsibility.[45]

5   A Ticket of Leave

Sheerness, where Croaker was taken by wagon, was reckoned one of the unhealthiest places in England.[1] The town was built on a swamp, on the northern edge of the Isle of Sheppey, and if the Dutch had not invaded the Thames Estuary in 1667 it might never have arisen from the rushes. Its strategic importance at the mouth of the River Medway earned the town a royal dockyard, wherein lay the hulk *Retribution*, Croaker's temporary destination. A more dispiriting place, when strafed by the north wind of winter, could scarcely be imagined. This harbour, between November 1815 and April 1816, was Croaker's unenviable home.

Hulks, within the confines of the royal dockyards, had been for nearly 40 years before Croaker's conviction the regular prisons of England, supplementing the town and county gaols in which the accused were held on remand.[2] Essentially, they were old vessels, sometimes captured warships, moored or beached, stripped of their superstructure, and hollowed into a cage. In airless and insanitary conditions, pushed pell-mell together, men reverted to a kind of atavism. In the worst hulks, under a blind and brutal regime, gang violence, murder, suicide and sodomy punctuated a timeless, twilight existence in medieval squalor. Even the thief James Hardy Vaux, seldom lost for words, found the description of conditions in the *Retribution* almost impossible: 'nothing short of a descent to the infernal regions can be at all worthy of a comparison'.[3]

Fortunately for Croaker, this was not the same hulk, despite the name, and in the five years which had elapsed since Vaux's (second) incarceration, conditions had generally improved, thanks to a select committee of the House of Commons. This committee, sitting in 1811–12, found that life in the hulks was sub-human; and as men were often released in a more depraved state than when they had entered, the idea was counterproductive.[4] The reforms which followed led to prisoners being more closely supervised, with every deck of the hulk being divided by a passage, flanked by rows of cells, each holding between ten and sixteen prisoners still, of course, kept in irons. A further advance was that convicts were segregated according to the nature of their crime. While this had a disadvantage, in that a burglar, for example, could learn better tricks of the trade from his cell-mates, it meant that a non-violent criminal like Croaker was now in less danger of humiliation from the ruffians. It is also possible, as happened at Woolwich,[5] that prisoners of a clerical disposition were found jobs ashore in the dockyard, escaping for a few hours the reeking 'tween-decks which no amount of parliamentary concern could improve to acceptable standards.

After such a long time on remand in Dover gaol, where conditions were perhaps no less noisome than those on the hulks, Croaker was tough enough to endure the winter. There is no reason to think his health was seriously affected by his imprisonment, or this would have been a further argument in the petitions for royal mercy which were submitted in February 1816, co-ordinated by John Sivewright. Instead, the petitions were based on the injustice of Croaker's bad treatment by Sackett, and the destitution which had now resulted for Susannah and the children. It is probable that the three of them, evidently living in London, were staying with Susannah's sister-in-law. Once every three months, on a Sunday afternoon, Croaker could have received visitors. On that basis, he probably saw Susannah twice during his time at Sheerness. They were also entitled to exchange letters, although the service was unreliable.

The damning reaction of the trial judge, Kenrick, to Croaker's appeal is reflected in the conclusion to his report: 'if ever there was a case in which the Law ought to be permitted to take its course, this is one which requires that it should so be done'.[6] And so, rightly or wrongly, it *was* done. On 12 May 1816 Croaker, with 59 other men from the *Retribution*, was transferred to the *Mariner*, a ship of 449 tons built at Whitby in 1807, and chartered for the carriage of convicts and a few free settlers to the penal colony of New South Wales. The ship had already taken 85 prisoners from the hulk *Justitia* at Woolwich, and was to take on another one at the Cape of Good Hope. With crew, guard, and other necessary personnel, the *Mariner* sailed with a total of 225 people, its full complement under the regulations of the day, and a small cargo of unspecified freight.[7]

By this time Croaker had heard the best news to come his way for some eighteen months: Susannah and the two children were to join him in New South Wales. There is no reason to believe the love for his family, stated in that desperate letter to Sackett of 17 January 1815, was insincere, and the prospect of reunion in the colony would have fortified him for the voyage. At another level, he must also have been gratified, as it was no small achievement for a wife to be allowed to go. Such magnanimity from the Colonial Office seems, on the face of it, unlikely, as more requests for a passage were refused than were accepted. In May 1816, it was stressed that 'every precaution' was taken in selecting wives of convicts allowed to travel. The criterion was to choose those 'who appeared most likely not to become burthensome to the Colony upon their arrival'. Lord Sidmouth confirmed that permission was granted only 'under very particular circumstances',[8] which certainly squares with the rebuttal given a few years earlier to the wife of the convict James Hardy Vaux. He wrote in his memoirs that the Secretary of State was unhelpful 'on account of the bad reports received of those women who had already been suffered to go out free with their husbands'.[9] No record has been found of Susannah's application. This might simply indicate, as it evidently does in Vaux's case, a missing file. When all the circumstances are weighed, the conclusion seems inevitable that she and the children were granted a special concession. To understand this it is necessary to revert to Croaker's petition to Lord Sidmouth, written in Dover gaol on 21 October 1815, soon after his conviction.[10] This document, drafted in the nadir of despair, complained bitterly about the arrangement dishonourably abandoned by Sackett and sought leave for his wife and family to join him. There was no direct plea for the quashing of his sentence, as he must have considered his case was hopeless.

In February 1816, when Sivewright organised the despatch of this petition to Lord Sidmouth, with the one from Susannah and the two depositions, the thrust of the appeal had somewhat altered. The case now appeared so strong (thanks to the depositions—especially Baker's), that the aim was nothing less than royal mercy, in other words an annulment of the sentence. This outcome, however, became impossible when Croaker's cause was so summarily dismissed by Kenrick. But if Lord Sidmouth no longer had a reason for bothering the Prince Regent, he might still have been troubled by the general injustice. It seems, therefore, that Sidmouth took the middle road.[11] The sentence would stand, but the substance of Croaker's petition of October 1815, that his wife and children be allowed to join him in New South Wales, was granted.

As Susannah had irrevocably assigned her personal estate to Sackett, in the mistaken understanding that it would settle her husband's legal and moral debt for his misdemeanours, the further question arises: how did she afford to travel? Her outlay included the cost of provisions on board, reputedly 'no small item of expense'.[12] As Sackett had relieved Susannah of any assets which might have been realised for the journey, it is likely she received some kind of charity. Her husband's parents can be ruled out as a source, as they had difficulty fending for themselves. It is also doubtful whether John Abbott, keeping his distance from Croaker after the brewery scandal, made any subvention, and the most probable provider of money was Garrett, whose mind was ill at ease. However, the Kemp family, large and widely spread, could well have seen it dutiful to look after their own. It is regrettable that no insight is possible into their assessment of the Croakers' position. Was Susannah an innocent victim of her husband's dishonesty, or did they see her, from their fuller knowledge of her character, as corruptible? The answer would affect the motive for seeing her go, rather than the decision to make it possible.

The only certainty about Susannah's departure is that she had little time to prepare. She and the children were assigned to the *Elizabeth*, a ship of roughly the same size and age as the *Mariner*, but scheduled to receive its convicts from the hulks at Portsmouth, rather than the Thames Estuary.[13] The *Elizabeth* began its journey at Deptford, on about 30 April, and it is possible that, in the few days at her disposal, Susannah organised her luggage to go on board at the outset. Her own embarkation, with the children, was probably at Portsmouth in mid-May, a straightforward journey from London by mail coach, but again a significant expense.[14] And so it was that husband and wife in different ships, he in irons, she with some dignity, found themselves pitching down the English Channel at much the same time, heading for a society which bore little resemblance to the traditions and values to which they had been accustomed.

The details of Croaker's voyage are to some extent known, because the ship's surgeon, John Haslam, wrote about his experiences. As a literary genre, the journals of ships' doctors are not uncommon, and the Public Record Office has many manuscript accounts of sickness and suffering on the open seas. Haslam's account, by contrast, was published in 1819, and for that reason it appears, rather curiously, to have been overlooked.[15] In any event, *Convict-Ships. A Narrative of a Voyage to New South Wales in the Year 1816 in the Ship Mariner, describing the Nature of the Accommodation, Stores, Diet, &c. together with an account of the Medical Treatment and Religious Superintendence of these Unfortunate Persons* differs markedly in content from the works of his professional colleagues. The rambling title prepares the reader for something more philosophical than a log, based on medical incidents, and the little work—only 23 pages—is basically an essay in what Haslam termed 'moral therapeutics'. The arrangement is distinctly layered. Indeed, if the structure is compared, at some risk of flippancy, with a sandwich, then the slices of bread are medical while the filling is moralistic to the point of overt religion.

Haslam's work is reproduced as Appendix I.[16] His narrative begins with ten factual (and very useful) pages on the ship's provisions, medical supplies, and conditions for the convicts. He then moves abruptly over the next dozen pages to describe and justify his 'grand object' of turning inveterate sinners into practising Christians—and has to confess with some bitterness his total failure. He made not one convert, and the deceits of those whom he had trusted wounded him to the core. There was one young man of good education who listened to Haslam's words, kept himself apart from the dissolute gangs, helped with divine services and studied the Bible, yet picked the first unguarded pocket on shore at Port Jackson. Even before the main voyage had begun, Haslam was downcast and bewildered. Anchored in the Downs, off Deal, the ship was visited by the wife of one of the convicts, a decent-enough man to all appearances, who was given a loving farewell and some comforts for the voyage. She was rewarded, in the final embrace, by a sleight of hand which saw her money and wedding ring transferred to her husband. When challenged, he feigned innocence and would not see her again for fear of over-taxing his emotions. In this instance, as in others, Haslam's evangelism had not the least impact and in case such pathetic failure should discredit him, he was at pains to end his narrative on an up-beat note. At New South Wales, he landed 'all of them [the convicts], without a single exception, in good health, and fully capable of executing any labour that the Governor might direct them to perform'. Thus, if he failed in his personal crusade, at least he got his job right.

It is worth digressing from the main narrative to make a judgement about Haslam's importance. As a medical log, his work is of no consequence, when set against the wider literature in this subject.[17] As a diary of the voyage, it is little better—only a few incidents are recounted and there is no sense of the tension which often arose between master and surgeon, aggravated by the ill-discipline of crew and guard. However, in two other ways, mutually contrasting, the book has a value. At a practical level, Haslam made a clear and succinct description of the convicts' diet and the ship's provisions, while on a psycho-analytical plane he peered into the convicts' minds. In the latter respect, he is open to a charge of ingenuousness, and he openly admitted his 'inexperience' with criminality. But the fact that a naval surgeon should even attempt a kind of moralistic psychiatry is interesting and invites a closer enquiry into Haslam's background and career.

His full name was John Haslam junior, therefore his father was called John, and the *Dictionary of National Biography* conveniently lists a Dr John Haslam (1764–1844).[18] This eminent man worked for many years at the Bethlehem Hospital in East London, a lunatic asylum, and was one of the best-respected psychiatrists of his day. His many published works include *Considerations on the Moral Management of Insane Persons* (1817), so he was strongly principled and a religious dimension to his work can be easily deduced. Dr Haslam had two sons educated at Merchant Taylors' School, in the City of London, one of whom was called John, a pupil from 1806 to 1808.[19] He, surely, was the naval surgeon. The registers of Bethnal Green, where Dr Haslam worked, reveal the baptism of John Haslam junior on 25 November 1792; he was therefore 23 when he embarked on the *Mariner*. As he entered the *Navy List* only on 17 August 1815, his youthfulness is confirmed. This would have been his first voyage on a convict ship, and he tackled his responsibilities with a verve and idealism inherited from his father.[20]

Haslam makes clear the conditions under which Croaker sailed. On coming aboard, the convicts were each issued with a change of linen and new clothes, including a blue kersey jacket and waistcoat, two pairs of trousers, and two checked linen shirts.[21] They were provided with 'good flockbeds, and blankets', but slept four men to every six-foot square; thus any antisocial proclivities of one were an obnoxious reality for the other three. The bedding was brought on deck each morning to be aired, while the prison quarters were washed and cleaned. During daylight hours two fumigating lamps, holding vinegar, were hung above the beds, while fresh air penetrated the prison by a permanent system of pipes and a wind-pump. The convicts themselves were allowed on deck in rotation for two hours at a time, from six in the morning until nightfall, weather and security permitting. Haslam set great store by hygiene, which met fully the standards expected by free emigrants. In fact, the convicts were better off, in his view, because their cleanliness was enforced. Three times a week, he and the captain inspected each man's clothing.

For meals, the convicts were divided into messes, each of six men, where the menu rotated strictly on a seven-day cycle. The only constant allowance was bread, rationed theoretically at 4 lbs a day. On Sundays and Fridays the men received 8 lbs of beef, and on Wednesdays there was 6 lbs of pork. On three days there were 4 lbs of flour, on two days 4 lbs of rice, and on four days 3 lbs of peas. The only fruit was raisins, of which 1 lb was allowed on three days. Four other ingredients made up the diet—butter, oatmeal, sugar, and a very small quantity of suet. If Croaker found all this boring, at least he could look forward to half a

Typical conditions in a convict ship in the early nineteenth century (by permission of the National Library of Australia)

pint of port wine twice a week; and occasionally the food could be enlivened by mustard or lemon juice, of which the ship had large stocks. It also held 206 lbs of 'Portable Soup'. Items such as tea, chocolate, tapioca, ginger and pepper were aboard as well, but regarded more as medicines. Generally, the range of comestibles seems reasonable, although Haslam would always have been concerned by the possibility of scurvy among convicts or crew.[22] As regards portions, it should be appreciated that deliberately short measures, and pilfering by the military guard, meant that convicts often received less food than their entitlement.

Croaker was not the only convict aboard with a middle-class vocation. His fellow criminals included an attorney, a schoolmaster and a clerk.[23] But Haslam made no distinction by profession in his bitter dismissal of their collective worth. He blamed 'premature commerce' with women for corrupting them. And 'if education in some instances had diminished the temptation to crime, it had also augmented the facilities to its commission'. In other words, literacy was no path to honesty, unless acquired against a moral and essentially religious background. The schoolmaster was at least of some use to Haslam, even if his character were irredeemable: he translated the 'flash' language of the convicts into a vocabulary which the surgeon understood.[24] By inference, Croaker was in no way disassociated from the general depravity. It was probably open to him, had he wished, to seek a clerical position within the ship, which would have made the passage more congenial.[25] But Haslam would have mentioned it, searching as he was for any an action in the least degree altruistic.

In Croaker's favour, it is difficult to accept Haslam's unqualified condemnation of the convicts, if only because the modern mind does not make religious sensibility the ultimate yardstick of human worth. There must have been some convicts less obnoxious than others. When the ship was caught in a bad storm off the Cape of Good Hope, there is no reason to place Croaker among the blaspheming few who shouted down the surgeon's panicky prayers and laughed at the thought of their own destruction. Nor was Croaker, in all probability, among the mutineers who 'hourly meditated' the seizure of the ship, and came within an ace of success on the night of 28 September, when they cut through from the prison to the hold in the course of a furious gale.[26] As Croaker was perhaps the only man in the ship who had his wife and children sailing out to the colony at much the same time, it was not in his interests to act in a way which might prejudice his freedom on arrival—still less to join forces with conspirators who would have sailed the ship elsewhere.

When the *Mariner* reached Sydney Cove on 12 October 1816, Croaker found that his wife and children were already there. The *Elizabeth*, a slightly larger vessel, had made the journey in 123 days, arriving on 5 October.[27] No incidents are known about her voyage. The ship had been carrying 153 convicts, the usual complement of crew and guard, and some interesting passengers.

Susannah Croaker found herself in the company of men who were to have a lasting influence on the management and direction of New South Wales, and in particular on the judiciary. The three most distinguished passengers, all destined to figure prominently in Croaker's later life, were John Wylde, his lawyer father Thomas Wylde, and Joshua John Moore.[28] John Wylde, a 35-year-old lawyer educated at Cambridge, was the colony's newly-appointed judge advocate. He was to be knighted in 1827. Wylde was accompanied by his wife, Elizabeth, their 3-year-old son, and two servants. His father, who had left a prosperous London practice,

A LIST of STORES shipped on board the
Mariner —— Convict Ship,
Thomas Herbert, Master, for the Use of
145 Male Convicts, Guard, and Passengers, during their Voyage to New South Wales;
and of Clothing for the Use of the Convicts
upon their arrival at the Colony.

ansport-Office,

Articles of Comfort for Use during the Voyage.

Mustard	150 ℔
Soap	1056 — 27 large 27 small
Combs	10 No.
Razors	
Hone	1
Strop	
Portable Soup	266 ℔
Lemon Juice	81 Gallons

Articles in Case of Sickness.

Tea	36 ℔
Sugar	173 —
Chocolate	9 —
Sago *(Tapioca)*	15 —
Scotch Barley	300 —
Ginger	12 Ounces
Black Pepper	3 ℔
Allspice	6 —
Red Port Wine	132 bottles
Rice	28 ℔
Pearl Barley	18 —

Fumigating Articles.

Tar	1 Barrel
Brimstone Crude	45 ℔
Vinegar	60 Gallons
Fumigating Lamps	
Extra Wicks	2 Sets
Oil	4 Gallons
Oil of Tar	

Hospital Furniture.

Canvas Jackets	
Trowsers	pairs
Calico Waistcoats	98 pairs
Cotton Hose	18 No.
Pocket-handkerchiefs	18 —
Nightcaps	18 —
Towels	15 pairs
Sheets	

Provisions for convicts aboard the *Mariner* (Public Record Office CO 201/82, pp. 40–2, AJCP Reel 38)

Calico Pillow Cases .... *15 pairs*
Pewter Bed-pans .... *2 No*
Urinals *2*
Spitting-pots *2*
Close-stool-pans and Chairs .... *2 of each*
Tin Tea Kettles .... *3 No*
Ditto Saucepans of Sorts .... *9 "*
Ditto japanned drinking mugs .... *18 "*
Knives and Forks .... *18 of each*
Water Purifier .... *1 No*
Charcoal for ditto .... *54 Bushels*
Bathing Tub .... *1 No*
Pails .... *4 "*
Airing Stove .... *1 "*
Ventilating Stove .... *1 "*
Kegs .... *25 "*
Spare Bedding ....

Clothing for the Use of the Convicts upon their arrival.

Yellow ~~Blue~~ Kersey Jackets .... *145 No*
Ditto Waistcoats *145*
Raven-duck Trowsers .... *145 pairs*
Ditto ditto for use during the Voyage *145*
Shirts .... *135 No*
Stockings .... *290 pairs*
Shoes .... *145 "*
Woollen Caps .... *145 No*
Beds complete .... *210 No*
Cotts .... *8 "*

Articles for the Security of the Convicts.

Bazzels with Chains .... *145 No*
Oak Blocks, with Iron Plates and Rings .... *2 "*
Stakes *2*
Hand-hammers with Handles .... *2 "*
Chissels .... *4 "*
Punches .... *4 "*
Handcuffs .... *31 pairs*
Extra Rivetts .... *6 dozen*

Medicines as per List transmitted. *to the Surge*

Sydney Cove and Town, New South Wales, with the *Mariner*, *Elizabeth* and *Willerby* at anchor: view believed painted between 12 and 29 October 1816 (From an album of watercolours relating to the East India Company and the *Mariner*, kindly provided from the private collection of Tim McCormick, antiquarian Australian arts dealer, Woollahra)

became clerk of the peace and Crown solicitor in his son's office. Moore became John Wylde's clerk, and was also his brother-in-law.

It is fascinating to ponder Susannah's shipboard status in such illustrious company. Small children, of course, are ignorant of social distinctions, and the young Wylde must have played openly with the young Croakers. For the parents it was, on the face of it, quite a different matter. The Wyldes represented the Establishment, not to mention the law, and would have thought a convict's wife beneath their dignity. But 123 days in a very small space in a limitless sea was a melting-pot for land-based conventions. Furthermore, Susannah was personable, noted in later life for her 'clever lady-like deportment'.[29] This implies that she was neither socially inhibited nor lacking intelligence. After several weeks at sea, in the boredom of the doldrums, a listless John Wylde would have been receptive to the account of her husband's skills and competence, perhaps even sympathetic to the tale of unjust conviction. In this way Susannah was probably instrumental in securing Croaker a placement in Wylde's office, soon after his arrival in Sydney.

Croaker himself had to loiter on the *Mariner* for six days before being taken ashore, although Susannah and the children had already disembarked. In that interval, the convicts were questioned as to their treatment and food on the voyage, their state of health, and their occupation. What they could see of the colony, from shipboard, was hardly prepossessing. Sydney looked a scattered, unlovely town with only a few buildings of any consequence. The scenery was more reassuring, with wooded creeks reminiscent of southern England and weather distinctly warm for early October. But clearly they were arriving at a place which was little better than a garrison. This was an upstart community, living by its wits, materialistic, and set within a regime so authoritarian that it possessed, according to Wentworth, 'neither a council, a house of assembly, nor even the privilege of trial by jury'.[30] The overall population was about 15 000, of whom one third were convicts. Men predominated, accounting for roughly half the total population, while about 20 per cent were adult females and some 30 per cent were children.[31]

To be more precise, society existed at four levels. The first class of citizens comprised senior officials, high-ranking military officers, and the richer merchants; next came free settlers, many of whom set up in trade; thirdly, other householders and traders who had once been prisoners; and lastly, free labourers and convicts.[32] The Croakers could aspire, in the short term, to the third level, but a feature of life in the colony was a considerable and enduring tension between free settlers and pardoned convicts. Lachlan Macquarie, who had become governor in 1810, set about energetically to improve amenities, commerce and communications;[33] but he was less successful in arguing the basic morality that a reformed convict was potentially as good a citizen as a person with no criminal record. It was a fact of life that many convicts in New South Wales, with their variety of trades and professions, were indispensable for the development of the colony. There was no case for retaining them as prisoners unless they continued to offend. The involvement of convicts in civil matters was certainly *faute de mieux*, and no doubt failed to meet the concept of retribution which some free settlers thought desirable; but without it the economy had no means to expand.

Governor Macquarie was distinctly liberal in promoting the interests of convicts who were potentially recruits to the scanty middle class. He was empowered to issue a concession called a ticket of leave, which basically exempted the holder from compulsory public labour, letting him work for his own benefit and acquire property. This was offset by

A ticket of leave (reverse side opposite) of the type granted to Croaker (State Records of NSW, SZ 1051.3, reproduced by kind permission)

restrictions as to residence, reporting obligations and a duty to attend church. The ticket of leave was a controversial concession, branded at the time as 'pernicious and indefensible',[34] not least because Macquarie ignored his own guidelines.

He should have waited three years in every instance, during which time the convict would have exhibited good behaviour. In fact, between 1813 and 1820, Macquarie granted 1716 tickets of leave of which 450 were issued immediately on arrival, especially to convicts who were physically weak, or showed 'pretensions to gentility'.[35] This liberality had

DESCRIPTION.

Standing No. of Prisoner.

Name ....

Native Place..................

Trade or Calling............. *Laborer*

Year of Birth................. *1805*

Height............................. *5 ft 4*

Complexion ....

Hair .... *Brown*

Eyes .... *Hazel*

General Remarks............

1. "Holders of Tickets-of-Leave for the District of Sydney, residing within the Town, shall be Mustered in the Parishes in which they reside, under the inspection of a Police Magistrate, upon the first day of every Month (or the second, if the first shall fall on a Sunday), at such place and hour for each Parish as the First Police Magistrate shall appoint."

3. "If a Ticket-of-Leave Holder shall quit his residence for another, in the same Parish, he shall within twenty-four hours report in writing to the Wardsman the place to which he removes, or, if the removal be from one Parish to another, he shall report in like manner his removal and actual residence, both to the Wardsman whose parish he quits, and to the Wardsman within whose parish he takes up his new residence. Any neglect of this regulation will cause an immediate Cancellation of his Ticket."

4. "Holders of Tickets-of-Leave residing without the Town of Sydney, but within the District for which Petty Sessions are held at Sydney, shall be Mustered Quarterly in Sydney, under the inspection of a Police Magistrate, on the first days of January, April, July, and October in every year, (or the second, if the first should fall on a Sunday,) at such place and time as the First Police Magistrate shall appoint."

5. "Holders of Tickets-of-Leave in the other Districts of the Colony shall be mustered Quarterly, on the days mentioned in the preceding Regulations, at the Court House at which the Petty Sessions for such District are held, by a Police Magistrate, where such is stationed in the District, or otherwise by the Clerks of Petty Sessions, under the inspection of a Justice of the Peace acting for the District."

8. "The Magistrate Superintending the Muster will, whenever he thinks it necessary, interrogate the holder of a Ticket-of-Leave respecting his means of subsistence and manner of life, and if he shall not be satisfied that the Ticket-of-Leave holder subsists honestly, he will render a Special Report of the case to the Principal Superintendent of Convicts, for the Governor's information."

an ulterior benefit, in that it meant fewer people to be maintained at public expense. Later, the abuse of the system was curbed by statute, imposing a minimum wait of six years for a 14-year sentence,[36] but in 1816 Macquarie was at his most munificent and Croaker could benefit. He, and perhaps seven others from the *Mariner*,[37] were granted an immediate ticket of leave. Of the other convicts, 82 were taken to outlying settlements for distribution to the farms of free settlers, or other duties; and the remainder, more than 50 strong, were allocated to Government work gangs in Sydney.[38]

Susannah also had an enviable concession. She and the children were placed by Macquarie 'on the stores' for a period of six months from about 15 October 1816.[39] This was an early and rarely-awarded form of state benefit, entitling Susannah to draw free rations from the commissariat. Suddenly, for the whole family, the privations of the journey must have seemed almost worth while. The brash colony was no substitute for the land and the life they had forfeited, but the irons were unlocked, the Governor was looking distinctly paternalistic, and the stigma of conviction was fading in the heady hopes of a new beginning.

For the first time in some 21 months, the Croaker family could reunite. They set up home somewhere in George Street, Sydney, which ran southward for about two miles from the harbour's edge to a square near the site of the present Central railway station.[40] At the harbour end the houses were of good quality; but the respectability decreased as the street gave way to one-storey, windowless cottages and ramshackle commercial yards. It was a time when Macquarie was trying to put some order and purpose into the infrastructure, which had grown haphazardly in the wake of long and liberal leases.[41] Possibly, George Street was chosen more for Susannah's sake than John's, as it contained the school for young ladies of Mary Greenway, wife of the ex-convict and architect Francis Greenway.[42] Susannah might have been employed there, before setting up on her own account.

After their middle-class life in Kent, the Croakers would have found the ambience of Sydney a test of their resilience and capacity to improvise. The cost of living was high, due partly to a poor wheat crop, and refinements were very limited. It was not a question of what was fashionable, but of what was available. People in the lower social orders ate what they could get, which was not necessarily what they liked, nor what they were used to. Sydney market, open three days a week, was a good source of fruit, vegetables, poultry and butter for the better-off, [43] while the colony's fauna gave scope for the skills of the amateur huntsman. Soups made from wallaby or possum bones[44] challenged the British palate, while household utensils and furnishings were nothing if not basic. The art of master craftsmen was most evident in imported goods, which were best taken out from England on the same ship as the emigrant. It is possible that Susannah brought with her certain items of furniture, but her baggage was more likely to have been clothes and soft furnishings. Such worldly goods as the family possessed at Margate, which were not necessary for the maintenance of a basic lifestyle, were probably sold over the winter of 1815–16 when she and the children were technically homeless, and perhaps living with a relative in London.

The social tensions mentioned above would have restricted the ability of the Croakers to integrate with the Sydney *monde*, such as it was. There were many men roaming the colony with a ticket of leave in their pocket, pretending to be free, variously breaking the law and affecting the reputation of the rest. In any case, there were few distractions from the business of making money, or simply a living. There was little time for the fine arts, when the rhythm of life in Sydney was set by 'the humming of a spinning-wheel, the dashing of a churn, or the grinding of corn in a steel mill'.[45] The theatre and annual races were dying on their feet, as the populace 'was not sufficiently mature' to appreciate them.[46] Subscription balls were held several times a year, and dinner parties were common, but they were both limited to the highest levels of society. The major relaxation for Sydney's population lay in numbing the mind with liquor, not expanding its cultural parameters. Nevertheless, as befitted a bank clerk and a school mistress, the Croakers could have strolled genteely with their children through Hyde Park in Sunday-best clothes, listening to the band of the 46th Regiment mellowing the twilight.

In the census of October 1816, as well as on his ticket of leave, Croaker was described as a 'dealer'.[47] This term, in the vernacular of the time, was applied to someone who made a living buying and selling a commodity, or any variety of commodities, at a retail level. In some respects, dealers were akin to hawkers or chapmen. They were quite distinct from merchants, who were large-scale operators usually involved in substantial importing and trading at both retail and wholesale levels. At this period, imports from Britain were being supplemented by increasing trade with India, China, and the Pacific Islands. From 1819, trade with the homeland was further affected by the requirement of a minimum size (350 tons) for merchant ships, which had the result of maintaining commercial cargoes aboard the convict ships.[48]

It seems strange that Croaker should have opted for this career so soon after his arrival. For one thing, he had little or nothing to trade in, unless Susannah had managed to put certain commodities aboard the *Elizabeth*. It is interesting that the ship's cargo for that voyage included a box of paint brushes, as well as linseed oil, paint and turpentine,[49] because John Croaker senior and his wife were at that time supplying a large number of brushes to St Dunstan's church, Canterbury. It has been suggested in an earlier chapter that John Croaker junior might have been involved in the book-keeping for that minor enterprise, and the possibility that he now envisaged his parents' brushes and associated items as underpinning a new career as a dealer is at least worthy of speculation.

Within a month or two of his arrival, and in parallel with his venture into dealing, Croaker found himself employed in the office of John Wylde, the judge advocate, as 'second' and 'public' clerk, on a salary of £50 plus stores for himself. The exact timing of this appointment is difficult to establish, but it took place before 17 April 1817.[50] As Wylde began employing Joseph Hyde Potts, a convict off the *Elizabeth*, on 3 December 1816,[51] Wylde was probably forming his team before the end of that year. Croaker's job was to provide clerical support to Wylde in his administration of justice in the colony. The judge advocate presided over the courts of criminal, civil and military jurisdiction, participated in committal proceedings, drew up indictments, executed judgements, acted as a notary public, and registered various legal transactions. Croaker assisted in clerical matters such as legal fees, writs and warrants, petitions, character references for defendants in criminal cases, minute-taking, administration of quit-rents, listing of sequestered goods, and correspondence.[52]

Wylde sought permission from Macquarie, as early as 1 May 1817,[53] to promote Croaker to principal clerk, so it can be assumed that he had shown himself a nimble-minded and conscientious recruit. As his thinking became attuned to legal niceties, memories of his own trial might well have kept Croaker awake. Although the judicial system had been different, it would have occurred to him that if he had known at Dover Sessions what he knew now in the colony, he could have made a better fist of his own defence. It must also have occurred to him that if he retained the confidence of Wylde, he might realise a future which could more than compensate for the career he had squandered.

6   Poacher into Gamekeeper

By good fortune, Croaker arrived in Wylde's office exactly when the judge advocate was pondering a project which overstepped the confines of judicial administration. As this stratagem concerned the colony's first bank, Croaker had an immediate chance to redeem himself and recover some self-respect. It is a matter of opinion whether Croaker took full-enough advantage of the new opportunity. If he did not, then at least he gave the project the benefit of his knowledge, and the colonial economy became more efficient, in the long term, as a result of his advice. Clerical ability could never elevate him to a public pedestal, but what mattered for Croaker was that it kept him in contact with the men of influence. Rarely had a convict been presented with such a rewarding prospect after so brief a sojourn in the colony.

As well as Wylde, the promoters of the Bank of New South Wales were Governor Macquarie, and his close associate and secretary, J. T. Campbell.[1] Wylde, at Macquarie's instigation, wasted little time after his arrival in October 1816 in formulating plans to establish the bank. Within seven weeks he had convened the first public meeting, and in December 1816 he played a major part in several more. Another influential figure at this early stage was Thomas Macvitie, who had just set up as a merchant in Sydney. Macvitie, who later also became prominent in the Bank of Australia, had lived both at the Cape of Good Hope and Mauritius, where banks had recently been established.[2] Wylde, probably with advice from Campbell and Macvitie, drafted the bank's charter, and continued his active involvement until the day of the opening in April 1817.

The staff of the judge advocate's office played significant roles in the establishment and initial operation of the bank, which used the double-entry system of book-keeping.[3] By arranging for Croaker, Joseph Hyde Potts, and Thomas Wylde to be employed there, Wylde formed a small team with varied experience and skills. It seems likely they were privy to

John Wylde, judge advocate, who employed Croaker as a clerk in 1817 (by permission of the National Library of Australia)

developments, and familiar with some of the judge advocate's thinking. Two of the first three public meetings were held in Wylde's chambers, giving his staff ample opportunity not only to keep abreast of events, but to take an active role. This involvement paid dividends for each of them. Thomas Wylde was elected 'Law-Solicitor' to the bank on 12 February 1817; he also served as a founding director. Potts, who was said to have 'gained knowledge in England in office work and accounting', was also renowned for his penmanship and had a 'penchant for mathematics'. He was appointed 'porter and servant' to the bank on 15 February, proved useful in preparing official documents, and subsequently served as the bank's accountant from 1829 to 1839.[4]

As for Croaker, his precise role is conveniently recorded in the minutes (p. 40) of the meeting of the bank's directors on 12 February, almost two months before the opening:

> Mr. Croaker of George St., Accountant, being called in, was informed that the Directors declined accepting his proposal for the situation of Principal Book-keeper, when he expressed his readiness of serving the Directors in any subordinate situation relative to the forming and opening of the Books of the Bank, which position was acceded to by the Board.[5]

Croaker's proposal, which showed initiative and self-confidence, was received three days before the first advertisement placed by the bank's directors in the *Sydney Gazette*, seeking to employ a 'Cashier' and a 'Principal Accountant'. The timing, therefore, is significant, suggesting that Croaker was aware of the discussions about staffing. Use of the term 'Accountant' in respect of Croaker is also of interest, as there are few earlier instances of any person in the colony being described as an 'Accountant' or 'Accomptant'.[6]

The setting aside of Croaker's 'proposal' is unsurprising, for the board would have found itself in a difficult position with a recently-convicted embezzler as a salaried employee, despite his ticket of leave. The bank's promoters were aware of the problems which could arise by too close an association with persons who were either emancipated convicts or not 'absolutely and unconditionally free'. The seventh clause of the bank's initial constitution, passed controversially at a general meeting of subscribers in February 1817, was designed to prevent emancipists (convicts who had served their term) from becoming directors. Some were nevertheless elected, but the general message—that some ex-convicts were not welcome—was clear enough.[7] John Wylde subsequently alluded to the bank's dilemma and the 'unpleasant consequence' if free persons were to note too close a link between the bank and 'those whom they might have possibly and very recently seen, on the passage to the colony, wearing the badges of conviction'.[8] Thus, it is understandable that the board chose to avail itself of Croaker's services discreetly, using him as a backroom adviser. Croaker certainly 'proved very useful in helping to establish the [bank's] bookkeeping system',[9] so much so that on 20 May 1817 the board approved a 'handsome remuneration' of £30 to him for his 'service rendered to the Bank in its Establishment . . . his services not being further required'.[10] At its next meeting, on 27 May, the board received a letter from Croaker 'acknowledging his receipt of Thirty Pounds (ordered last Board-day for his Assistance in opening the Books of the Bank)'.

Croaker's engagement preceded by over a fortnight that of E. S. Hall (the foundation 'Secretary and Cashier') and Robert Campbell junior (the foundation 'Head Accountant, Clerk of Discount, and Principal Book-keeper'). Unlike them, he had enjoyed first-hand experience of double-entry and his capability was unrivalled. The biographical profiles[11] of Hall and Campbell suggest that neither was equipped to devise a double-entry book-keeping system. Nor would they have been able to implement such a system, in a banking environment, without guidance from an experienced practitioner. Indeed, both reputedly 'had to learn their occupation virtually as they went', failed to distinguish themselves in their position within the bank, and had interests in other directions. Their ability to produce the necessary bonds (£1500 and £500 respectively) as surety probably had as much to do with their appointment as anything else.[12]

Croaker appears to have been so highly regarded that, when the Bank of New South Wales suffered financial mismanagement several years later, it turned to him for help. He duly assisted, early in 1821, after the departure of the secretary and cashier (and former accountant), Francis Williams, who had bled the bank of almost all its capital. Williams' book-keeping was a shambles:

> there was a shortage of £12,000 in his accounts, caused by his having entered unpaid bills as paid, crediting his friends with amounts not deposited to their accounts and permitting them to overdraw, and accepting presents, usually quite insignificant ones—as, for instance, a couple of fat chickens—from customers whose cheques he would accept and hold until there was enough money in their accounts to meet them.[13]

On 8 February 1821 the bank's directors appointed Croaker to 'assist the cashier until a proper person can be obtained'.[14] The bank set up a committee of proprietors and empowered them to 'enquire into and examine the Minute Books, Accounts, proceedings and management of the bank as well as the state of capital, expenses, dividends, debts and credits thereof'. The president of the bank, John Piper, recommended to this committee that they 'avail themselves of the services of Mr. Croaker, at present a temporary and voluntary assistant in the Bank'. The same bank clerk who had been disgraced in England was now the troubleshooter in New South Wales for misdemeanours no less unacceptable than his own. Croaker must have found this change in his fortunes, from poacher to gamekeeper, both ironic and amusing.

Croaker appears to have steered the bank through its predicament until the appointment of John Henry Black as 'accountant and assistant cashier' on 12 February 1821. He was awarded a payment of £10 in April for 'services rendered', but he would have seen his greater reward as the respect and approbation which his intervention engendered. This goodwill in the context of the bank, could be turned, he suspected, to his material advantage. Thus, in November the same year, when he successfully petitioned the governor to grant him the 'indulgence of an Absolute Pardon', he stated proudly that he 'was at the opening of the Bank of New South Wales'.[15]

Croaker's role in establishing double-entry book-keeping resulted more from his being in the right place at the right time than from any exceptional ability. His competence in double-entry was that of a trained bank clerk, rather than a self-professed expert. He was probably no better and no worse at it than any other English bank clerk who had endured a long apprenticeship, and felt the discomfort and irritation of having a more senior clerk standing over him, eyes narrowed in the expectation of some inexcusable error. He was simply well placed, by coincidence and circumstance, and as a result of Susannah's promotion of his skills, to apply an empirical solution to a problem which, in his absence, might have been tackled by men with no formal training.

In a wider context, the entitlement of Croaker to be regarded as Australia's first double-entry accountant, seems at least a match for the claims of others. Three such possibles, Andrew Miller, John Palmer and William Broughton, were employed at various times in the colony's store, the commissariat, although the term 'accountant' was not used before 1817 to describe the occupation of any of its 30 or 40 employees. Miller, the colony's first commissary (1788–90), was believed responsible for the initial entries in the commissariat accounting records,[16] but his work appears to have been single-entry list-keeping. Some accounts prepared by the colony's second commissary, Palmer, have survived from May to October 1792, and these, in the opinion of at least one commentator, 'enable a suggestion' that he 'understood some of the principles of double-entry bookkeeping'.[17] But there is no mention of Palmer's familiarity with the double-entry system in the *Australian Dictionary of Biography*, and his education and career argue otherwise.[18] As for Broughton, who held senior positions in the commissariat between 1810 and 1815 and described himself as an 'accountant', there is a total lack of evidence as to his book-keeping skills. He was referred to by Macquarie as 'a very clever and correct accountant',[19] but there is no reason to believe his work was other than single-entry. It was not in the interests of the commissary, and officers of the New South Wales Corps, to adopt a book-keeping system which allowed their (often dubious) entrepreneurial activities to be examined too closely.

There are certain other claimants about whom less is known. One Michael Hayes described himself as an 'accomptant' in advertisements to secure work, published in the *Sydney Gazette* in 1803. He was employed briefly, shortly afterwards, by the Sydney merchants Bishop and Bass. The 'quarterly accounts' he prepared for them have not survived. The term 'accountant' appears only once in the *Index of the Sydney Gazette, 1803–1826*, in respect of a 'work wanted' advertisement placed by Thomas Ayliffe Gee on 17 December 1814. But although Gee extolled his knowledge of 'accounts', and sought a job in that field, he himself did not use the term 'accountant'. In any case, his contribution to the book-keeping history of the colony was slight as, four months later, convicted of an unspecified crime, he was transported as a secondary punishment to the closed penal settlement of Newcastle, where he languished. Yet another pretender might be Robert Jenkins, a self-styled 'competent bookkeeper' who, to settle a law suit, was engaged to audit the accounts of a partnership of Sydney merchants in 1813.[20] But those accounts were single-entry, and none of the above claimants is impressive. From the midst of the throng, Croaker's head peeks noticeably, if without bravura.

It is unwise to be dogmatic about absolutes, but the case for the bank's system to have been the first in the colony in double-entry looks quite strong. No earlier system by this method has so far been discovered,[21] despite analysis of the books of leading figures, including T. Abbott (for 1805–11), W. H. Mansell (1809–19), and D'Arcy Wentworth (1812–20).[22] Traders in the colony had little incentive to embark on double-entry, as commercial activity was small-scale. If larger merchants, like Simeon Lord and Robert Campbell senior, ran 'counting houses' from around 1810, this should not be taken as evidence of sophisticated practice.[23] Most colonial merchants had only a rudimentary knowledge of accounting, and a less-than-thorough grounding in commerce: 'the range and variety of [merchants'] activities defied careful bookkeeping'.[24] There is little here to challenge the bank's title to have instituted a new procedure.

A limited case can be argued for Croaker's indirect involvement in the drafting of the charter of the Bank of New South Wales. The fifty clauses were largely the work of John Wylde,[25] probably aided by J. T. Campbell, who apparently had significant experience in the operational side of banking. Campbell was Macquarie's secretary, and without him the governor would have had no first-hand expertise to draw upon in the long run-up to the establishment of a bank. Campbell had served briefly with the Bank of Ireland, where he was a 'runner' in 1793 and an assistant in the discount office in 1795.[26] Later he 'had a principal part in the Establishment and conduct of the Bank at the Cape of Good Hope'.[27] The thought emerges briefly that Campbell—the only other man reputed to have had experience of banking—might have instituted the book-keeping procedures in the Bank of New South Wales, but this seems unlikely. Only by serving a banking apprenticeship was Campbell likely to have acquired the discipline of book-keeping, and his training in the Bank of Ireland was not in that area. His expertise in New South Wales was at a different procedural level, probably linked to determining the bank's terms of reference, and rules for the discounting of bills. Secondly, even the facts of Campbell's first-hand association with banking, especially at the Cape, are not without challenge. His biographer, Holder, admits that Campbell's past was 'obscure', and the historical record of his background might be unreliable and exaggerated.[28] Recently, new evidence has come to light about Campbell's career at Dublin, but it is still disturbing that the standard history of South African banking[29] does not refer to him.

There is much to be gained by examining the foundation charter of the Bank of New South Wales, as if through Croaker's eyes. The bank was a joint-stock company, incorporated with limited liability by a charter granted by the governor for a term of seven years. These few words encapsulate the extent to which the bank's constitution was beyond Croaker's experience. In England at that time there was only one joint-stock bank, the Bank of England itself, established by charter in 1694, following an Act of Parliament. In Scotland there were three chartered joint-stock banks, the Bank of Scotland (1695), the Royal Bank of Scotland (1727), and the British Linen Company (1746), while the Bank of Ireland was established by charter in 1784. From these various precedents, and from banking activities in Cape Town and Mauritius, the Bank of New South Wales drew its inspiration, improvising to meet the needs of an economy fettered by the uncertain status of many of its customers. The term of seven years was a tighter restriction than the periods granted initially to the British banks,[30] while the limitation of proprietors' liability to the extent of their shareholding was an arrogation by Macquarie of a privilege normally reserved to letters patent from the Crown.[31] The principle of limited liability among British banks in general was not authorised until 1858, and even then many bankers and indeed shareholders were reluctant to adopt it.[32] Another peculiarity of

Macquarie's charter was the amount of space devoted to the minutiae of the bank's business. The practice in royal charters was to take great pains establishing the rights and duties of the proprietors and directors, but to let them get on with the business of banking as they thought fit. Predictably, Macquarie's tight and idiosyncratic charter was disapproved of in London, to the extent of being deemed invalid, but in the remoteness of the colony this made little difference. The Bank of New South Wales, constituted to the satisfaction of the locals, was in business.

The banks with which Croaker had been associated formerly, far from being chartered, were probably conducted without written terms of reference. Provincial joint-stock banking was illegal in England until 1826, and the myriad private firms which facilitated the rise of the Industrial Revolution were governed, if at all, by articles of partnership. Typically, these stated the length of the agreement, and the respective share of profits among the principals, but if the bank had only one boss, such as Garrett in Ramsgate and Sackett in Margate, it could be set up without paperwork, able to trade at the whim of its sole proprietor. The only interference from Government was in the form of a stipulation, in force from 1808, that bankers had to apply for an annual licence from the Stamp Office to issue promissory notes for money payable to the bearer (i.e. banknotes) in every town where they (the bankers) had an office. However, it was unwise for the formalities to end there. A sensible bank made some public and very precise statement of the service which it intended to provide, or it risked doing no business at all.

Few of these statements have survived, but one lucky exception is the public notice issued by the Canterbury Bank of Gipps, Simmons and Gipps, on 5 July 1788.[33] This notice can be regarded as indicative of the business also conducted by the banks of Garrett and Sackett. It gives notice of the range of activities envisaged, principally the receipt of money on deposit, the provision of banknotes, the discounting and sale of bills, the remittance of money to London, and the purchase of stock—activities which were typically within Croaker's duties. If these functions are examined against the charter of the Bank of New South Wales, Croaker is shown to have been sufficiently knowledgeable to influence procedures. Of the 50 clauses,[34] however, the first 29 were largely restricted to questions of capital, strategic management, and the payment of dividends to shareholders, all matters which had eluded his experience. The exception was clause 26 which stipulated, in effect, a double-entry book-keeping system. While Croaker would have been unfamiliar with the secondary stages of report and approval which were necessary for the accounts of a corporate body, the basic task of balancing the books on a half-yearly basis had been central to his work in Kent, and he could have taken it in his stride.

Clauses 30 and 31 dealt with the issue and denomination of bank-notes, and their registration within the bank. Here, also, Croaker would have been comfortable. He knew all about these functions, as the banks at Margate and Ramsgate were note-issuing; at Margate at least, he would have maintained the banknote register, subject to Sackett's occasional scrutiny. The only aspect which would have surprised him, to the point of amusement, was the range of tiny denominations, as low as 2s 6d—a sum more suited in England to the realm of tradesmen's tokens.[35]

The clauses from 32 to 50 are described as 'General Rules' and they weave in and out of the limits of Croaker's familiarity. Number 33 for-bade the discounting of bills of exchange with more than three months to run, a restriction which Croaker would have considered unexcep-tional, as few bills in the English market exceeded that duration. More interesting were the clauses 34–36, which governed the size and duration of loans on landed property, and advances against deposits of bullion or plate. English bankers generally fought shy of offering any kinds of loan in their statement of function, although of course they needed them to earn good profits. The risks were considerable. Loans were tailored to the merits of each applicant and the security available, and were negotiated in the privacy of the 'parlour'. They were very much a favour for the influ-ential few, and not a matter to be broadcast on a public poster. Thus, Croaker would have been surprised at the way the rules for loans were spelt out, but not unfamiliar with the details.

Clause 37 enabled the bank to take valuables into safe custody, but apparently only items belonging to shareholders. Again Croaker would have been comfortable with this general procedure, but of course the paperwork had more to do with the keeping of a safe-custody register, and what bankers refer to as 'Out and In' controls, than book-keeping in the conventional sense. Most items deposited with English banks were of documentary rather than intrinsic value, for instance title-deeds, per-sonal papers, and share certificates. There was again a certain reluctance among English country bankers, certainly in Canterbury, to publicise the service, and from much the same coyness as restricted the advertisement of loans. The bank was prepared to take the valuables only of those whose wealth or status suggested a good line in ancillary business. The emphasis on intrinsic value, with the Bank of New South Wales, suggests a desire on the part of the directors to have as much of the colony's specie as possible under their own control, in order to underwrite their note issue. Therefore, the clause was as much for the wider benefit of the bank as a service to its proprietors.

The limitation of 10 per cent on the charging of interest, or the discounting of bills (clause 38), would have sent Croaker pondering usury. This figure, 2 per cent above prevailing rates, created a new benchmark, but rates went even higher in some private transactions. The going rate in East Kent for discounting was 5 per cent, and this was also the general rate fixed since 1746 by the Bank of England—a figure which until 1822 failed to respond to the exigencies of the market.[36] Clause 39 stipulated another ceiling, this time for loans, which in any one case were not to exceed £500; while clause 40 prohibited loans against the deposit of bank stock certificates. The statement of an absolute limit would have been unfamiliar to Croaker. It is impossible to know the size of the loans which were agreed by Burgess and Sackett, but certainly a restriction of £500, even at one time, would have found little sympathy with the partners of the Canterbury Bank, who lent £4600 to Flint's Brewery.[37] Other large loans to the same concern were noted in chapter 1, where the rival Canterbury Union Bank was seen to have advanced no less than £7100.

The Bank of New South Wales, by virtue of clause 41, prohibited the payment of interest on deposits except by special arrangement. Furthermore, the money could not be withdrawn inside three months. In those cases where an arrangement was authorised, interest was not to exceed 8 per cent. All this Croaker would have found fascinating. If nothing was given in return, no English banker would have expected to receive any money on deposit, yet the inflow of surplus capital from the customer base was essential to provide liquidity for loans. The public notice of the Canterbury Bank invited deposits of not less than £100, for which the bank paid interest at 2.5 per cent. The investor also received a note for the amount of the capital, payable at sight after thirty days, but in an emergency the money could be reclaimed at any time, less a penalty. Thus, assuming always that the Canterbury procedure was broadly similar to that elsewhere in East Kent, the length of deposit being demanded in the colony would have struck Croaker as severe. As for the 8 per cent ceiling on interest, he would have regarded that as beyond possibility— no more than a generous and unreal compromise between the need to keep the directors in check and the flexibility to which they were entitled to meet a changing market.

Following a clause forbidding the directors to contract debts by bond, bill or note, without express authority (a matter not to hold Croaker's attention), article 43 empowered them to 'keep running Accounts', which could not be overdrawn. These were, in modern language, current accounts, which sat at the heart of the business of any bank. Most of Croaker's time in England had been spent maintaining the ledgers of such accounts and summarising the figures to produce balanced statements of profit and loss which, enhanced by proceeds from other areas of the bank's activities, gave his boss a bulletin on the health of the business. However, the absolute prohibition on overdrawing would have been new to him, underlining in his mind the cultural gulf between the society he had been used to and the one he was living in. The point deserves elaboration and again the parallel with the Canterbury Bank is instructive.

The first paragraph of the Canterbury Bank's public notice offered current account holders 'printed Checks', on which they could draw for 'real' money, local banknotes, or drafts payable in London. In other words, current accounts offered a local banker the best route to an expansion of his business. Not only did the banker receive working capital, on which he paid no interest, but if the account-holder withdrew sums in the form of local banknotes, then shopkeepers and others were more or less obliged to accept the bank's paper, which could lead them to opening an account. In the matter of overdrafts, it was often worth the banker's while to carry a modest excess if the customer could be trusted, because the short-term deficit could act as a loss-leader for the acquisition of new business. The bank could also charge interest, or a fee, for its indulgence, although the ledgers of the Canterbury Bank suggest that the partners kept their attitude flexible. The overriding impression is not of an overdraft for the privileged few, but of an overdrawn account being almost a matter of routine.[38] Against this background, the dour restriction in the Bank of New South Wales would have struck Croaker as the measure of how far the crime-ridden and immature society he had entered differed from the conventions and gentility of middle-class southern England. It is important, of course, not to be simplistic as to the differences: the banking system in England was as prone to charlatans and fools (on both sides of the counter) as it was anywhere else. But New South Wales lacked the base of clergy and hereditary landowners, as distinct from entrepreneurs, who were important to English banking and shaped its sensibilities.

If clause 43 gave Croaker nostalgic memories, the next one brought home to him the reality and uniqueness of the economy in which he now worked. Current accounts could be opened in the new bank by the deposit of store receipts, or bills on the Treasury in London. The former, replaced at intervals by the latter, were receipts issued by the commissariat store in payment for the purchase of local produce, and they circulated like banknotes.[39] The new bank was expressly recognising that both instruments were 'to all intents and purposes Cash', a self-evident but also self-centred decision, as it wished to replace them with its own banknotes. The fewer the store receipts and bills in circulation, the less the risk that any rival institution could use them to underwrite a note issue. Croaker would have found it novel that such liquidity could be awarded to 'virtual' money, as the accounting he was used to saw cash as one thing and bills as another.

Croaker's experience was also unequal to clause 45, which forbade the bank's cashier, on pain of dismissal or fine, to pay or debit drafts (in modern terms, cheques) without sanction of the directors. As a senior bank clerk in England, it would have been entirely within Croaker's competence to process a cheque, as long as he was satisfied with the circumstances of its presentation and the identity of the drawer. The clause is therefore further striking evidence of the cultural divide which then existed between Britain and its colony. The very strength of the prohibition highlighted the dismal and deep extent to which the society of the latter was corrupt. It was no doubt this corruption, at least in part, which influenced the next clause (no. 46), which prohibited the officers of the bank from having any other trade or business. Indeed the bank as a whole was 'absolutely and altogether' barred from trading beyond the activity of banking (no. 47). At this point the normal practice of realising security in the case of bad debts warranted a specific dispensation in the charter, a refinement which Croaker would have found most curious, as it was no more than a necessary banking procedure. The final three clauses dealt with questions of conduct or capital which concerned only a joint-stock enterprise, and Croaker would have had no view as to their pertinence.

The examination of the charter as a whole through his eyes has revealed significant areas where he would have felt experienced and comfortable, even if the procedures were to alter. It has been necessary to make the comparative analysis with the Canterbury Bank to penetrate the wall of doubt which stands between Croaker and his acceptance as a significant and neglected figure in the economic history of New South Wales. It has been shown that the transition from private to joint-stock banking would not have disconcerted him, as in many ways the activities overlapped. It was the scale of the new bank which brought it within Croaker's experience. For all the rigmarole of joint-stock incorporation, and the need to foster international connections, it was essentially a bank to serve a population no greater than the hinterland of Canterbury and the Isle of Thanet. It needed to keep its operation as uncomplicated as possible, and in this respect Croaker could help. He had first-hand knowledge of best practice, in the minutiae of banking, even if his track record suggested he had not kept to it. To that extent, the possibility of Wylde seeking his view, in questions of registration, custody, training and procedure, look perfectly tenable. No grander role for Croaker can be postulated. He made no speeches, presented no reports, and argued no philosophy. But he could set up a banking-hall, he knew the language for paperwork and the headings for ledgers, and the evidence is that he put these skills to good use. He was there at the beginning, he helped lay down the method, and for once in his life he got something right.

7   A House of Cards

The dealers, to whose ranks Croaker was aspiring, had a thoroughly bad reputation.[1] In a colony where a good reputation was as rare as summer snow, and melted away at the same speed, this was not in itself remarkable. Even Governor Macquarie, in many people's eyes an enlightened administrator, was by no means without his critics. It was he who had created a class of ticket-of-leave convicts out of men whose character and integrity he had no means of knowing and every reason to mistrust. It was Macquarie, also, who had favoured emancipists with large grants of land and appointed them to high civil office. Even the magistracy was within their grasp.[2] Many free settlers felt resentful and insecure. It was a question more fundamental than the abuse of social conventions, or competence to hold down a job. The unique New South Wales system of penal indulgence was arguably effective, but was it right and proper? There needed to be recognition of where, in the words of Commissioner Bigge, soon to be sent from England to investigate the colony's affairs, lay 'the moral ascendancy'.[3]

In the early months of 1817 the ascendancy which interested Croaker was distinctly worldly. It might have bothered him later that dealers were characterised as vultures who 'prey upon the living victims who are sinking around them',[4] but his need in the short term was to make a career. The future seemed promising as he was advancing on three fronts. He was salaried in Wylde's office at £50 a year, in May he received £30 from the Bank of New South Wales for his help in setting up the book-keeping, and the dealing was achieving a turnover, if not a profit. Furthermore, the whole family, by separate concessions, was victualled from the Government stores, and it is at least possible that Susannah was earning an income. But he was not doing what he really wanted, which was to make a lot of money as fast as possible. It is an interesting commentary on the ethics of New South Wales that Croaker, while a civil servant in the judicature, was unconstrained as a dealer.

What the laxity of the colony allowed Croaker with one hand its jealousies took away with the other. He already knew, and had probably accepted with good grace, that the Bank of New South Wales would not want to employ him in his status as a ticket-of-leave convict; he would have been less pleased that they would not open him an account; and he was soon to feel humiliated that they would not even discount a bill which he presented, although there was nothing personal in the refusal. The business case for this aloofness made little sense, and the legal position was equally weak. There was nothing in the charter, a document which Croaker knew as well as anybody, which precluded him as a customer. He was a victim of the general irresponsibility of his peer group, and of the opposition of free settlers to persons who were not of their standing. Others might have taken offence, and rejoined the ranks of the miscreants. But Croaker played the game by its arbitrary rules and progressed to a largely honourable, if frustrating, association with the bank from the public side of the counter. What he did for the directors has already been recounted; what they could do for him, and indeed for other dealers, can now be discussed.

Although it is frustrating to be unaware of the commodities in which Croaker traded, his rocky path to moderate success does at least demonstrate, to some extent, how dealing worked. The system depended on the juggling of debts, and the trick was to balance the interests of the owed and the owing. The strength of the new bank was that it created a marketplace for the subtleties of documentary credit, which existed at two levels. The less formal instrument was the note of hand, or promissory note, which was effectively a recognition of debt made from A to B— something very like a modern cheque, but with a restriction against immediate payment. As B could not claim the money until the lapse of a specified time, the note could be discounted. In other words, B could sell it to C (usually a bank) for something below its face value, while C, at the maturity of the note, sought the full value from A. In practice, there was usually another tier: B assigned the note to C, to whom he or she had a debt, and it was C who sold it to the bank, who thus became D. Other intermediate assignees were quite possible. This process made a promissory note similar to a bill of exchange, the instrument at the other 'level', whose workings have already been discussed. The distinction was further eroded by the custom of drawing promissory notes 'value received'.[5] Indeed the Bank of New South Wales summarised both instruments as bills. The directors' minute books, however, show an important change in wording.[6] A promissory note was drawn A *to* B; but a bill of exchange was drawn A *on* B, which meant the debt was from B to A, and therefore the other way round from a promissory note.

With these arcane distinctions in mind, the 37 transactions, between April 1817 and September 1820, in which Croaker was successfully connected with discounting (Appendix II), become more meaningful, at least at a procedural level. However, the list is preceded by a complication, which is the rebuff alluded to above. W. H. Moore had made a promissory note in favour of J. J. Moore, who endorsed it to Croaker, who presented it for discount on 15 April 1817. The period of credit (probably two months)[7] was not minuted, nor was the sum in which the note was drawn. The bank declined to co-operate on the grounds that 'Mr Croaker was not qualified to present Bills for Discount, he not being free in the Colony'. It is unwise to speculate on an underlying commercial deal, as the presentation smacks of a collusive action between the Moores and Croaker, by which the latter could test his acceptability in the eyes of the bank. Injured pride apart, the rejection would have struck Croaker as ridiculous. The real issue for the bank was the reliability of W. H. Moore, from whom the directors would be seeking their money. As long as they were satisfied with his liquidity, the status of the presenter was a commercial irrelevance. Moore, the drawer, was a free man, one of the colony's two solicitors of the Crown, sent to New South Wales in 1815 by Earl Bathurst.[8] As his credentials were hardly in doubt, and he must have known both the endorsers of his note, the snub to Croaker was all the more bewildering. If the bank was to place 'moral ascendancy' above business acumen, its future profitability would have seemed to Croaker in some doubt. But he was soon to learn that discounting in the colony had its unique pitfalls, and the bank knew what it was doing.

The directors' refusal to discount Croaker's promissory note happened exactly one week after the bank opened for business. On that occasion, 15 April 1817, five notes were presented, but only the fifth was discounted. The first was refused for technical reasons; the second was Croaker's; and the third and fourth were declined as they were payable to bearer, not to order. The bank was making it clear that sloppy presentation would not be tolerated. Croaker was the first person to be rejected on the grounds of his ticket of leave, and the fact that he was in the vanguard of would-be presenters testifies to his familiarity with the banking process, as it had evolved in England. He had the unwelcome distinction of being the precedent against which convicts of his ambivalent status were to be treated. He was not rejected because he was John Croaker, but because he represented a class of entrepreneur with which the bank had no wish to associate. After what he had personally done for the bank, it is to be hoped that the directors came to their decision only after considerable debate, and that their consciences were disturbed as they voted him inadmissible.

Later in 1817 Croaker received two promissory notes drawn in his favour, one for £45, the other for £50. As with all such transactions, the maturity dates are not recorded in the minute book, but again a credit of two months is very likely. The surnames of the drawers, respectively, were Reib(e)y and Moore, and in both cases Croaker endorsed the notes, passing one to J. J. Moore, and the other to R. Jenkins, an agent and merchant, who thus became entitled to the money. It is possible to interpret these transactions in different ways. In the first place, Reiby and Moore as drawers could have been paying Croaker for whatever commodity he supplied them, or they could have been lending him money. In either case, J. J. Moore and R. Jenkins could simply have been acting as intermediaries, to allow Croaker to get his money early (less what the bank deducted as a discount). Thus these actions would have been, once again, collusive, agreed for Croaker's benefit as he was barred from presenting the notes himself. If the prospect of so much collusion seems unlikely, then an alternative interpretation is very possible: the endorsements can be seen as a simple means for Croaker to pay J. J. Moore and R. Jenkins what he happened to owe them, without the need to find real money.

Unfortunately, two further complications arise. The bank would not discount *any* promissory note (as distinct from a bill of exchange) unless it was endorsed by an 'accredited' person. This was introduced for the bank's protection, and was in line with its stated aim of reducing the amount of untrustworthy paper in general circulation.[9] As the accredited person was not necessarily a party to the underlying transaction, the bank's rule could only have blurred still further the outlines of mutual indebtedness between dealers, and between dealers and their customers. For the historian, the problem surfaces when the bank's lists of discounted 'bills' are examined, giving three names—the drawer, the payee, and the endorser. It is probable that the last-named was also a party to the debt, but he might simply have been there to facilitate the discounting. An even more imponderable situation was created by the bank's custom to list only these three names, that is, not necessarily to mention all the endorsers. It is evident from legal papers that a three-month promissory note could have at least six endorsed signatures before the bank received it for discounting, and the assumption must be that each endorser owed money to the next.[10] In summary, it is a brave person who seeks to demonstrate the finer workings of the colonial economy on the evidence of the bank's minute books. At this remove, the knot of dealers' debts can never be satisfactorily unravelled.

If Croaker was to make a success of his dealing, he needed a more logical relationship with the bank, centred on his acceptability as a drawer and presenter of instruments of credit. This meant an elevation in his status and John Wylde was the man to arrange it. Croaker was proving his reliability as a legal clerk. Wylde was also the beneficiary of Croaker's dealing, as £59 went out of his bank account in Croaker's favour, between April and December 1817.[11] It was on 8 December that Wylde, known for his 'friendly and placable disposition',[12] took the unorthodox step of petitioning Macquarie, as a personal favour, to grant Croaker a conditional pardon.[13] The ostensible aim was to secure Croaker's continued service in the judge advocate's office, and indeed that squares with Wylde's attempt, soon afterwards, to have Croaker promoted to principal clerk. Wylde argued that Croaker's status was 'scarcely compatible or reconcilable' with his ticket of leave, and doubted whether the office could survive its heavy workload without him. But the notion that Wylde was acting at Croaker's instigation, to facilitate the dealing, makes good sense, and it is to the latter's credit that he did not abandon Wylde's office once he had his way.

Macquarie, on the other hand, was not to be rushed. To accede would have contravened his own guideline of 1813, that a conditional pardon should only be considered for convicts who had lived in the colony for at least two-thirds of their term of transportation.[14] Croaker's case was therefore some five or six years premature—which argues by itself for his historical importance. The brashness of Wylde's approach cut no ice with J. T. Campbell, Macquarie's secretary, who scribbled a note to the governor at the foot of the petition: 'Do not answer this 'till at perfect leizure. Should not have addressed you'. Macquarie, however, was more for than against. He took limited advantage of a suggestion by Wylde that Croaker should remain 'under positive Articles' for a further three years, if the petition were accepted. Six months later, in June 1818, when Croaker had continued to fulfil his duties conscientiously, Macquarie granted him a conditional pardon. In the language of the colony, he was now an emancipist.[15]

The effect was significant, as Croaker was two steps forward. He could get bills discounted himself, if need be, and the bank was prepared to accept his bills and notes as valid instruments. He still had no running account, however, and this deficiency is difficult to explain. His omission from the opening (and only surviving) ledger means he was certainly not a customer, if at all, until the end of 1820. There might have been reasons why an account did not suit him when he was working under a ticket of leave,[16] but, with a conditional pardon behind him, he had little hope of servicing his growing business needs without a repository for cash. Also, it was definitely in the bank's interests to have the money of its discounting associates within its own vaults. It created capital to underwrite loans, and funds could be withheld if the account-holder overdrew, or dishonoured a bill. Furthermore, the bank could not discriminate totally against emancipists or it would miss out on much of the colony's wealth. Given the directors' moral debt to Croaker in the first place—of which they were periodically reminded by the need to ask his guidance—the position makes little sense. Perhaps the directors simply felt he needed time to prove his reliability. If that really was their thinking, they were later to congratulate themselves on their perspicacity.

Croaker, meanwhile, felt a new confidence and launched ten promissory notes and three bills of exchange before the end of 1818. The notes pose the same puzzle as discussed above, in that they were all endorsed by the payee in favour of an intermediary, who presented them to the bank for discount. As Croaker was now an acceptable presenter in the eyes of the bank, the possibility of collusive action can be rejected. Each endorser was apparently a creditor of the payee. Only two conclusions seem possible: either Croaker was building up his stocks, or he was borrowing money. The bank, meanwhile, was exposing itself to an increasing risk. The ten promissory notes alone added up to some £867, which Croaker eventually had to honour. On the evidence of certain court proceedings, less than six months away, it would appear that his affairs were not always as liquid as he or his creditors would have liked.

Before long, the bank lost patience with the way documentary credit was being abused. It is unlikely that Croaker was the catalyst for its action, but he certainly played his part. The directors had been in the habit, from the beginning, of seeking from the endorser(s) the full value of the bill or note, if the drawer defaulted.[17] This was, of course, a main reason for them insisting that weak promissory notes needed strengthening by the signature of an accredited person. From 22 March 1820 any endorser who failed to meet a payment was debarred from presenting further bills for discounting. A proprietor of the bank, Thomas Middleton, had already suffered a different ignominy arising from the same problem. In November 1819 the directors retained £300 from his current account to meet a dishonoured bill in favour of James Hankinson, another proprietor.[18] By these tough and impartial measures the bank established order and authority. The value of bills discounted rose from £12 193 in 1817 to £81 672 in 1818, with another 20 per cent rise in the following year. Commissioner Bigge was mildly surprised at these impressive totals, and concluded that they were caused by a low ratio of bad bills.[19] In reality, the proportion was probably higher than most British banks experienced, but the directors' effective steps to secure payment by other means ensured they had few bills to write off, and therefore the balance sheet stayed respectable.

It was not until September 1818 that Croaker exercised his new right to present a bill of exchange for discounting. This was a bill which he had drawn on 'Moore' for £65 12s 11d. The very precise sum seems to indicate 'value received', in which case he really had supplied goods to Moore, and this was not an accommodation bill to provide Croaker with a short-term loan. This was the only occasion, in all Croaker's activities with the bank, when a bill of exchange did not involve three parties before discounting, and indeed only on one other occasion (16 February 1819) did he present a bill himself. Strangely, no bills of exchange were ever discounted in which Croaker was the acceptor—that is, the party who had to pay at maturity.

Croaker's banking transactions which involve discounting seem to offer a cautious insight into his turnover, and maybe profitability, as a dealer. The position is complicated by the negotiable nature of the notes and bills, and the conditions laid down by the bank, but an analysis of the documents literally at their face value suggests that his affairs were healthy. If bills drawn by him, notes drawn in his favour, and a bill endorsed to his order are regarded as credits, then in the three years between September 1817 and September 1820 his dealing earned him around £1345. If notes made by him are interpreted as debits, then he paid out about £883, which indicates a balance in his favour of some £462. But it must be recognised that an unknown number of notes was circulating, drawn by Croaker but never discounted by the payee; as some were definitely dishonoured,[20] further caution is required when assessing Croaker's profitability from this angle. Another consideration is that barter was common in the colony, and while this would have had little impact on evidence of profit margins, it could distort an assessment of volume of business.

An alternative glimpse into Croaker's dealing is afforded by the running accounts of those among his clients who were also customers of the bank. Considerable sums of money were paid to Croaker, with April 1818 being something of a pivotal month. Before then, he received 21 individual payments totalling £527. But from April 1818 through to

August 1819, transactions became more frequent, and much larger. There were then 35 individual payments, totalling £2191. Furthermore, the clients were different. His associates in the judicature, like John and Thomas Wylde, and J. J. Moore, no longer featured prominently. He was now dealing with an assortment of publicans, merchants, auctioneers and landowners, many of them prominent and long-established citizens, and proprietors of the bank. During 1818, for example, he was paid £171 by James Hankinson, merchant and publican. But the fact that Croaker made promissory notes in favour of Hankinson in the same period totalling £277, shows that a merchant who was his customer could also be, in terms of another commodity, his supplier.

If the goods in which Croaker dealt are unknown, they can at least be reckoned, from the number of his contacts and the variety of their interests, to have been broadly based. He was a middle-man who bought wholesale from the importing merchants, or at auction, and sold retail to the people at large. As items imported from England sold at a mark-up of 60 to 100 per cent, there was ample room for profit at different levels. His type of business was further encouraged by the colony's lack of basic money, of which the importing in 1813 of £10 000 worth of dollars from Madras (punched out to create a rim and centre of different nominal values) was symptomatic.[21] For sums above 5 shillings, however, there was still inadequate provision, with store receipts and promissory notes providing a rough-and-ready currency until the Bank of New South Wales, having proved its stability, could offer its own banknotes as a reliable alternative.

Conditions favoured a class of entrepreneur—the dealer—who could negotiate credit terms for himself with his suppliers, while prepared to allow rather less credit to his trustworthy customers. If most of the obligations thus contracted could be settled on paper, by an exchange of bills and notes within the two or three months before they matured, only a minimum of 'real' money was ever needed to square one person's debt to another. Indeed, there was no need to settle the debts at all, unless a dealer or merchant allowed his affairs to get badly out of balance. If Hankinson, say, owed Croaker £30, and had just received a promissory note from Jenkins for £50, he could endorse it to Croaker, who was thus instantly converted into a debtor to Hankinson for £20. This would also have altered the creditor–debtor relationship between Jenkins and Croaker. With so much paper changing hands, it is hardly surprising that some individuals lost control of their book-keeping. For a dealer like Croaker, who could not open a bank account, the acquisition of too much hard money was simply uncomfortable. Was he to place it under the mattress, or in a hole in the gum tree at the bottom of the garden? Far better for him, with so many recidivist convicts around, to keep his money as illiquid as possible, and invest in what could not be stolen.

Within six months of his arrival in the colony, Croaker's ability to balance what he owed and what he earned, while keeping a modest float of ready money, came to grief. On 2 March 1818 he drew a promissory note in favour of one George Williams, promising to pay him £25 in two months time.[22] Williams endorsed the note, and gave it to Robert Campbell junior, who thereby became entitled to the money. When the note matured, Croaker failed to honour it, although Campbell overlooked the debt for several weeks. This leniency seems compatible with Campbell's character. 'Convivial and charming, with the flair of a bon viveur', he claimed to have made between £20 000 and £30 000 in the years 1811 to 1813.[23] He was also connected in various ways with the new bank, which could have made him reluctant to put Croaker in court. He therefore let a modest debt ride, and he and Croaker continued to do business. As for the latter, litigation was unhelpful in his public position, and in June he endorsed in Campbell's favour a promissory note for £50 drawn by J. J. Moore. This seems to have been an attempt by Moore to keep Croaker out of trouble, perhaps at the instigation of Wylde. Despite this, the debt had allegedly reached £200 by September 1818, and Campbell's tolerance was exhausted.

Campbell sued for his money in the Supreme Court of Civil Jurisdiction. It was common practice in litigation roughly to double the claim, to allow for costs and unclaimed interest at high rates.[24] But as long as the defendant admitted the true gross debt, the plaintiff had no case for pursuing the artificial total. Croaker, as a clerk in the judiciary, did the sensible thing in an awkward position, and confessed the debt at £110 11s (presumably the capital sum, interest, and a legal fee), which Campbell then accepted, and the claim for £200 was abandoned. To cover further costs, the amount was increased to £124 9s, which Croaker was wholly unable to meet. A writ of *fieri facias* was therefore issued, instructing the provost marshal to levy the sum from Croaker's goods, which happened by 21 January 1819.[25] In an eleventh-hour attempt to stave off his embarrassment, Croaker assigned two bills to Campbell in that same month. But they would have made less than £40 together after discounting, and the law took its course. Thereafter, with honour satisfied on both sides, the two men immediately resumed their business connections. In February a bill for £50 drawn on J. J. Moore was endorsed by Campbell in Croaker's favour, thus returning the compliment of the previous June, and in May Croaker assigned to Campbell a promissory note from Francis Greenway for £20.

The relationship between Campbell and Croaker endured, because there was nothing fundamentally wrong with the latter's position. He had allowed his trading account with Campbell to enter the red, but he was not insolvent. Given enough leeway, he could probably have earned the money to balance the debt. With nowhere to keep working capital, he could only borrow long and lend short, and hope that his customers were good for their money. Evidently he miscalculated, or was badly let down, and so the profitability cautiously deduced above from banking records is revealed as an accounting chimera. It existed in one sense but not in another, because when Croaker really needed hard money, it was sometimes not in his pocket. Soon there was to be another flutter of law suits against him, for much the same reason. But Croaker was getting worldly-wise, and his attitude towards the litigants, and his reactions to the writs, was soon to harden.

No dust had settled on the Campbell file before Croaker was again in court.[26] The circumstances are less fully preserved, but the gist of the litigation is clear. The case is also, indirectly, the key to Croaker's rather painful co-existence with the bank which he had helped to organise on the most efficient book-keeping principles. Towards the end of 1818 Croaker drew two promissory notes in favour of Robert Hazard, a Sydney merchant, for a total of £177. Both notes were endorsed by Hazard and given to Thomas Underwood, who successfully presented them to the bank for discounting on 8 December. The underlying transaction cannot be established. When the notes matured, apparently three months later, the bank went to Croaker for its money, but it can be deduced that he dishonoured them. The bank immediately exercised its contingency plan, and claimed the full amount from one or other of the endorsers. Which of the two paid is unknown (perhaps Underwood was simply the third party required by the discounting rules), but the bank had been satisfied by someone and was therefore uninvolved in the subsequent law suit. Hazard, on the other hand, was back where he started and sued Croaker for some £360, roughly double the debt as usual. Again Croaker admitted his liability, and the true total of capital and interest, with further fees, was reconciled as £195 1s, which the provost marshal had to levy from the defendant's effects. The debt was eventually settled on 1 May 1819.

In parallel with this hearing, Croaker was sued by Edward Eagar, a Sydney merchant and lawyer, for £100.[27] As payment was agreed at

£53 11s 8d, the original capital debt was doubtless £50. No circumstances are known, but this was presumably a dishonoured promissory
note. Again, the provost marshal was set to work, and levied goods from
Croaker worth £57 16s 8d (i.e. the gross debt, plus further fees and
expenses). This plaintiff was also satisfied on 1 May 1819, so during the
first five months of the year, Croaker was deprived of goods to the value
of more than £377. Within a few months, on 22 November 1819, he was
back in court.[28] The reasons are again obscure. This time the plaintiff was
Thomas Arndell, who had entered the original plea at some £72, to secure
repayment of roughly £36. There seems to have been an accommodation
whereby the provost marshal levied only £20 13s 7d from Croaker's
estate, which was paid to Arndell as late as 1 November 1820.

Other law suits were brought against Croaker in 1820, but it is useful
to pause here and study those so far cited, in relation to his wider
activities and the rough and tumble of dealing. During the four instances
above, he worked for John Wylde as a clerk in the judicature, authorising
his colleagues (Thomas) 'Wylde' or (Joshua John) 'Moore' to plead on
his behalf, with or without other attorneys, in at least three of the cases.
While he was being sued for debt, he was drawing his salary of £50 a year
and being supported, along with his family, from the government stores.
Such a conflict of interests in England would have cost Croaker his job,
and it was a fairly uncomfortable situation even in New South Wales. But
as long as he stayed within the law, and avoided total insolvency, his
predicament was acceptable to his superiors, at least in the short term.
What caused an eventual re-think of Croaker's position was the searching
enquiry by Commissioner Bigge, who was already in the colony in 1819.
The four law suits mentioned above were initiated before Bigge got his
knees properly under the desk. Croaker had little time in which to make
the best of his lot.

The fact that the provost marshal had to raise money for Croaker's litigants by distraining four times upon his goods should not be seen as the
enormity, or humiliation, which such an action would suggest today. In
1818–19 Croaker was good for his money, in kind if not in cash, and the
lawsuits were simply a consequence of his inability, or disinclination, to
satisfy any given creditor at any given time. Civil proceedings were an
expensive rigmarole, but they were inevitable once the balance of debts
was out of control, or when the plaintiff's affairs were so generally embarrassed that he had to seek money wherever it was owed, regardless of
the normal tolerance in dealer–merchant relations. The English notion
of dishonour attaching to debt was absent. It was possible to be in the
most straitened circumstances in the colony and still command prom-

inence. This truth is demonstrated by the career of Edward Eagar, who is worth closer analysis.[29] His suit against Croaker was the third case cited above.

When he took Croaker to court, Eagar was chronically in debt. This was far more than a temporary set-back, because he owed two sums of £600 to the Bank of New South Wales.[30] Thus in May 1819 the small amount he received from Croaker was absolutely necessary to help mitigate his debt to the institution he had helped to create. The likelihood is that, with his affairs in average order, Eagar would have let Croaker's minor obligation annul itself in the ordinary course of trading. But there is still deeper insight to be gained from Eagar's plight. He was assigned two promissory notes in the summer of 1819, both drawn by James Hankinson, another merchant with whom Croaker had dealings. These notes totalled more than £500, and Eagar endorsed them in favour of the bank, no doubt relieved at the prospect of an end to his impecunious state. But Hankinson, unfortunately, refused to honour his own notes when the bank asked him for its money in October. The directors then had no option but to seek redress from Eagar, as the final endorser. The last thing Eagar wanted was to be visited with Hankinson's debts as well as his own, and he no doubt found a way to indicate his displeasure. With regard to the bank, he could do nothing but default in these further payments, and the directors had no option but to sue him.

The complicated manoeuvres from that point onwards are not relevant to the Croaker story. What matters is that Eagar's apparently desperate state made little impact on his career. He had recently received an absolute pardon, and had moved from law into commerce, with eyes on Tahiti.[31] His proposed monopoly of trade with King Pomare II of Tahiti is evidence of increasing commercial interest in the Pacific arena, and the loosening of connections with Britain. In 1819 Eagar was also secretary to the committee which drew up an important petition to the Prince Regent about civil and commercial disabilities in New South Wales. He was soon to tackle Bigge about the colonists' problems, and he went to London shortly afterwards to argue with some success for emancipists' rights. Here, then, was a man of stature whose career eventually overcame the stigma of his felony. The fact that he had been grossly in debt, had dishonoured commercial obligations, had been sued by his bank, and taken his grievance against the directors to Commissioner Bigge, seems to have been no impediment to his ascendancy. In England any one of these infelicities would have spelt his social ruin, and probably his bankruptcy. In New South Wales they were apparently unfortunate, but nothing more. It is interesting that Eagar's conspicuous debt of

1819, and his legal battles with the bank, are not mentioned in his profile in the *Australian Dictionary of Biography*.

There is a lesson here to help with the understanding of Croaker's position. The circumstances were not quite the same because Croaker, unlike Eagar, was a civil servant, but the parallel is nevertheless revealing. Once he had been blooded by Campbell, and realised how the system worked, Croaker would have viewed the suits against him with only limited concern. If Bigge had not been raising to the masthead the flag of propriety, even the few qualms he did feel would have been further reduced. It was in Croaker's interests to be passive. Let those sue him who wished. Let the writs of *fieri facias* be issued. Let the provost marshal do his job. Better the loss of a cow, some corn, or a crate of imports, than the thankless task of pursuing his minor debtors for ready money. If too many dealers called in too many debts, they risked the collapse of the house of cards, on which rested the economy of New South Wales.

There is proof that Croaker could have met his debts, had he wished. On 10 April 1819 he borrowed £500 from Thomas Middleton at legal interest (10 per cent).[32] Middleton was one of his regular dealing associates, but the arrangement had nothing to do with their usual exchanges of notes and bills. This loan was effected by a warrant of attorney, a non-negotiable instrument which allowed Middleton to have a judgement entered in his favour in the civil court, if Croaker defaulted. A promissory note, with its inflexible maturity date, would simply have dragged back the arrangement into the arena of commercial debt. The warrant of attorney left Croaker with more latitude for repayment, but if he persisted in dishonouring the obligation, Middleton could expose him to a clinical remedy at the hands of the provost marshal. The purpose of this loan, as will be seen, was to allow Croaker to develop a focused business interest, in which Middleton himself was involved. Thus for Croaker, at this period, dealing debts were a tiresome distraction. He knew where he was going, and it is time to follow on his heels.

8   Land and Liquor

May and June of 1818 were probably the happiest months which the Croakers spent in their short time as a family unit in New South Wales. They had come to terms with the colony and learnt how to make the best of its opportunities and frustrations. Susannah was now pregnant, her husband had received a conditional pardon, and it was time for the Croaker ménage to acquire the trappings of respectability which befitted a clerk in the office of the judge advocate, and his wife who had an independent profession. It was also a convenient opportunity to invest surplus money received from the business of dealing for which Croaker, with no deposit account at the bank, lacked any alternative outlet.

The family moved to Perroquet Hill on the outskirts of Sydney, to the north of Parramatta Road. The locality had been named by the French zoologist, François Péron, who visited it in 1802, remarking that the silence was 'interrupted only by the singing and chirping of the richly plumed paroquets and other birds which inhabit it'.[1] Tastefully dotted with pleasant villas, the area was home to some influential people, among them John Harris of Ultimo House, a former naval surgeon, magistrate, and a founding director of the Bank of New South Wales.[2] The Croakers had the benefit of a government servant called Joseph Gunston, who had also been transported on the *Mariner*.[3] The exact date when they counted Harris as a neighbour is a matter for conjecture. Perroquet Hill was certainly their address by September 1817 when Croaker was raided by Bartholomew Roach. He stole three cows and two calves—already reduced to two hindquarters, six feet and four pieces of skin by the time Roach was arrested at dead of night on the Sydney road.[4] It is likely, from the following evidence, that the house and lands were leasehold.

On 14 August 1819 the *Sydney Gazette* carried an advertisement from Joshua Palmer, a George Street baker, seeking to let his farm at Perroquet Hill in the following year. It consisted of some 25 to 30 acres, cleared and fenced, centred on a weatherboard dwelling-house. The site 'was peculiarly adapted either for a Gentleman's occasional country retreat, or otherwise for a Gardener, the ground being as rich as the situation engaging'. The property was then 'let to a respectable tenant at £30 per annum, whose lease expires next May [1820]'. It is tempting to see this person as Croaker, who was unwilling to continue the tenancy. The reasons for that can be discussed later; at this stage it is necessary to establish Croaker as the lessee. Press notices suggest that Palmer advertised the tenancy roughly every two years.[5] The notice which appeared in the *Sydney Gazette* of 6 July 1816 was too early for Croaker, but he could have taken over the lease in, say, 1817, and before the next normal renewal date. It can be assumed that Croaker and Palmer, both from George Street, knew each other quite well and the absence of a press notice for the letting in 1818 points to the Croakers being already in residence.

Susannah Croaker gave birth to her third child, Thomas Lawrence Pennel, on 23 February 1819.[6] The infant was baptised at St Philip's Church, Sydney, on 21 March. It is probable that, before and during her pregnancy, she ran a private day school to which she later returned. A submission to Commissioner Bigge, dated January 1821, indicates that she taught ten girls at that time and the only question is when she began.[7] It is interesting that a wife was not considered automatically tainted by the sins of her husband. Bigge's unmistakable discomfort with the rise of emancipists did not prevent his endorsement when necessary of the inherent good character of their spouses. He was quite happy, for instance, to concede that the matron who supervised the girls' orphanage at Parramatta 'was a person of respectability, the wife of a convict who resided in the house, and who assisted also in its management'.[8] She was, therefore, employed in her own right and, to that limited extent, a woman's good character was able to make amends for her husband's conviction.

The importance of this in the context of the Croakers was that Susannah would have been regarded by free settlers, as well as by emancipists, as a fit person to teach their children. Her prestige would have been boosted by friendship and even some business link with her friend Mary Greenway. The latter was in an especially strong position as her husband, the forthright architect Francis Greenway, was one of the very few emancipists for whom Bigge had a good word.[9] It is likely that Susannah and Mary had a reciprocal arrangement whereby, when one of

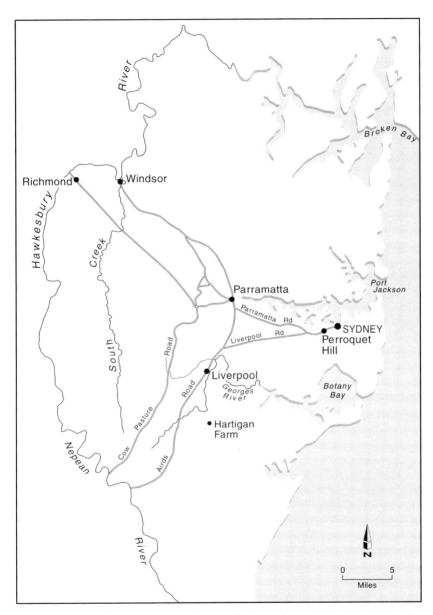

The settled area of New South Wales in 1817 (redrawn from AO Map No. 1123 with permission)

them entered confinement, her pupils were taught by the other. It was important that recognition as a teacher, once gained, should not lapse. The social disadvantage normally felt by a male emancipist in the company of free settlers could be side-stepped by his wife, if she had a professional vocation. The result for her was a status little different from that which she had forfeited in England, usually by no fault of her own, and this could only have helped the aspirations of her husband. There are indications that this worked for the Croakers. When he was being sued for debt, his description was never lower than 'gentleman', and was even cast as 'settler' in October 1818.[10] A position in the judicature enhanced his standing, but the literate Susannah, no doubt socially ambitious, was a conspicuous asset.

The property at Perroquet Hill raises the enduring and important issue of Croaker's role as a farmer. In assisting the Bank of New South Wales he had been working wholly within his training; in setting-up as a dealer he could have used his knowledge of business, acquired through banking, to some limited advantage; but as a farmer he was green. This was a significant drawback as the acquisition and management of land, the only commodity in the colony not in short supply, was an obvious route to wealth and influence. Much of this land was granted by the governor, sometimes in very large acreages (subject to a quit-rent), both to free settlers and emancipists. The bigger plots were developed into grazing for cattle and sheep but the smaller acreages provided little more than subsistence farming, with the opportunity to sell surplus produce to the government stores.[11] Often these plots were held by free settlers of modest means, people who were sometimes illiterate and picked up the skills of farming as they went along. A settler was often aided by a convict labourer, fresh from the ship, whose aptitude and experience was usually no better than his master's. All this was a fascination for Commissioner Bigge, who took evidence from professionals like Gregory Blaxland and Robert Dunn.[12] What was the cost of clearing the ground? How long did it take to reach profitability? What were the conditions in this place or that?

Another dimension to this issue, pertinent in the study of Croaker, arises from the role of the dealer. A common practice was to supply goods to outlying settlers against the security of a mortgage. When the debtor, from the absence of hard money or for other reasons, could not pay, the dealer foreclosed and acquired the land. 'This system', complained W. C. Wentworth, 'of buying goods, and afterwards selling them at an almost arbitrary profit, the greater part of which is thus converted into landed property, is daily gaining ground'.[13] Wentworth, too indignant to notice his own pun, was expressing a widespread resentment against dealers which struck at the root of the antagonism between free settlers, on the one hand, and convicts with a ticket of leave, or conditional or free pardon, on the other. Bigge got wind of these practices, and asked one of his witnesses, P. Hart, whether he could cite an instance of a settler 'being sold off by a [merchant *deleted*] Dealer in Sidney [*sic*] & becoming his Tenant afterwards?'[14]

Hart certainly could. He had been owed £146, including interest and expenses, by a man called How. As Hart was insisting on payment, How transferred his debt to one 'D. Cowper' (probably Daniel Cooper), who paid off Hart and thereby had How at his mercy.[15] An estate of 40 acres was made over from How to 'Cowper', who let the former remain on the land at a rent of £46 a year, 'being allowed a horse & cart to work it'. This was virtually a descent into serfdom, a general point not lost on Wentworth. 'They [the dealers] constrained these poor wretches to cultivate as tenants, the same soil which lately belonged to them, and exacted from them in return, a rent too exorbitant to be paid.'[16] Another contemporary, James Atkinson, explained that when the provost marshal offered a farm for sale, following an action for debt, it was usually bought by the creditor for about half its value.[17] As for Bigge, who can be pictured pressing his enquiry with ever-narrowing eyes, he was curious to know whether instances of this kind were common in New South Wales. 'There are a great many', confessed Hart, with some embarrassment. It was he who had forced How into his predicament in the first place.

It is a tantalising question as to whether or not Croaker picked up the dealers' worst practices. He might have dispossessed an existing tenant of Palmer's in this way to get the property at Perroquet Hill. That he became a substantial landowner early on, by one means or another, is not in doubt. Returns to Commissioner Bigge in 1820 include lists of those who held real estate, arranged by locality: 'J. Croaker' is entered for 120 acres in the district of Sydney.[18] That was a snapshot figure in October and there is no way of knowing how it compared with his holdings in the preceding two or three years, nor what element was represented by the property believed leased from Palmer. The only other information given in the return was that Croaker's land was acquired by purchase and not by grant. This is helpful if only to suggest that he made no big impression on Macquarie. But what did 'purchase' mean? Was it simply the catch-all alternative to 'grant' or did it mean, very precisely, the secondary acquisition of land which had originally been granted to someone else? In other words, could the buying of a leasehold interest, or the kind of deal explained above between How and 'Cowper', be construed as 'purchase'?

The conclusion must be that they could be construed in this way. The list of landowners of which Croaker is part, clinical as it is, speaks whispered words. It distinguishes between those free by servitude (59 names), those with free and conditional pardons (19 and 31 names respectively), and those with a ticket of leave (only 9 names). In every case it explains whether the land was held by grant or purchase. Many of these people were dealers at one stage or another in their careers and must have acquired at least some of their property deviously, as Wentworth and Atkinson reported. The high incidence of purchase is enough to implicate each class of convict, if not an individual, in sharp practice. Those free by servitude held nearly 23 000 acres by purchase, but fewer than 7000 by grant. Of those with a free pardon, the ratio was 2415 to 1535 acres. Among those with a conditional pardon, who included Croaker, the proportion was 2360 acres to 1530. In his class, Croaker was 7th out of 31 in acreage, although a long way short of the leaders. The largest estate among his peers was held by Solomon Levey at 1000 acres (all by purchase),[19] followed by two at 400 acres (all by purchase, bar 50 acres), one at 300 acres (200 by purchase), and two at 250 (mostly by grant). It is significant that one of the 400-acre landowners was Daniel Cooper, who seems to have dispossessed How. It is difficult to accept that such large estates were not acquired partly by devious means. Most convicts with a conditional pardon, however, held fewer than 100 acres and as little as 10, and nearly all these lands had been granted to them. This sub-class was evidently the most restrained. Particularly vulnerable, on the other hand, to the charge of profiteering from antisocial practices are the ticket-of-leave men. All nine of them held their lands, totalling 635 acres, by 'purchase'.

Whether or not the Perroquet Hill property was included in Croaker's total of 120 acres, it can be assumed that he had acquired some, if not all, of his land while living at that prestigious address. On 11 July 1818 he tendered to supply the commissariat in Sydney with 4000 lbs of fresh meat.[20] As he lacked the capital, time and expertise to set up a cattle property, he must have bought into or otherwise acquired an existing business. Perhaps it included the horse and cart listed in another return to Commissioner Bigge.[21] The likelihood is that Croaker bought his property with the early proceeds of dealing, while leaving it in the hands of a herdsman such as Jacob Winter (another convict off the *Mariner*), who was described as a part-time employee when Roach stole Croaker's livestock.[22] Rearing cattle in the colony was 'simple and economical' according to Wentworth,[23] but still well beyond Croaker's capability. The other possibility is that he engineered control of the property from a debtor, but in the absence of any evidence he is entitled to the benefit of the kinder alternative. In any event, his heart was never in cattle rearing. He does not feature in lists of cattleowners submitted to Bigge and on the only other occasion when he is known to have supplied meat to the commissariat—in October 1820—the quantity was reduced to 363 lbs.[24] This suggests that he had considerably scaled down his involvement in livestock, which fits with growing evidence of his interest in crops.

Croaker probably knew no more about arable farming than the management of cattle, but the question needs analysis in the light of his wider objectives. It must have dawned on Croaker that there was a deficiency in the colony of good ingredients for the manufacture of beer. If there was one business he really knew about, other than banking, it was brewing, and in that area there were fewer impediments of status to hamper his progress. It was not the case that New South Wales had no breweries but rather that the beer was so disgusting that porter and ale were imported from England.[25] For this reason, and for lack of wine or cider, most people who drank alcohol were addicted to spirits. Croaker was later to hedge his bets by involvement in the retailing of liquor. But for the time being he made a determined sortie into beer, not as a brewer but as a provider and co-ordinator of ingredients which would improve the quality.

The two crops in Croaker's mind would have been hops and barley. The former grew strongly in the area of Port Jackson where the brewers had several plantations.[26] They could also be shipped from England without detriment to quality, and as Kent was the hop county *par excellence* there is no doubt that Croaker was well placed to arrange a supplier. The bigger problem by far was barley, needed to make malt. Commissioner Bigge found barley was little in demand and therefore seldom sown. In its absence, some brewers used malt made from maize, one of the two most favoured cereals in the colony, the other being wheat.[27] Barley joined oats and rye among the lesser crops. The strain was known as 'Cape' or 'Skinless' barley, which could yield up to 42 bushels per acre on good soil, but it ripened capriciously and too fast.[28] Gregory Blaxland had dabbled briefly in malting but found that his barley germinated too quickly; furthermore, the malt was 40–50 per cent lower in saccharine content than its English equivalent.[29] Wentworth was no less gloomy. While criticising brewers for a general 'want of skill', he specifically blamed barley for the bad quality of the beer. In his view, a brewer with

£5000 at his disposal would succeed either at Sydney or Hobart, but 'he should understand the process of making malt, since there are no regular maltsters yet in the colony'.[30] Atkinson agreed that this was the crux of the problem: 'good malting samples of barley will always sell readily'.[31]

It is likely that Croaker was excited by the commercial possibilities with this product. At Canterbury, where the maltster May Inge (Susannah's brother-in-law) plied his trade behind Abbott's brewery, the young Croaker would have been fascinated by the deep and silent mysteries of the process. The smell of malt on the kiln is sweet and powerful. More especially, he knew why malt mattered. No one could successfully adulterate beer without understanding why it tasted as it should and Croaker, it seems, had been implicated in the Canterbury scandal, at least as a book-keeper. Now, in a curious role reversal, he was aiming to produce the proper, palatable beer which was eluding the brewers of the colony. This meant growing and harvesting the barley and perhaps seeking to import from England a strain better suited for malting. The temptation, therefore, was to enter ever more deeply into farming, about which he knew little, and the siren voices of cheap land, low labour costs, and potential wealth were not to be ignored.

To pursue his ambitions, Croaker teamed up with a brewer, Nathaniel Lawrence of Pitt Street. It may not be fanciful to see the Lawrence element in the name of the Croakers' baby as complimentary to their new associate. The evidence for this business connection will be shown to lie in 1820, but it is reasonable to bring the date forward to 1819, when (on 3 July) Croaker was assigned the lease of 1 Upper Pitt Street, on the corner of Park Street, some one hundred yards from Lawrence's brewery.[32] The assignor was Robert Cooper, who later became a distiller. This was a complicated transaction, as on that same day Croaker mortgaged this property, along with 2 Upper Pitt Street, to Cooper for £250 repayable on 3 January 1821.[33] This presumably meant no. 2 was already, somehow, in Croaker's possession and the mortgage was effectively a loan by which the two properties could be united for business use. Such a conversion required an imponderable amount of ready money and so Croaker's unwillingness to meet his debtors' claims over the spring and summer of 1819 becomes increasingly understandable. The importance of Middleton's loan to him of £500, in April, is also seen in sharper focus. It was needed as venture capital in the absence of any support from the Bank of New South Wales, to whom Croaker made no application. Middleton was also developing business interests on his own account. He ran the 'Wellington' brewery in Pitt Street and stood to benefit directly from the improvements which Croaker was planning.[34] Other shadowy figures in the consortium are likely to have been Daniel Cooper, and Edward Eagar who had an interest in 3 Upper Pitt Street.[35]

The site which Croaker developed was probably the south-western corner of the junction of Upper Pitt Street and Park Street. In 1827 it consisted of 'a front dwelling together with a brewing-house, a three-storied granary and stores, with the various other erections needful for a brewery establishment', on land which measured 32 × 140 feet.[36] Croaker seems to have been partly responsible for the conversion of this area into an adjunct to Lawrence's main brewery, with a retail outlet. The component properties, nos 1 and 2, remained distinct, while each contributed to the working success of the whole. No. 1 was occupied by Miles Fieldgate, who moved there from Sydney Market in May 1819,[37] although his brewing licences (none between 1818 and 1821) were for the Bull's Head in George Street. He died in 1822, but well before then—certainly by November 1820—Croaker was giving 1 Upper Pitt Street as his business address.[38] As Joshua Palmer readvertised the farm at Perroquet Hill on 14 August 1819, it is possible that the Croakers moved from there to Upper Pitt Street at around that date, although the living accommodation would have been cramped for a growing family with pretensions to dignity. It is, perhaps, safer to see the Croakers returning at this point to George Street, where they were certainly domiciled a year later.[39] As for 2 Upper Pitt Street, this was described in March 1822 as 'a newly erected well-built cottage' of four rooms. Behind it was a yard, a two-stall stable, and 'a well of excellent water'.[40]

The various sub-tenancies are difficult to disentangle, but it seems that Lawrence was the ultimate landlord when he died in 1826, while Middleton and Daniel Cooper retained significant interests.[41] The comprehensive nature of the brewing site indicates that it contained a malthouse and this can be construed as Croaker's particular contribution to Lawrence's expansion. When the latter petitioned for the renewal of a wine and spirit licence on 23 February 1820, he claimed to have 'lately at the expence [sic] of about £1600 erected a Granary, Drying House malthouse etc'.[42] The location was not given, but it is convenient to see this as a reference to Upper Pitt Street, confirming Lawrence's seniority among the partners to the enterprise. It appears also that Lawrence made the greatest investment in the scheme, although some of Croaker's money might have been represented in his statement. The malthouse element required only a modest outlay. Apart from barley, the only raw material necessary was a supply of clean water, which the premises clearly enjoyed from the well. An alternative supply was from the Tank Stream, if its purity could be relied upon.

The actual process of malting required little equipment but an understanding of the rules and rhythm of nature. Barley-corn arrived at one end of the building and was immersed for a few days in a 'steep' of water, so the grain could swell. After draining on the 'couch', the grain was spread over the malting floor to a depth of a few inches, where it lay for about a week. During this time the grain began to germinate and the maltster's art was to judge the critical point when this germination should temporarily cease. The conversion of the starchy content of each grain into sugar had to take place in the brewery's mash tun, and not on the malthouse floor. To arrest germination, the maltster removed the grain to a kiln, where it was heated and dried to evaporate the water content.[43]

It follows from this description that a malthouse was generally a long, low building with a cistern at one end and a kiln at the other. The conversion of outbuildings from storage to malting would be possible with the money at Croaker's disposal following the mortgage to Cooper and the loan from Middleton. The other expenses of the site would have been met by Lawrence. There is no difficulty in believing that Croaker, the son of a brewery manager, had the basic knowledge to design and accomplish the bricks and mortar of this project, although he was not to be described as a maltster. It was to be Lawrence and Middleton who handled the 'manufacture' of beer through all its stages. The importance of Croaker to the brewers was threefold: he knew the procedures of the ancillary trade; he could establish contact with maltsters, hop-growers and brewers in East Kent; and he had land not too distant from the new enterprise on which barley—perhaps of a new, imported strain—and hops could be harvested.

The question of land re-opens the vexed discussion of how far Croaker operated as a farmer. It has been established that he owned 120 acres in 1820 in the Sydney district which may or may not have included his leasehold acreage at Perroquet Hill. It is known that his involvement in livestock decreased and a rising interest in arable farming took its place. In the nature of things, this is difficult to quantify as the crops he was producing were intended for his own use and therefore no statistics need have existed, for the eyes of Bigge or the governor, of the harvest yield. When Croaker did produce a cereal crop for the commissariat, there was, of course, a record of it. In July 1819 he delivered 316 bushels of wheat into store in Sydney.[44] This could have been produced from as little as 15 acres of land so he had much spare capacity for barley, hops or indeed vegetables. In view of his other commitments, not least his basic job in the office of the judge advocate, he must have employed labourers to prepare the ground and manage the crops. Much of this work was seasonal, but at least one skilled man would have been necessary all the year round. It is because of this, and the attendant expense, that doubts re-emerge as to Croaker's moral title to his land. If he had pulled off a dealer's coup, as 'Cowper' had done with How, he not only got a sitting farmer but one who paid him rent.

The problem of Croaker's real estate crystallises in the district of Airds, about one mile from Campbell Town and 35 miles south-west of Sydney. On 3 March 1821 a farm of 40 acres, originally granted to Dudley Hartigan in 1816, was advertised for sale in the *Sydney Gazette*. Twenty-six acres were 'clear and in cultivation, with newly erected stock-yards, calf-pens, &c. and a very extensive and desirable run for cattle, being always supplied with water in the driest seasons.—Application to be made to Mr. J. Croaker, No. 1, Upper Pitt-street, Park-street'. The descent of title to this small farm over only five years is an object-lesson in the complexities which bedevil the study of colonial landholding.

Hartigan, the original grantee, had been dispossessed by Edward Eagar in 1817 after an action for debt.[45] The farm was then taken over by Patrick Devoy, probably installed by Eagar. Friendly relations had once existed between Eagar and Devoy, as the former had acted as a trustee for Mary McDonough whom Devoy married in 1813.[46] No doubt in accordance with the trust deed, Eagar transferred to Devoy, on 10 November 1817, the title to two houses on the corner of Pitt and King streets in Sydney which he (Eagar) had been holding on Mary's behalf.[47] Within a few months, however, the relationship had soured and Devoy was facing two court actions, one brought by Eagar and both presumably for debt.[48] Neither litigant was satisfied and Hartigan Farm was advertised for auction in the *Sydney Gazette* on 18 April 1818. One of the Pitt Street houses (no. 38) and a farm known as Mary Redman's at Botany Bay were sold at the same time. All three units were described as the property of Devoy. In June 1818 Eagar registered his new title to 38 Pitt Street and Redman's Farm, bought by him at the auction, but not to Hartigan Farm,[49] which suggests that he had no further interest in it. It is tempting to see Croaker as the purchaser in April 1818, if only to soak up the proceeds of dealing, but at that time he was still on a ticket of leave and restricted to the area of Sydney. Besides, there is no record of him, or indeed of any other party, registering the title. It is best, therefore, to see Hartigan Farm as unsold in 1818 and reverting to the ownership of Eagar, by default, with Devoy as a tenant 'by daily labour'.[50] If Eagar did not particularly want the farm and had no plans to keep it, he would not have bothered to register his title.

Why, then, was Croaker advertising the farm for sale nearly three years later? The two possibilities seem to be that he had bought it in the intervening period, or that he was an agent for the true proprietor. The problem is further compounded by subsequent events. A few weeks after the advertisement of 1821, Croaker was seeking 'a steady man to superintend the management of a farming concern', which could well have been the 40 acres at Airds.[51] On 15 March 1822 Croaker again advertised the farm for sale in the *Sydney Gazette*.[52] Thus the point is established that his involvement with Airds was not an isolated incident, but the facts, as far as they are known, paint a picture which is far from complete and may be misleading.

It would be natural to seek a solution to this impasse through the affairs of William Redfern, by far the biggest landowner in the district. Redfern had trained as a surgeon before joining the navy, where he was implicated in the mutiny at the Nore.[53] Reprieved from a death sentence on account of his youth, he arrived in New South Wales in 1801 and won the support of successive governors. Given a free pardon in 1803, he established his credentials as a doctor and acquired vast amounts of land, much of it in the Campbell Town region, where he eventually owned 6296 acres. He was a founding director of the Bank of New South Wales and played a full part in the colony's philanthropic institutions. Macquarie appointed him magistrate for the district of Airds in November 1819, a decision which upset Commissioner Bigge, who succeeded eventually in getting Redfern removed from the bench. Although Bigge admired Redfern's ability as a farmer, the antipathy between them resulted in no adequate return being made of land held by convicts in the district of Airds. It was Redfern's responsibility to organise the survey and send the list to Robert Lowe at Bringelly, who would then add it to certain other returns before transmitting the whole to the secretary to the commission of inquiry. Redfern's dignity was offended by this oblique role and he declined involvement unless he were written to officially.[54] Whatever the outcome of this tantrum, no landholders at Airds were included in Lowe's return to Bigge (which nonetheless kept Airds in its title) and no other list has survived among Bigge's papers.

This stubbornness by Redfern has resulted in the absence of conclusive evidence as to whether or not Croaker bought Hartigan Farm after the grant of his conditional pardon. It is possible that he did, because he paid Redfern around £50 in the summer of 1819, yet on no other occasion does the latter feature in Croaker's activities with documentary credit.[55] This would mean Redfern himself had bought the farm at the auction of April 1818, which makes some sense as he was expanding rapidly in Airds during that year. Furthermore, he was very well acquainted with Edward Eagar in whose interests the farm was being sold. Redfern could have stepped in to ensure that his friend, who had severe money worries of his own, acquired reasonable proceeds. However, why Croaker should have wanted the farm a year later is yet another question. It was clearly geared to cattle and there was no reason why he should have been interested in this aspect once his attention had turned to brewing. Furthermore, he would have needed to pay a farm manager and perhaps labourers, and the expense and logistics seem to be problems he might well have avoided. The most attractive conclusion, therefore, is that Eagar or Redfern owned the farm after 1818 and Croaker was some kind of agent, seeing to matters which could only be resolved in Sydney.

In January 1821 both Redfern and Eagar committed themselves to a long stay in England to argue better rights for emancipists. They set sail in October. Redfern returned to the colony in July 1824 but Eagar never returned, dying in London in 1866. Croaker's management of Hartigan Farm therefore fits the circumstances of either absentee but looks better in the context of Eagar. Owning so much land, Redfern must have made a comprehensive provision for the management of his farms and it would have made little sense to isolate one insignificant property for the attention of Croaker. On the other hand, Eagar was not a big landowner in Airds and his connection with Pitt Street is proven—another link with Croaker.

An apparent complication is the law suit Eagar v. Croaker of 1819, already discussed. Eagar was critically in debt and the provost marshal had to distrain from Croaker's goods to recover some £50 which Eagar was owed. Was it then likely that Eagar and Croaker would have continued to do business? Indeed, it was. It has already been argued that lawsuits in the colony between people engaged in commerce were entered into without prejudice to business associations. The law was a clinical procedure when the balance of debt became out of control, and no stigma attached to the defendant. The connection between Croaker and Robert Campbell junior demonstrated that a writ was not a knife to cut the bonds of the marketplace. By the same token, no animosity should be assumed between Eagar and Croaker as a result of litigation. But, for that matter, there need not have been friendship. Each did business with the other for what he got out of it and there was, no doubt, some benefit foreseen by Croaker, albeit a long way ahead, in keeping on the right side of Eagar.

Thus Croaker's business career reached a plateau, rather than a pinnacle, of success. He had arrived at a certain altitude but was now to lose sight of the upward path. He had shown resourcefulness, and some ingenuity. He had prestige and standing, due in no small part to Susannah. He was also alive to the challenges and risks which the colony presented. Unfortunately, events to a large extent beyond his control were about to deny him the success which he might reasonably have expected.

9   Decline and Disgrace

If the birth of Thomas Lawrence Pennel Croaker in February 1819 had marked his father's aspirations for a new and rewarding career, the birth of the next son, Charles William, coincided with his rapid decline. This third son entered the world in December 1820, so the peak of Croaker's achievement can be measured in months rather than years. By a combination of bad luck, poor timing and a touch of ineptitude, the sands of success ran quickly through his fingers. Yet, even in that short interval, he raises many interesting issues which strike at the heart of the colony and its culture.

The first quarter of 1820 was marked by a shift in Croaker's position both as a businessman and a civil servant. If the diminution of his discounting activities is anything to go by, his dealing days were largely at an end. Henceforth he focused on his enterprise in Upper Pitt Street and his fortunes were linked to the vicissitudes of brewing. It was also time for him to leave the judicature and find employment which would entail a commensurate salary and no loss of prestige. This would free Wylde from the embarrassment of a clerk whose involvement in litigation was threatening to undermine the credibility of justice. As Commissioner Bigge became increasingly aware of the colony's imperfections, so Macquarie felt obliged to curb the worst abuses. It was time for people to distinguish between what Bigge called 'the pursuit of civil [public service] and mercantile occupations', resisting in the former role the 'great temptations of profit' in the latter. In his report to the British government, Bigge believed such duality had 'been openly discontinued, yet it is known still to exist'.[1] Croaker personified the problem. He had renounced dealing but remained in a civil position with a sideline in the brewing trade. With such double standards endemic, it would take more than a commissioner and a change of governor to rehabilitate the system.

On 1 April 1820 Croaker was transferred to the police office where he became principal clerk on the recommendation of William Minchin, the superintendent.[2] The move was little more than a side-step as his salary had been paid all along by the police fund. This fund met the expenses of such public works and institutions of the colony as were not otherwise paid for by England. His annual salary was now £45 (£5 less than before) but in this post, as in his earlier one, real income was considerably enhanced by the appropriation of fees. Bigge was very much alive to this practice and reported that clerks in the law offices at Sydney 'derived emolument from the fees that they took upon the issue of summonses in small causes under 40s'.[3] There was also income from many other fees and charges but Bigge was unable to quantify the proportion converted to private gain. He did, however, instance 'the convict clerk of Mr. Wylde, sen.' who, on one occasion, had appropriated a fee of ten shillings.[4]

While Bigge was unhappy with these perks of the job, he refrained from condemning them in so many words. In the colony it was a question of making the salary appropriate for the job without draining official resources. Bigge reserved his accusation of 'highly improper practice' for the custom of magistrates' clerks to allow accused persons to see the prosecution file on payment of a fee.[5] But it was the principle of disclosure which offended him more than the pocketing of the money. It was difficult for Bigge to grasp the extent of the practice as there was a grey area between the police and the judicature in the collection of fees for beer and spirits licences. Thomas Wylde, as clerk of the peace, complained to Macquarie in October 1821 that the fees had wrongly gone to the chief clerk of William Minchin, superintendent of police, while he (Wylde) was on official business in Van Diemen's Land.[6] In other words, they had gone to Croaker. Wylde was unabashed in telling Macquarie, in what must be considered a post-Bigge environment, that he regarded the fee of 5 shillings per licence, along with other fees, as being a legitimate supplement to his own salary.

The question of fees, although a fascinating reflection on the colony's culture, has little impact on the analysis of Croaker's prosperity. Even if the money had doubled his pay, which seems improbable, he was dabbling in extramural matters where the risks and rewards dwarfed the gross of his clerical income. The importance of his time in the police office is that it brought him to public attention. His was the name in the *Sydney Gazette* which banned carts from the racecourse in Hyde Park and sought applications for the renewal of their licences from butchers, brewers of beer, and retailers of beer and spirits.[7] It was Croaker who

POLICE OFFICE, SYDNEY, 27th August, 1820.
NOTICE is hereby given, that all Persons found driving Carts along the Race Course, in Hyde Park, will be prosecuted, agreeably to His EXCELLENCY the GOVERNOR's Orders on that Head ;—And all Constables are charged to strictly carry this Order into Effect. (By Order of W. MINCHIN, Esq Principal Superintendent of Police),
J. CROAKER, Principal Clerk.

Croaker warns against carts using Hyde Park racecourse. (*Sydney Gazette*, 26 August 1820)

supplied Bigge with lists of licensed carts, bakers, butchers and watermen in Sydney.[8] In recognition of his status, he was officially assigned a convict, one John Mayo, as a servant, while Susannah was assisted by a free maid named Mary Coppinger. The Croakers' family residence was now, once again, in George Street. It suffered a disharmony in August 1820 when Mayo, with two henchmen, robbed Coppinger of her money and some clothing. He was convicted and sent to Newcastle for fourteen years.[9]

There was an advantage for Croaker in being close to the centre of regulations over liquor, and before long his senior colleagues in the police office were to evince a personal interest in these areas which nicely supported his own. When William Minchin died in March 1821 he was succeeded as superintendent of police by D'Arcy Wentworth, who had resigned from the same post in April 1820, on grounds of ill health—exactly when Croaker was recruited. Wentworth epitomised the colony's unique ability to turn logic on its head and appoint to responsible office a man who, on his record, seemed wholly inappropriate.[10] Although not technically an ex-convict, and a surgeon by profession, Wentworth's four acquittals on indictments of highway robbery were no compliment to the efficacy of English justice. The best which can be said is that his decision to sail to New South Wales, on a voluntary basis, retrieved some sense of honour for an ancient and respected family. Once in the colony, Wentworth sided with the emancipist cause and was on good terms with successive governors, Bligh being a conspicuous exception. Macquarie thought particularly well of him and Wentworth was 'noted for probity in his commercial transactions'.[11] He was, nevertheless, a rich and large-scale dealer in spirits, and the conflict of interests which this fact represented was compounded by his reluctance to convict those who sold spirits without a licence.[12] In this insouciance for propriety, without breaking the letter of the law, Wentworth and Croaker were not dissimilar.

Another aspect of Wentworth was his philandering, and it is an extraordinary possibility that one of his women in England, Mary Wilkinson, was related to Croaker's mother. In any event, Croaker would have known William Dodd's farm in Leaveland, where Mary Wilkinson had apparently worked.[13] While these associations might only have come to light, if at all, after Croaker had transferred to the police office, it is arguable that Wentworth was aware of the link all along and had earmarked for Croaker a place in his department. It was more by accident than design that Croaker began at the police office exactly when Wentworth temporarily left it, especially as there is nothing to show any link between Croaker and Minchin, who had been a military officer. That Croaker's new job was brokered by John Wylde is certainly a possibility, but a small degree of connivance between Wentworth and Croaker should also be considered. When Thomas Middleton, who was implicated in Croaker's Upper Pitt Street venture, is added to the equation (he became assistant to the superintendent of police on 30 September 1820) a three-man cabal was eventually created, treading both sides of the invisible line between duty and abuse of privilege. It should not be assumed, however, that Wentworth had any dealings with Croaker on a social scale, or that he regarded him as anything more than a reliable vehicle for enhancing his own wealth.

With this coherent team assembled, it was a misfortune for Middleton and Croaker that the enterprise at Upper Pitt Street was proving less than a goldmine. The year 1820 had begun well enough, with Nathaniel Lawrence sailing to England in March 'for the purpose of purchasing hops and utensils for the establishment of a Porter Brewery in this Colony'.[14] There is no difficulty in believing that Croaker provided him with letters of introduction and, in February 1821, Lawrence returned to the colony with 45 pockets of hops (each around 168 lbs) and a variety of equipment.[15] During his absence he had 'appointed a most competent agent' who might well have been Croaker.[16] There is certainly evidence of Croaker acting in that period in such a role. In November 1820 he was 'authorised to treat for the sale' of the Chelsea Pensioner hotel, then newly erected in Charlotte Square, Sydney.[17] The proprietor was William Ikin, who had been a free passenger on the *Mariner*. Croaker was taking every opportunity to ingratiate himself with those who had a vested interest in the production and retailing of beer, and this could have been one of Lawrence's tied houses.

While Lawrence's journey was evidently successful, the outlook in the colony for brewing was beginning to look bleak. There were several problems and the first of them centred on the cost of a licence. Bigge was content that licences for the retailing of liquor were such as the traders could afford; but it concerned him that the £25 required for a licence to brew 'operates as a restraint upon the production of a good and whole-some substitute for spirits, and upon the competition [by] which its quality would be improved'.[18] He recommended that the fee be reduced to £5. It would not have escaped Croaker and his associates that sym-pathetic noises were emanating from Bigge's office and these could only have encouraged them to sink much of their energy and resources into a better quality of beer. But, unfortunately for the Upper Pitt Street con-sortium, Bigge's attitude was ambivalent.

In December 1821 Sir Thomas Brisbane succeeded Macquarie, and the focus of interest moved to distilling. Already, in February of that year, the *Sydney Gazette* had carried a notice stating the new rules under which distilling in the colony could be practised, with effect from 1 August 1822.[19] Bigge was happy with this development because it called for distilleries to be opened in rural areas, thus preventing the exodus of country people to Sydney simply for the sake of buying liquor. His own view was that 'the Bengal spirit', an established favourite in the colony, would maintain its market share despite the extra duty; but at the same time he was sanguine that the colonists could improve the quality of their own product.[20] As for the farming lobby, they were assured that distilling would take place 'from grain grown in the colony, and from no other grain whatever'. The farmers could not hold the distillers to ransom, because the latter could use fruit as their raw ingredient if the price of wheat at the Sydney market exceeded 10 shillings per bushel on two con-secutive days.[21] There was nothing in these developments to cause Croaker anything but anguish. If the colony maintained its interest in spirits, there would be little call for the production of hops, and growers of barley would find it more profitable to revert to wheat.

The plight of the brewers was further affected by Brisbane's abolition of retail licences to each of the four breweries, effectively ending a system of tied houses. In a memorial to the governor, the brewers linked their own difficulties with the potential detriment to farmers, if the demand for local malt were curtailed. These farmers, it was claimed, were ben-efiting directly from an increased production of malting barley, while hops were being grown 'to great perfection'. With apparent magnanimity,

POLICE OFFICE SYDNEY, JAN. 17, 1822.

NOTICE is hereby given, that the LICENCES for SELLING SPIRITS and BEER, and for the BREWING of BEER, for the Year 1821, will expire on the 19th Day of February next;—Such Persons who are desirous of obtaining Licences for the current Year, are to apply for the same, by Memorial, at this Office, on or before the ensuing 13th Day of February next ; and those who may be approved of, will have it notified to them on the 17th, and will be required to attend, with their Sureties, on the 19th, to enter into the necessary Recognizances.

By Order of D. Wentworth, Esq. Supt. of Police,
J. CROAKER, Principal Clerk.

Croaker solicits applications for liquor licences. (*Sydney Gazette*, 25 January and 1 February 1822)

the brewers petitioned for an increase in the duty on imported malt liquors, so as to maintain the viability of 'the Agriculturist'.[22] But it was not the farmers who were uppermost in their minds. One of the colony's main malting enterprises was probably managed by Croaker, whose fortunes were linked to their own, and it was vital to keep production alive. Ideally, the brewers wanted malt for beer but, if a downturn in consumption were inevitable, then the production of malt for local distilleries could at least generate some income.

Given these events, it will be no surprise that Croaker's attention turned slowly from beer to spirits between 1820 and 1822. But before this conversion is considered, the story must revert to the early months of 1820 when, with his resources committed irrevocably to Upper Pitt Street, he began to suffer further pressures on his liquidity through action in the civil courts. The first man to worry him was Robert Cooper, the dealer to whom he had already mortgaged his business. As the suit opened in March,[23] Croaker's transfer to the police office in April could only have gladdened the heart of the judge advocate, and perhaps the case precipitated the departure of his errant clerk. The circumstances of the debt are unknown but the instrument was a warrant of attorney; its non-negotiable nature emphasised the seriousness of Croaker's commitment. The penal debt was £665, but the parties agreed a figure of some

£333 payable over two years. This was probably the actual debt, to which a crippling 8 per cent interest per annum was added for every £100 unpaid. As Cooper made no subsequent legal claim for the £250 which Croaker still owed him on mortgage, it can be assumed it was incorporated in the newly agreed figure. Now, for the first time, Croaker was on the receiving end of the formidable and lawful instrument (the warrant of attorney) by which men of his former calling could reduce their clients to virtual penury. In the short term, he continued to go about his affairs with all outward signs of prosperity. He would have been worried about his debts, but he clearly had money to hand for the time being, as he lent at least £30 to one John McEwen, in Sydney, on 13 June 1820.[24]

The career of McEwen (also spelt McOwen and McKeon), an illiterate Irishman, was to be a classic sacrifice of naivety at the altar of the crafty and rapacious. He arrived in the colony on the *Atlas* in 1802. He is difficult to follow over the ensuing years as the inconsistencies in the spelling of McEwen make it impossible to be certain of identities. He appears to have been farming a 40-acre plot in the Bunburry Curran district of Airds in 1811, or soon afterwards, with an interest in cattle and arable farming.[25] In 1814 this farm was mortgaged to Patrick Cullen of Sydney for £70.[26] While this debt was unresolved, and another one had been contracted to Edward Redman, McEwen was granted another farm in 1816.[27] Both Redman and Cullen took him to court, but he had no money to repay them.[28] McEwen's house, main farm, mare, cart and harness were auctioned by the provost marshal, but he and his family remained where they were. The explanation must be that his debts were settled by another party who retained McEwen as a sitting tenant in 'a state of vassalage'.[29] His adjacent 20-acre farm was increased in size during 1817 when a neighbour, John King (clearly also in desperate straits), sold part of his own farm for £1 per acre.[30] The money presumably came from McEwen's 'master', who might have been Thomas Dunn, chief constable in the Sydney police office.

On 29 April 1819 McEwen leased 'Hyde Park Farm' in Airds, then containing 27 acres, to Dunn for 999 years at a nominal rent.[31] This deed, which in England would have been known as a demise, was tantamount to a conveyance, used when the vendor's title was too suspect for a freehold grant.[32] The next day McEwen put his mark to a bond in £40 in favour of Dunn.[33] It appears that Dunn had paid McEwen £20 for the 27-acre farm but, the title being insecure, feared for his investment. The bond, therefore, was to force McEwen into seeking a confirmation, within five years, of the grants originally made in 1811 and 1816 but never, it seems, registered. On 17 August 1819 the original 20-acre and 40-acre farms were registered as new grants, as of that day.[34]

If McEwen avoided the penalty in the bond, he was nevertheless in consistent trouble. The seasons conspired to deepen his misery. In the dry year of 1818 the harvest failed, with wheat at Airds cropping at three bushels to the acre, a fraction of the normal yield.[35] Within two years McEwen was destitute and succumbed to the dealer's classic manoeuvre. On 12 June 1820 the 40-acre farm at Airds was assigned to Daniel Cooper without consideration or power of redemption.[36] From that time, McEwen was not a man but a commodity. It was the next day when Croaker lent him money, presumably to support the subsistence farming in which McEwen was still engaged, on land which now belonged to Dunn and Cooper.[37]

As McEwen's new debt was acknowledged by a warrant of attorney, witnessed by Daniel Cooper, this was no charitable move, and Croaker meant business. But business for whom? There could be little doubt that McEwen would default, but Croaker had no hope of getting any land as it was committed to other parties. It is quite possible that McEwen's debt to Cooper exceeded the value of the 40-acre farm and that Croaker, in collusion with Cooper, lent McEwen the money to make up the difference. But what was in this for Croaker? As McEwen had no possible security to offer, there was every likelihood that Croaker would lose his money—which was exactly the outcome. In keeping with the mysteries surrounding Hartigan's Farm, there was a wider Airds dimension which history has not disclosed.

For the remainder of 1820 Croaker's affairs marked time while he awaited a clearer vision of the future of brewing. He was tumbling ever more deeply in debt, although the exact circumstances cannot be known. He was finding it difficult to meet the ready money for his obligatory payments to Robert Cooper. He became careless over debts to a Sydney butcher and publican, James Bloodsworth, to whom J. J. Moore assigned two of Croaker's promissory notes, each for £34 10s 3d and drawn on 11 October.[38] On that same day Croaker acknowledged two outstanding debts to Bloodsworth, each of £100. No doubt with the equilibrium of the colony in mind, Bloodsworth was as reluctant as Cooper to force Croaker into a corner, and there was no instant call for repayment once Croaker had admitted his liability.

With debt being a way of life for most of the colony's merchants, dealers, and tradesmen, Croaker's predicament was probably not apparent to most people, which in itself lulled him into phoney comfort.

ADVERTISEMENTS.

—oooo—

TO be SOLD by PRIVATE CONTRACT, all that capital FARM in the District of Airds, originally granted to Dudley Hartigan, and now known or called by the Name of Hartigan Farm, within about a mile of Campbell Town, containing forty acres, 26 of which are clear and in cultivation, with newly erected stock-yards, calf-pens, &c. and a very extensive and desirable run for cattle, being always supplied with water in the driest of seasons.—Application to be made to Mr. J. Croaker, No. 1, Upper Pitt-street, Park-street.

Croaker advertises the sale of Hartigan Farm. (*Sydney Gazette*, 3 March 1821)

Yet his ruin was inevitable and proceeded at a measured pace. The appointment, on 1 January 1821, of William Love as second clerk in the police office, at an annual salary of £25,[39] was to be a harbinger of the ultimate pathos in Croaker's career. Yet, in many respects, Croaker presented a front of normality. He had his salary and his prestige, and there were still those prepared to lend him money by an informal arrangement. On 16 January a Sydney merchant named Thomas Henry Hart lent him around £50, payable on demand, and was in no hurry for his money.[40] It was important for Croaker to maintain the dignity of his position, and with returns to make to Commissioner Bigge and official notices to send to the press, he appeared equal to his job. In February he assisted the Bank of New South Wales, as 'a temporary and voluntary assistant' while a replacement was sought for Francis Williams, and he subscribed to the colony's Benevolent Society in the same month.[41] Soon his name was to join the many others who signed a petition to the Prince Regent, seeking trial by jury for the colony and economic reforms.[42] It was time to push the limits of respectability as far as they would go, and take his emancipist state to its second and final level: in short, he pondered an application to Macquarie for a free pardon. A new governor might not be so accommodating.

While he canvassed for support, Croaker's legal affairs were deteriorating further. He was in no mood to treat his own debtor, John McEwen, with any leniency. The issue for Croaker was becoming survival. McEwen's debt, probably from punitive interest, was now around £100 and during May 1821 Croaker secured a writ of *fieri facias* against him.[43] But McEwen was penniless and the fragments of wheat which greeted the provost marshal's levy raised little over £10. There was nothing there to relieve his desperate creditor. Croaker's position was no less parlous. He watched with apprehension as past and present associates jostled him like carrion crows picking at a body. Suddenly, the butcher's name, Bloodsworth, must have seemed uncomfortably appropriate. Having waited a year for some £160 which Croaker owed him in total, he sued for his money at the end of October.[44]

By a paradox so eloquent of the colony's way of life, Bloodsworth allowed Croaker a loan of £130, acknowledged by warrant of attorney on 12 November.[45] He was thus giving with one hand and taking with the other. The money was needed urgently by Croaker to satisfy Thomas Middleton for the informal loan of £500 in April 1819, and it was apparently in Bloodsworth's interests to keep Croaker afloat. But the money was not enough, so Middleton, his colleague in the police office and associate in Upper Pitt Street, had recourse to law.[46] Croaker offered no defence and judgement was awarded to Middleton. The next logical move was the order to distrain. However, the writ of *fieri facias*, once viewed by Croaker with nonchalance but now with apprehension, was withheld. Middleton, even more than Bloodsworth, needed Croaker solvent and active. It appears that Middleton was never satisfied by Croaker, at least to the full extent of the loan, as he was creditor of the estate after Croaker's reported death.

As for McEwen, there was clearly not the least hope of assets from that direction and his personal distress became, for Croaker, a matter of indifference. The provost marshal was empowered to make another levy on his goods, chattels, lands and tenements, but came away with nothing.[47] This made McEwen an insolvent debtor, and Croaker, out of spite, anger, or despair, had him removed to prison in Sydney. The convention was for the creditor to provide maintenance for the prisoner, but Croaker was in no mood for the niceties. On 21 October McEwen wrote to the court that he 'should be actually starving were it not for the humanity of some Gentlemen Debtors confined here', who no doubt assisted him with the writing of the note. The court made an order for Croaker to contribute, which he ignored. On 5 November 1821 McEwen petitioned Judge Barron Field for release, as Croaker had not allowed him any maintenance. The court could not agree, but Croaker was reminded of his duty. By 26 December McEwen was *in extremis*. In a new petition he complained that, whereas Croaker had to supply the subsistence money (known as 'groats') at noon every Monday, nothing was paid until dusk.

For McEwen, however, the immediate misery was soon at an end. Another petition to Judge Field won the compassion of the court. McEwen was discharged from prison on 4 January 1822. He was a landless pauper, but at least he had recovered some self-respect. For Croaker, on the other hand, the humiliations were just beginning.

Within a few days of McEwen's release, Bloodsworth set about recovering £130 from the unmapped mountain of Croaker's debt. Almost immediately, Thomas Hart decided that he, too, needed repayment. Croaker was clearly looking immensely vulnerable and no creditor wanted his money taken by another. Now, some three years after the first distraint, Croaker was again on the wrong end of a writ of *fieri facias* and far less complacent about the outcome. Before 15 February 1822 the provost marshal was expected to raise some £250 from Croaker's assets.[48] But Croaker was no longer dealing and therefore had fewer commodities at stake. Likewise, he had retreated from cattle farming and had no livestock to lose. As for his arable farming, this probably offered only barley in any quantity, and that was not what the market wanted. The provost marshal found what he could, put it up for sale, but there were no buyers.[49]

As his affairs reached a critical state, but before the denouement, Croaker obtained his absolute pardon. The petition to Macquarie, in November 1821, was based on Croaker's services to the colony as a clerk in the offices of the judge advocate and the superintendent of police, which he claimed to have fulfilled 'without reproach'.[50] Wylde wrote in support of the submissions and attested to Croaker's good conduct. Another strong argument, discussed in a past chapter, was his statement to have been 'at the opening of the Bank of New South Wales'. It was some six months earlier that he had provided emergency help for the bank at the sudden retirement of its principal accountant, and the directors were in his moral debt. Two of them, John Piper and Thomas Macvitie, acted as sponsors and were also magistrates. Piper was then president of the bank, while Macvitie would have known Croaker from the days of the bank's inception, when each played a key role. The other two sponsors, George Johnston and George Druitt, are more problematical as both were from a military background.[51] Johnston owned property near Perroquet Hill and may have met Croaker as a neighbour. Druitt, another Perroquet Hill man, was the colony's chief engineer. In that capacity, he would have known Francis Greenway, who was one of Croaker's acquaintances and possibly a close friend. At one stage Druitt employed Mary Coppinger, the Croakers' maid, which might indicate contact at a social level between her masters.[52] All these sponsors were well known to and indeed well liked by Macquarie, and Croaker was granted his absolute pardon on 24 November 1821.[53]

The importance of a pardon to Croaker, at this critical juncture, was that he could now leave the colony if he wished. As his sponsors were more in the nature of character referees than business associates, the enormity of Croaker's position might not have been known to them. They would realise he had debts, but this was nothing unusual and need not reflect on his integrity. But if it had been known how rapidly the situation would deteriorate for Croaker in the early months of 1822, the free pardon might never have been granted. During the first week of February, Croaker appeared to be heading for bankruptcy and his position in the police office became untenable. On 25 January, and again on 1 February, his name appeared below the notice inviting applications for licences to brew beer, and to sell beer and spirits.[54] On 7 February the same notice appeared under the name of M. Robinson, principal clerk. Croaker had resigned or been dismissed. On the next day the *Sydney Gazette* carried notice of an auction of his household furniture and effects, to be held at 2 Upper Pitt Street on 12 February, to satisfy Bloodsworth and Hart.

Whatever the sum of money raised, it failed to liquidate the debt. Croaker had just a few weeks respite before the next writ would take its course. He retrenched his business to 1 Upper Pitt Street and, on 18 February 1822, the clerk who had invited others to apply for licences decided to follow his own advice. He made application to D'Arcy Wentworth, as a private citizen, for a licence to sell spirits.[55]

By this act Croaker renounced his interest in beer and brewing, changing allegiance from barley to wheat. He could still practise malting, but as spirits did not necessarily depend on malt, there was barely a living. Within two years a 'New Brewery' in Pitt Street, occupied by Thomas Middleton and owned by Daniel Cooper, was advertised for sale at £1000.[56] This was not the downfall of Middleton, as he had another brewery about to open in Bent Street,[57] but it was the end of the Pitt Street consortium. If Croaker was not the main figure in the enterprise, he was nevertheless the linchpin, and with the loss of his liquidity there was no way forward. For Croaker it was a personal disaster. Not only was his application for a spirits' licence at 1 Upper Pitt Street refused, but he stood to lose even the property he held at that address. On 19 April 1822 both 1 and 2 Upper Pitt Street, with their household furniture and effects, were auctioned to satisfy the unpaid debts to Bloodsworth and Robert Cooper.[58] As Cooper had provided the mortgage for Croaker's initial involvement in Upper Pitt Street, the wheel of fortune had completed

PROVOST MARSHAL'S OFFICE, FEB. 7, 1822.
In the Supreme Court.
BLOODSWORTH *v.* CROAKER.—HART *v.* CROAKER.
THE PROVOST MARSHAL will Cause to be Put up,
and Sold by Public Auction, on the Premises,
No. 2, Upper Pitt-street, on Wednesday next, the
13th Day of February Instant, at the Hour of Eleven
o'Clock in the Forenoon, by Virtue of Writs of Fieri
Facias issued out of the Supreme Court, All the valuable Household Furniture and Effects, the Property of
the Defendant; unless the Executions thereon be previously superseded.

The Croakers' personal effects are advertised for auction. (*Sydney Gazette,*
8 Febrary 1822)

one revolution. But even this sale failed to make amends. The provost
marshal raised £349 13s for Croaker's creditors, but there were other
judgements outstanding against him; after fees were deducted from the
balance, only £40 8s 10d was available to meet them.[59] Worse was to
come, as the provost marshal could identify no other property on which
to make a levy.

In July and August 1822 Patrick Garrigan, a licensed victualler of
George Street, Sydney, and Thomas Harper, a Sydney merchant, sued
Croaker for repayments totalling more than £100.[60] In the normal course
of events, they might well have waited for their money, but Croaker was
on his beam ends; if they did not act now, they might never see a penny
of what he owed them. This was a critical embarrassment for Croaker, as
the provost marshal knew there was nothing left to take. Croaker was
summoned to appear before the court on 15 August, or within three
days, to respond to Harper's plaint. He evidently failed to appear, as on
21 August the provost marshal was instructed to bring Croaker forcibly to
court, and keep him there 'until he shall then and there give security to
abide and perform the final Order of the Court'. On 3 September Croaker
was 'duly arrested', but discharged quickly on the authority of a note
from the plaintiff's solicitor. The plot, at this point, becomes obscure, but
there seems to have been an understanding among his creditors that it
was not in anyone's interests to push Croaker to extinction.

Croaker's application for a spirit licence (Mitchell Library, Sydney, Wentworth Papers, A765, p. 197, by kind permission)

On 23 September 1822 Croaker tendered 80 guineas for a one-year lease of the government mill.[61] This extraordinary evidence of resources in a quagmire of debt is further evidence, at two levels, of the colony's unique standards. A virtual bankrupt, Croaker retained a stature which enabled him to divorce the stigma of debt from the reality. At some point, he and his family had moved from George Street to Market Street, which might be regarded as an economy move, but he retained a servant (John Buxton) during the abortive attempts of the provost marshal to levy goods for sale.[62] Furthermore, the provost marshal appears only to have shown an interest in Croaker's business address. The system fought shy of distraining in the dwelling-house of a man with a free pardon, whose wife ran a highly respectable school, and who had four children for whom the colony would otherwise be responsible. In fact, that total was rising to five, as Susannah became pregnant again in the summer of 1822. As for the money (80 guineas), speculation as to the source is idle. It might have come from Susannah, it might have come from assets which Croaker, stubborn to the last, had denied to the court, or it could have been venture capital from other, perhaps new, partners who wished to tap Croaker's expertise in the processing of grain. A man who ran a successful malting might equally become a good miller, and wheat was another entry into the spirits trade, keeping alive Croaker's hopes in that direction. His tender was rejected, although lower than that of James Hankinson who won the contract.[63] Croaker was out of favour.

The options now open to Croaker were few and diminishing. There was no question of his ending up, like McEwen, in a debtors' prison, because this was not the way matters were arranged for those whose intellectual skills were needed in the colony and whose ruin threatened a serious jolt to its economic stability. His creditors, therefore, had no option, having gained what they could, but to desist from litigation and await Croaker's return to wealth for the balance of their money. He was now free to leave the colony and he saw no option but to do so. On 9 and 16 January 1823 the *Sydney Gazette* carried advertisements for a ship due to leave for England on 20 January via Rio de Janeiro, having loaded coal at Newcastle. The passenger manifest, on 8 February, carried the names of John Croaker and his eldest son, John Wilkinson Croaker, then aged ten.[64] There was no question of Susannah leaving as well. She had three children to look after, she was pregnant with another, and doubt-less had a school to run.

There is no evidence that the crisis caused antipathy between John and Susannah, although it must be a possibility. The fact that John Wilkinson Croaker was listed seems curious, as was the precipitate nature of the voyage. The next child was likely to be born in his father's absence. Some tension between husband and wife seems a reasonable conclusion, but the marriage had not broken down. Croaker was urgently travelling to England to alleviate his debt. If the scenario of hidden loot is too romantic, then he was travelling to rediscover old friends and contacts, and negotiate a deal in some context of the liquor trade. Lawrence and Middleton must have paid the fares, unless the money came from Susannah. It was a matter of self-esteem for Croaker to return to England as a free man. It would also be appropriate to introduce his son to those in the family whom he (John junior) could scarcely remember and, indeed, might never have met. Despite this, the presence of John junior on the ship is unsatisfactory. His parents would have had no illusions as to the dangers of the voyage, and his father was focused on serious business.

It only remains to speculate on the reasons for Croaker's failure as an entrepreneur. He was not lazy nor unimaginative, nor was he dishonest within the liberal parameters of the colony's moral code. He might well have been extravagant, but he had contacts in the right places, a career path to respectability, a wife to be proud of, and skills which were in demand. But he was committed to the wrong product at the wrong time. Beer was always an unattractive drink for the colonists and he put his money into brewing exactly when regulatory control was favouring spirits. It was impossible to extricate himself without forfeiting his salaried position in the civil administration, and the spiral was ever downward. And like many practitioners in the liquor trade, he probably drank more than was good for him.

There are also more specific reasons why Croaker failed. His commitment to brewing required farming skills which he did not possess. His crops were therefore at the mercy of such employees as he could muster to take care of them, who were themselves unequal to the vagaries of the climate and fluctuations in yield. Furthermore, he had never gained the confidence of Macquarie, for reasons which are not obvious. Macquarie seems to have looked at him with suspicion, as if unsure whether or not the initial concession of a ticket of leave had been too generous. Had they been on better terms, Croaker would surely have received some grant of land. Yet the departure of Macquarie and the arrival of Brisbane was an even worse event, because it heralded the decline of beer from its already indifferent position. And behind all these factors lay the enquiry by Commissioner Bigge. An investigation into the colony's probity of administration, and the legitimate limits of self-interest, was most untimely for a clerk who registered the process of law with one hand and took writs against himself with the other. Bigge removed the backdrop of tolerance which allowed Croaker to play the laxity of the system.

The ultimate blame must lie at yet another level. Arguably, Croaker was too impetuous for his own good, quick to stride the grand highway to riches while the safer, slower by-road was via salaried jobs and patience. A more significant failure, however, must be debited to the Bank of New South Wales. Beholden to Croaker for its book-keeping systems, eager to seek his help and advice when its own employees were found wanting, the bank allowed him no running account and no investment loan. For reasons obscure, the directors' trouble-shooter was *persona non grata* on the other side of the counter. Perhaps they were wise not to trust him with their money, but Croaker was entitled to bear a grudge. In England it was a bank which brought him down through his own misdemeanours; in the colony it was a bank which let him down for little fault of his own.

10   Outwards to Oblivion

The ship Croaker chose for his passage to England bore the same name as the convict transport which had brought him to Sydney in 1816: *Mariner*. But they were different vessels. The second *Mariner* was about 262 tons burthen, built in Philadelphia in 1810, owned and registered in England, and captained by James Douglass.[1] It was advertised as a 'fine fast-sailing ship' with 'excellent accommodation for passengers'.[2] Why Croaker chose another *Mariner* is interesting. He might have seen the coincidence as a token of his release from the stigma of conviction; on the other hand, he had weighty matters on his mind, and the name might simply have struck him, in an idle moment, as ironic. Whatever his reasons for booking the passage, Croaker had made a poor choice—one which would ultimately cost him his life.

The *Mariner* had a reputation for being unseaworthy. It had undertaken a 'large repair' in 1816 and other 'repairs' in 1818 and 1821.[3] When it sailed from London to Sydney in July 1821 a London agent wrote to Edward Wollstonecraft in Sydney advising him that the *Mariner* should be 'avoided' as she was 'a bad ship and owned by parties who do not know what they are about'. With prophetic accuracy, the agent averred that if the *Mariner* does 'get out [to Sydney], it is a doubt with me whether [it] will get back [to London] again'.[4] Mary Reibey, a prominent Sydney citizen, was one of the passengers aboard the *Mariner* when it did reach Sydney in December 1821.[5] Her diary, which recounts the frustratingly long and seemingly inexplicable delays in the ship's departure from England, is portentous and revealing. She portrays the *Mariner*'s owners as short of money, parsimonious, and generally unsavoury. Shortly before the ship sailed, one of the owners, a Mr Evans 'came on board and gave the mate a good scolding for giving the passengers their provisions . . . a great dispute arose amongst him and the passengers and on his leaving he was hissed and hooted not without deserving it for a more oppressive villain cannot exist'.⁶

By the beginning of 1823 the ship's plight could only have worsened. Voyages to the Isle de France (Mauritius) and Macquarie Island in 1822 had been followed by several months of idleness in Sydney Harbour.⁷ Repairs and maintenance were probably ignored or skimped for lack of funds and mistrust of the owners. It can be assumed that Croaker was unaware of this background or he would not have risked his own safety, and especially the life of his son, on such an unpropitious voyage. The ship's proposed route was via Newcastle, about 60 nautical miles north of Sydney, where it would load 270 tons of convict-cut coal for Rio de Janeiro, before proceeding to England. On 11 February 1823 the *Mariner* cleared outwards from Sydney Harbour.⁸ Strict regulations governed vessels heading for Newcastle, to ensure that convicts were not given an easy opportunity to escape, and that there was no unauthorised poaching of coal or cedar. The *Mariner* had to seek a licence from the governor's secretary to enter Newcastle Harbour, and Captain Douglass was required to sign recognisances of £100 for himself, and find two sureties of £25 each, to observe the very strict rules of the port.⁹ To reclaim his money, and be allowed to proceed overseas, Douglass needed to return to Sydney and complete customs formalities.

Croaker and his son were not required to board the ship until its return from Newcastle. This was very convenient, as Susannah was expecting her baby during March. On the 6th she gave birth to another son, baptised Philip Henry at St Philip's Church, Sydney, on 30 March.¹⁰ This timetable just allowed the Croakers a final opportunity to assemble as a family, before the ship set sail for Rio on 4 April. On board the *Mariner* were fifteen crew members—Captain Douglass, his mate, a boatswain, a carpenter, a cook, a servant, a steward, and the remainder seamen.¹¹ The two Croakers were the only passengers. The weather would be wintry but there was one concession to safety. The *Mariner* departed with the 188-ton brig *Angerstein*, commanded by Captain Thomson. Both vessels had loaded coal in Newcastle at the same time and were cleared outwards from Sydney for Rio on the same day.¹² The intent, by common practice, was that each ship would 'look out for the other' and provide assistance in the case of misadventure. But what happened after the two vessels disappeared over the eastern horizon off Sydney is clouded in mystery. The *Mariner* called at the Bay of Islands, as was normal, at the north-eastern end of the North Island of New Zealand in late April 1823.¹³ This appears to have been her last contact with the *Angerstein*. On 2 May the *Mariner* set sail, with course unknown: perhaps she sailed north-east for the safety of an intervening landfall at Pitcairn Island, or she may have ventured east-south-east across the hostile Southern Ocean, directly for Cape Horn.

While some crucial facts are known, the ultimate fate of the *Mariner* and most of those aboard is henceforth a matter of conjecture. The ever-fainter trail of information abandons the historian in a thicket of political, military and topographical entanglements from which there is no escape. The account which follows relies and builds upon four pieces of basic evidence on the *Mariner's* fate: *The Times*, 29 April 1824; *Lloyd's List*, 17 February and 30 April 1824; and the *Sydney Gazette*, 1 April 1824. Although not always consistent with each other, these sources reported accurately the information which came their way. The challenge is to develop the narrative further in the light of circumstantial evidence from a much wider arena. It is a fact that Croaker failed to complete the journey, having died 'on the passage to England in 1824'.[14] This is known from the application for probate to the Supreme Court in Sydney, in January 1825, and suggests death from illness. But where and in what circumstances?

One basic fact is that the *Mariner* did not reach the southern Atlantic Ocean. In late June 1823 the vessel 'could not effect the rounding' of Cape Horn 'owing to want of provisions, and unfavourable winds'.[15] Captain Douglass had little option but to steer northwards along the desolate western coast of Chile and seek a safe anchorage to revictual his ship. The nearest port, nearly 1000 miles away, was on Chiloé, a mountainous and wooded island about 120 miles long and 60 miles across at its widest point. But Douglass would have been reluctant to go there because at that time the Chilotans were embroiled in a bitter war of independence from Spanish rule. Chiloé was being defended by well-entrenched Spanish royalists, led by General Antonio de Quintanilla, against invasion by Chilean republican (or patriot) forces then operating principally from Valparaiso. Chiloé was an island of considerable strategic importance, as it held 'the key to the whole western side of the Pacific'.[16]

It seems safe to conclude that Captain Douglass, rather than proceeding to one of the anchorages off Chiloé, plotted a course northwards past the island, aiming for Valparaiso. This was the closest British-allied port where a welcome would be assured. As Valparaiso had been a projected destination for an earlier voyage of the *Mariner*, the ship probably had an agent at the port and Douglass might have been there before.[17] In any case, he would have heard reports of Valparaiso developing 'into a "coast town" of Great Britain, where English "tailors, shoemakers, saddlers and

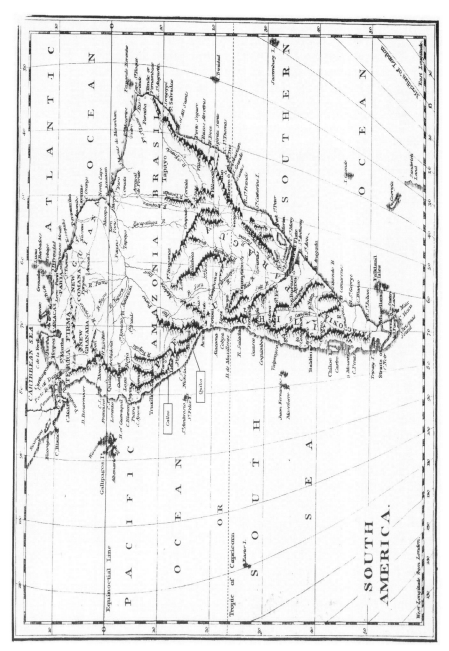

Places in South America relevant to Croaker's final journey. (From J. Walker, *The Universal Gazetteer* (London, 1815), with the towns Quilca and Callao added)

inn-keepers" hung out their signs in every street'.[18] There was no better port on the western side of South America, at that time, for a British vessel in difficulties.

Unfortunately for the *Mariner*, these difficulties got the better of the captain's intention. The area had a legendary reputation for the fiercest of weather.[19] Indeed, 1823 was a year of especially bad storms, with some 27 vessels, other than the *Mariner*, wrecked on the Chilean coast.[20] One of these gales probably engulfed the *Mariner* on its northward journey, and the ship suffered structural damage. There was no sensible alternative but to make for Chiloé, where 'it was found expedient to run the vessel on shore'.[21] On 1 July 1823, in the words of two sources, the ship was then 'unfortunately wrecked' and 'totally lost'.[22] This is a little unsatisfactory as two books on Chilean shipwrecks, both of them detailed and one centred specifically on Chiloé, make no mention of the *Mariner*.[23] There must, therefore, be at least a possibility that the ship was somehow salvaged, perhaps by locals without the owner's knowledge or consent, but for the purposes of this narrative it can be assumed that the wrecking was absolute. The ship was abandoned by its crew and passengers, but not without loss of life. At this point the evidence becomes graphic, but tantalisingly short of precision.

The report in the *Sydney Gazette* of 1 April 1824 was provided by Captain Wight, master of the ship *Medway*. As he returned to Sydney with a survivor from the *Mariner*, Wight was well placed to know what had happened. He reported that: 'Two of the crew were drowned, and one perished in the mountains, while endeavouring to gain the town of Castrao [now Castro]'. On 30 April 1824 *Lloyd's List* (which had reported on 17 February that the *Mariner* was out of touch), named the drowned crewmen as David M'Kaill, carpenter, and Henry Harding and John Owen, seamen. *The Times* (29 April 1824) agreed that 'three of the crew drowned', but did not name them. The basis of its report, in any case, would have been the same source as that available to *Lloyd's List*.

It is unknown exactly where the *Mariner* went aground. It is conceivable that the eastern, sheltered side of Chiloé, with its many land-locked coves free of ocean swell, was chosen by Captain Douglass if the storms permitted such precise navigation. Here, a ship could be 'laid ashore with facility'.[24] There were also flattish areas of the island on the western seaboard, but between there and Castro is a range of mountains. By great good fortune, another clue as to the ship's location appears to be given in Charles Darwin's published journal of exploration in Chiloé. Writing in 1835, the naturalist described his overland trip along the road from

San Carlos [now called Ancud] to Castro and his encounter with one of the Indian huntsmen who inhabited the higher part of his route. One of them

> by chance discovered, a few years since, an English vessel, which had been wrecked on the outer coast. The crew were beginning to fail in provisions, and it is not probable, that without the aid of this man, they would ever have extricated themselves from these scarcely penetrable woods. As it was, one seaman died on the march, from fatigue.[25]

This seems likely to be a reference to the *Mariner* and its survivors. The Indian's account tallies in three crucial aspects with that of Captain Wight: the route was across mountains; the men were short of provisions; and one of them died. The conclusion is, therefore, reasonable that the wrecking took place on Chiloé's outer, western coast, perhaps near Cape Metalqui. As the ship travelled north, so the possibilities receded of a successful beaching. The north-west coastline of the island was described by Darwin as 'exceedingly rugged and broken, fronted by many breakers on which the sea is eternally roaring', while just inland it was 'impracticable to proceed on foot'.[26] In addition, the north-west winds of winter were infamously violent, and a ship which lost its seaway was in immediate peril. There must have been something very wrong with the *Mariner* to induce Captain Douglass to attempt a beaching on such an inhospitable shore.

That any of the *Mariner*'s survivors reached safety must be due to their good fortune in meeting the local Indian. He had given the pathetic survivors advice, and perhaps some sustenance. Shocked, drenched and destitute, the party set out for Castro, a journey of between 20 and 40 miles, depending on the exact location of the beaching. The Indian must have been with them, or he would not have known of the death en route. The terrain was no less hostile than the sea. There were no roads, not even established tracks, over the forested mountains, where the higher peaks touched 3000 feet. Rain was incessant, with a driving ferocity which numbed the limbs and sapped all strength. Darwin himself had tried such a route—under circumstances of his choosing and with due preparation. His party

> became ensnared in a tangle of undergrowth, creepers and fallen trees so thick it was impossible to set foot on the ground. They had to crawl on hands and knees along the branches, often 15–20 feet above ground level, the seamen jokingly calling out 'soundings' as they inched forward. Having covered only 200 yards in 24 hours, they very prudently gave up.[27]

It would have been late July or even early August 1823 when the survivors straggled into Castro, on the eastern side of Chiloé. The going would have been difficult to the end, as the mountains and forests gave way to a damp and difficult bog. The town, with a population of about 8000, was the island's ancient capital, governed by a Spaniard named Colonel Don José Rodriguez Ballesteros, second-in-command to Quintanilla.[28] If the contemporary reputation of the Chilotans is correct, the bedraggled survivors were probably well treated.[29] Although there was no love lost between the English and Spanish at a political level, the little group would have been regarded as 'sailors in distress', and afforded the customary courtesies. But for logistical reasons, if for no other, it was in the Spaniards' interests to see the survivors taken elsewhere. The first step was to escort them nearly forty miles north to San Carlos, which was the headquarters of Quintanilla. As the last outpost of the Spanish empire in Chile, his forces had been isolated since early in 1822. Now, some eighteen months later, provisions were low.[30] The island was self-sufficient in little except water. Two privateers successfully harassed shipping and the resulting bounty was largely responsible for sustaining the garrison from 1823 to 1826.[31] These ships were the *Jeneral Valdes* and the *Jeneral Quintanilla*, operating out of San Carlos and preying on vessels of the Peruvian and Chilean independence (or patriot) forces.[32]

At this crucial point in the story, one last and vital piece of information is provided by the report of Captain Wight of the *Medway*: 'Captain Douglass remained at the island, intending to go to Valparaiso; but most of the ship's company entered on board one of the Spanish privateers'.[33] This can be taken to mean they enlisted as crew. The quoted words are puzzling, especially in relation to John, and John Wilkinson, Croaker. The first problem is 'most'. If Douglass was the only member of the ship's company not to board the privateer, it is odd that the report did not state 'the rest'. The second problem is that the Croakers were not strictly part of the ship's company at all, but fare-paying passengers. Yet references only to crew emerge from the slender evidence concerning the dead and the survivors. As regards Croaker himself, this is perhaps understandable. He was a grown man, sodden and disorientated like the others, and his status in those conditions was something of a nicety. But the total absence of references to a young boy is troubling; it is also worth pondering whether he would have been strong enough to survive a trek to safety which cost the life of a toughened, professional seaman.

The possibility must be considered, therefore, that John Wilkinson Croaker, despite being entered in the passenger manifest, was not on board the *Mariner* at the time of the wrecking. His parents might have had second thoughts as to the wisdom of the journey, and he withdrew at the last minute. Or he disembarked, for some reason, at the Bay of Islands and was escorted back to New South Wales. As far as evidence within the colony is concerned, the position is intriguingly balanced. When Susannah petitioned Governor Brisbane in September 1825, she claimed to be providing for *five* young children.[34] This raises two possibilities: that the boy had never left Sydney, or that he been returned to his mother, from the Bay of Islands or from South America, by that date. Repatriation was certainly possible in the timescale, but it seems likely that the poignancy of his return would have raised at least a column-inch in the *Sydney Gazette*. The absence of such a report, therefore, would argue that he had never sailed in the first place, or that he had continued to England. Further negative evidence is offered by the 1828 census of New South Wales, in which John Wilkinson Croaker was not recorded. Of course, he might have left the colony in the intervening years, but his absence in 1828 would be consistent with the theory that he survived the wreck and continued his journey, successfully, to England. As it can be shown that his father, on the other hand, did *not* complete the journey, there can be no certainty about any aspect of John Wilkinson Croaker in relation to the fateful voyage. Much depends on exactly when and where his father died. As this death was in 1824, and therefore at least five or six months after the wreck, the second stage of the journey might have been so far advanced that it was more practicable to send the boy on to England than to attempt his return to New South Wales. The narrative now continues on the assumption that the two Croakers were together, but the reader should be aware that counter arguments exist.

The Spanish privateer which the survivors boarded was likely to have been the *Jeneral Valdes*. Named after a royalist hero, this was a former English-flagged brig which had earlier sailed as the *Puig*.[35] The captain was probably called Mitchell, a name corrupted by the Chilotans to Milches or Michel. This ship appears to have been the 161-ton *Bahia Packet*, registered in Sunderland, and captained by 'J. Mitchell'. The *Bahia Packet* arrived in Valparaiso from Liverpool in September 1822, in Valparaiso from Lima on 6 January 1823, and in Lima from Valparaiso on 23 January 1823.[36]

The *Puig* (*Bahia Packet*) sailed subsequently for Rio de Janeiro with supplies from Don Luciano Murrieta, the Spanish head of trade at Arequipa in southern Peru, and was returning with a cargo for the royalist cause. The ship arrived at Chiloé in the autumn of 1823, armed with 18 cannons and carrying 23 royalist officials who had escaped from detention in Buenos Aires. Also aboard were two friars who had fled from Lima in 1821 to take refuge in Brazil, and who were no doubt influential in renaming the vessel *Puig* after a martyr to the Inquisition.[37] Captain Michel had called at Chiloé to obtain naval intelligence about the state of the wars between royalist and patriot forces. Having been informed of blockades ahead along sections of the coast, Michel reconsidered the wisdom of maintaining the *Puig* as a merchantman.[38] Instead, he took letters of marque from Quintanilla, renamed his ship the *Jeneral Valdes*, and became a privateer in the service of the Spanish royalists before venturing further north. The other privateer, the *Jeneral Quintanilla*, was the former merchant vessel *Cinco Hermanas*. It was commanded by a Genovese 'desperado', infamous for the betrayal of his former master.

It makes more sense to see the survivors leaving Chiloé on what was essentially an English ship, with an English captain, than on a Genovese vessel commanded by a man of proven treachery, who spoke another language. The assumption, therefore, is that the Croakers and surviving crew members sailed from Chiloé on 23 August, on the first of the two departures which the *Jeneral Valdes* made from that island in 1823, beating the patriot blockade.[39] The difficulty lies in establishing what happened next. It would have been pointless for Captain Michel to carry the survivors any further than he had to, and Valparaiso would have been a logical point to set them down. There was so much British shipping there—apparently some twenty vessels in port at any one time[40]—that the survivors hardly needed to go ashore. Furthermore, the *Mariner* probably had an agent there, and it was, according to Captain Wight, the intended destination of Captain Douglass once he had left Chiloé. It can be assumed with some safety that Douglass had lingered on the island to ascertain whether his ship was a write-off. On being told, rightly or wrongly, that it was, he duly made his way to Valparaiso and despatched a report to London. This was, in all probability, the basis of the accounts which appeared in the English press.[41]

But did the *Jeneral Valdes* put in at Valparaiso? Captain Michel would have wished to avoid contact with ships of the patriot navy, at least until he had delivered his cargo (loaded when the vessel was still the *Puig*) to the Spanish-Peruvian authorities in the region of Arequipa. As the main port in that region, Quilca, was not well placed for the onward despatch of destitute seamen, a likely intention of Captain Michel was to disembark them at Callao, the port for Lima, in early September. This was a necessary port of call, to deliver and receive military intelligence between Quintanilla and the royalist command. Another argument against Valparaiso is the way Captain Wight of the *Medway* phrased his report back in

Sydney. He appeared to be making a distinction between, on the one hand, Captain Douglass whose intended destination was Valparaiso and, on the other hand, those who were simply taken on board a Spanish privateer. If their destination had also been Valparaiso, Wight might well have said so.

At some point, the journey of the *Jeneral Valdes* must have crossed that of the *Medway*, to which one survivor transferred and became Captain Wight's informant. This man alone wished to return to New South Wales and it is interesting to ponder where he might have separated from the rest. The *Medway* is unlikely to have called at Chiloé in view of the blockade but, if it did, then the word 'most' in Captain Wight's report makes immediate sense: it was this man, as well as Captain Douglass, who did not board the privateer. For military reasons, however, it is better to conclude that this seaman was picked up either at Valparaiso or Quilca. The *Medway* definitely cleared from Valparaiso on 20 January 1824, heading for Sydney. One theory, therefore, would have him waiting at that port for the first available ship. This is a tenable proposition, but weakened by the wording of Captain Wight's report: by that time the man would have been more aware of the fate of the other crew members, not to mention the Croakers. The *Medway*, moreover, is known to have loaded a cargo of gold, silver and copper somewhere on a voyage south from Lima in the second half of 1823.[42] The mineral-rich Arequipa region of southern Peru and the nearby silver mines of Potosi were an obvious source for such a cargo, and Quilca was the closest port.[43] It was conceivably at Quilca, therefore, that one of the seamen took advantage of a return voyage to New South Wales. For this theory to hold, the two ships would have needed to cross in late August or early September 1823. The record of shipping movements in *Lloyd's List* appears to sustain this. The *Medway* arrived in Lima 'between 25 and 30 June 1823' and on 3 July 1823 'sailed (with troops) from Lima', said to be 'for forty days, on a secret expedition', but known from other sources to be Quilca. Thus, the *Medway* can be placed comfortably in Quilca, free of its cargo of Royalist troops and loading gold, silver and copper, at the end of August or the beginning of September. As further confirmation, *Lloyd's List* reported the arrival of the *Medway* in Valparaiso on 27 September 1823.[44]

The rest of the crew probably sought work on other vessels, leaving the two Croakers to pursue their intention of reaching England by one of the established routes of communication. The options open to Croaker were threefold. The most obvious choice was all the way by sea. There was an established route from Peru and Chile to England via Cape Horn, with ships calling at Buenos Aires or Rio de Janeiro. It seems doubtful whether Croaker could have afforded a passage on a merchant ship, and equally unlikely that the captain of such a ship would have agreed to carry two extra people to England simply out of charity. If Croaker had been landed at Valparaiso, however, he might have used his clerical skills to earn money for the next stage of the journey. Had the Croakers been taken aboard a British naval vessel, or applied to British representatives for money to continue their journey, some indication of this might be traceable in official records. The fact that ships' logs and consular reports are silent on this issue does not rule out the possibility that some sub-vention or practical assistance was afforded, because the evidence is not comprehensive: but it must weaken the likelihood. That opportunities existed to leave Lima on British warships is indicated by the departure of HMS *Blossom* from Callao in early December 1823.[45] The ship called at Valparaiso on Christmas Eve before reaching Rio on 8 March 1824, and Spithead on 8 June. As the Croakers were not among the super-numeraries, they must have already made other arrangements.

A second possibility is that the Croakers attempted an overland passage to the Atlantic coast. Unless the survivors had been landed at Valparaiso in the first place, this would have entailed a voyage south from Callao, between which ports there was plenty of commerce. The established mail route between Chile and England began at Valparaiso and took between 14 and 18 days by mule and horseback to reach Buenos Aires. From there ships travelled north to Rio de Janeiro, con-necting with packet-boats sailing for Falmouth.[46] The whole journey took about 65 to 70 days. There were many dangers and hardships on the overland stage: the ascent of the Andes, which were crossed by several passes of similar difficulty at around 20 000 feet, was not for the faint-hearted, nor the infirm. With 'cold so intense that steel shatters like glass', a traveller could die of exposure or altitude sickness, or tumble with his mule into the depths of a rocky ravine, before reaching the rela-tive safety of Mendoza.[47] Most narratives of the crossing are from east to west, provided by travellers from England anxious to take three weeks off their journey time and avoid Cape Horn. Despite all the dangers, with good luck and good weather the crossing of the Andes, however frighten-ing, could be achieved without incident. The Englishman Robert Proctor made the journey in late April 1823 with his wife, small son, two female servants, and one manservant. All survived uninjured, although at one point, they travelled along a path eighteen inches wide between, on the one hand, a drop of 300 feet to a river and, on the other, an overhanging mountainside studded with loose rocks. Proctor was made of stern stuff and found 'the narrow passes so much exaggerated by those who have passed them, and so much dreaded by those who have not'.[48] The morale of the rest of the group would not have been raised by the continuous line of small, wooden crosses, each marking the spot where a mule and its rider had parted company with the path.

If Croaker had landed at Valparaiso in early August 1823, he is unlikely to have contemplated the land crossing—if it appealed to him at all—until the worst of the winter weather was at an end. If he had landed at Callao, and then contrived a trip south for himself and his son, his wait at Valparaiso would have been that much shorter. It is, therefore, possible that he died early in 1824 by some accident or illness high in the Andes, and that his son was then taken back to Valparaiso and eventually re-patriated to New South Wales. This is unlikely to have happened, as there seems no way by which he could have supported himself and his son for so long at Valparaiso unless, as already suggested, he was able to find some kind of temporary employment as a clerk. It would ease the time problem slightly to suggest that he had set out earlier and was killed on the Pampas (having crossed the Andes) by some marauding band of Indians. But this option is presented without conviction.

The third route open to Croaker, if he had landed at Callao, was to proceed northwards. On 13 November 1823 HMS *Aurora* sailed for ports including Panama, destined for Acapulco and San Blas in Mexico.[49] There were also merchantmen plying the same route. It was practicable to cross the Panamanian isthmus, and then find a boat for Carthagena,[50] now in Colombia, which had a regular communication with Kingston, Jamaica.[51] If this was Croaker's intention, they would have disembarked at Panama, spent a day or two hiring mules and muleteers, and set out on the day's journey to Cruces. The narrow track through a forest of 'primeval luxuriance', impenetrable on either flank, would have re-minded Croaker, uncomfortably, of western Chiloé. But then it was whipping rain and debilitating cold; now it was enervating heat, and clothes made rancid with sweat. After an overnight stop in primitive con-ditions, the Croakers would have hired canoes to take them, over two days, down the Chagres River to its small, eponymous port, opening to the Caribbean Sea. Dangers and miseries lurked, with threat of constant ambush. The river was rocky, eddying and foaming with hidden ridges which could rip out the bottom of a boat. If the occupant were not drowned immediately—the kinder fate—then alligators were on the watch for a richer menu. Even at Chagres there was no relief. The town bordered an immense tract of swamp and the inhabitants looked 'very yellow and ill'.

It is idle, in the absence of definite evidence, to speculate too far on the circumstances of Croaker's death. Another shipwreck seems the least likely reason, as the odds were surely against it. Furthermore, such a fate would almost certainly have been revealed in the application to administer Croaker's estate. Some form of accident or illness springs more readily to mind. It would be in keeping with the litany of misfortune which was Croaker's existence if he were felled by a humble banana— one of the central American variety which, when eaten in combination with spirits, produced hallucination and death. Perhaps he caught malaria, or yellow fever, between Panama and Chagres and was too sick to proceed with his journey. Or maybe he staggered on as far as Carthagena or Kingston, a stinking, hollow-eyed shadow of a man, awaiting the squalid death of a stranger with no money and no status, agonising over the safety of a dependent son. But, equally, he might have died with dignity just a few days sail from the English coast. He might even have taken his own life. In the absence of the slightest evidence, the historian arrogates the privilege of a coroner's jury and enters an open verdict.

Epilogue

Susannah would have had no news about her husband and son until the arrival of the *Medway* in Sydney at the end of March 1824. She can be pictured, in agitation, seeking out the crewman for more information about the wreck of the *Mariner*. The details were hardly reassuring, but could have been much worse. As for John's death, the news must have broken in Sydney about nine months later, because probate proceedings were instituted in January 1825.

Croaker died intestate, and the Supreme Court granted letters of administration to Thomas Middleton, as the principal creditor.[1] The estate was valued at nearly £200, and consisted largely of household effects. Thus the debtor who had been sued so repeatedly, to the apparent frustration of the provost marshal, had goods all along. Even after death, Croaker exposes the charade of colonial litigation. Middleton, along with James Hankinson, auctioneer, and James Foster, gentleman, undertook to hold the property in trust for the Croakers' children. The ages of the four who were definitely in the colony at that time ranged between eighteen months and ten years.

It was a mark of Middleton's magnanimity that he did not seek to offset, albeit in this small way, the mass of Croaker's irrecoverable debt. It was also a measure of his concern for the widow and family of a friend. This adds a rare humanitarian dimension to a narrative which has necessarily been focused on the more clinical aspects of business. Whatever provision had been arranged for the upkeep of Susannah and the children while John was away was proving unsustainable. There was some income for Susannah from her boarding-school, but the upkeep of her own children and her ability to maintain a middle-class standard of living were under threat.

In September 1825 Susannah petitioned Governor Brisbane for a 'grant of land in trust for her children, and for their future support and advancement in life'.[2] As had happened in England, some ten years earlier, her literate letter to higher authority was disregarded: the petition was marked 'contrary to regulations'. Her plight, however, attracted attention less altruistic than Middleton's. In April 1826, at St James's Church, Sydney, Susannah married William Love, described as a 'writer'.[3] Shortly afterwards, she and the children moved into his house in York Street. Susannah had known William Love for some time: he had arrived in Sydney in 1820, transported for 14 years, and in February 1821 was appointed second clerk in the police office, where Croaker was his superior for about twelve months.

Love had also had interests in the liquor trade. In 1823 he opened a brewery in Liverpool, but could not make it pay.[4] In 1825 he was penniless, and confined to debtors' prison in Sydney.[5] In many ways Love was Croaker in another guise. His career pattern had such echoes of Croaker's slide to disaster that it was only natural, perhaps, that he should aspire to Croaker's widow. He seems to have jilted an existing fiancée on the way.[6] It is less obvious why Susannah should have been attracted to another unsuccessful entrepreneur. But Love had 'business-like manners', and was still in favour at the police office.[7] In May 1827 he was appointed to Croaker's former position of principal clerk, no doubt through the influence of Middleton, still the family friend.

Susannah had two more children: Clarissa Augusta, born in 1827, and Emily Susannah, born in 1832. Early in 1828 she re-established her school, now known as 'Lovedale' and operated jointly with her husband at their 'country residence, at Concord', some eight miles west of Sydney.[8] They owned 50 acres of cleared land and a house with eleven rooms. There were nine servants in residence, and fourteen female pupils, between the ages of nine and eighteen.[9] Love was soon in debt again, but the enterprise prospered, being known in 1845 as 'Mrs. Love's School'.[10] Widowed again in 1853, Susannah died of 'disease of the heart' in September 1866, aged 76. She was buried at Ashfield, in what is now an inner suburb of Sydney. Her tombstone bears the legend 'Looking unto Jesus, the authorised finisher of our faith', which suggests that she held, throughout her life, a strong Christian conviction. Neither husband appears to have done likewise.

Susannah left a considerable real and personal estate, all to her youngest daughter Emily. The elder daughter by her second marriage had already been provided for, and continued the interests so manifest in her mother. In 1852 Clarissa was described as 'so steady', and 'an excellent teacher', while employed as a governess.[11] As for Susannah's children by Croaker, they were unmentioned in her will, with the exception of Mary

Ann. She had been a witness at her mother's re-marriage, and was bequeathed £20 as 'the wife of Richard Tress'. The conclusion is inevitable
that Susannah's sons were out of favour, having inherited the more dishonourable characteristics of their late father.

John Wilkinson Croaker had probably reached England in 1824, and
was no doubt cared for by members of the family. No record of this
sojourn has survived, but it would be reasonable to suppose that the
circumstances of his father's death had been relayed to New South Wales
on the authority of John junior's first-hand account. For some eighteen
months, from January 1836, J. W. Croaker was postmaster at Yass, 200
miles south-west of Sydney,[12] which strengthens the assumption that he
had returned to the colony about 1834, having reached his majority. In
1857 he married Annie Connell, and lived for many years near Young,
raising eight children on an extensive farm called Burramunda. In April
1862 the Croakers were threatened, taunted and robbed by a notorious
group of bushrangers, members of a gang led by Frank Gardiner
although he was not among them at the time.[13] To add to the humiliation, Mrs Croaker was forced to prepare them a meal and provide musi-
cal entertainment.

In later years John Wilkinson Croaker led a rough and violent life of
which his mother was evidently ashamed. He was constantly at odds
with his neighbours, and is alleged to have formed a gang who set upon
the selectors. From among the weapons of his men, so it is said, derives
the place-name of Cudgell Creek. In 1876 J. W. Croaker mortgaged his
property, and in 1881 was declared bankrupt.[14] Like his father before
him, he was forced to uproot and re-establish his life in more humble
surroundings near by. At 'New Burramunda Troy', he died of 'disease of
the heart and senile decay' in 1885, aged 72. He was buried locally. Little
is known of the fate of his brothers.

Fortunately, the more acceptable attributes of Croaker were not lost
in the excesses of his eldest son. A book-keeping gene, triumphal and
dominant, has descended to the modern-day accountancy firms of
C. R. Croaker & Co. in Bundall, Queensland, and John Croaker & Co., in
Bathurst, New South Wales. The partners of this surname trace direct
descent from the subject of this memoir. Such a warm, living link
contrasts with our imperfect perception of the qualities of Croaker
as a human being. In the absence of personal letters and diaries, the
subtleties of his emotions and the conflict in his mind between right and
wrong cannot be analysed with confidence. His feelings are glimpsed
indistinctly, as if through frosted glass, from his mistakes and misde-

meanours and from the actions of others. His morality appears blurred, creating neither hero nor villain and a paradox of values. He brought misery to his wife, but it caused him pain. He was careless with legality, but not a recidivist. He was maladroit in business, but not ingenuous. His was a brief, rather gauche career trapped in the destiny of its own misfortune. An astrologer might have studied the heavens at Croaker's birth and found the planetary aspects rather worrying.

Appendix I

CONVICT-SHIPS

A

NARRATIVE

OF A

VOYAGE TO NEW SOUTH WALES,

IN THE YEAR 1816,

IN THE

SHIP MARINER,

DESCRIBING THE

NATURE OF THE ACCOMMODATIONS, STORES, DIET, &c.

TOGETHER

WITH AN ACCOUNT

OF THE

MEDICAL TREATMENT

AND

RELIGIOUS SUPERINTENDENCE

OF THESE

UNFORTUNATE PERSONS

BY JOHN HASLAM, JUN[R.]

SURGEON IN THE ROYAL NAVY

Caelum, non animum mutant, qui trans mare currunt. –HOR.

LONDON:

PRINTED FOR TAYLOR AND HESSEY,

FLEET STREET

1819.

NARRATIVE, &c.

The accommodations afforded to convicts during their transportation from this country to New South Wales, together with their medical treatment and moral superintendence during the voyage, having been very differently reported and understood; I take this opportunity of communicating to the public the result of my own observations and experience on this important subject. With conflicting opinions as they may possibly arise from the zeal of contending parties, I have no concern: a narrative of the simple truth is my object; and the accuracy of the following account does not rest on the strength of my individual assertion, but can be confirmed by documents which are still existing.

It may be proper to state that I am a Surgeon in the Royal Navy, and have derived some experience from the exercise of my professional duties in the service of my country. On the 6th of April, 1816, I was appointed Surgeon to the ship Mariner, 446 tons, hired for the conveyance of convicts to New South Wales. On Monday 6th of May, 85 convicts were received on board from the Justitia Hulk at Woolwich. On the 12th of the same month 60 from the Retribution at Sheerness, which, with the addition of one who was sent on board at the Cape of Good Hope, amounted to 146, and of these there were 28 who were under 20 years of age. They were allowed for sleeping a space of six feet square for every four persons, and they were provided with good flock-beds, and blankets. Their diet consisted of the following articles.

Rations of provisions for each mess of six convicts for seven days successively.

Days of the Week	Bread pounds	Flour pounds	Beef pounds	Pork pounds	Peas pints	Butter pounds	Rice ounces	Suet pounds	Raisins pounds	Oatmeal pints	Sugar ounces
Sun.	4	4	8					—	1		
Mon.	4				3	—	4			2	2
Tues.	4	4						—	1		
Wed.	4			6	3	—					
Thurs.	4	4						—	1	2	
Fri.	4		8		3	—					
Sat.	4				3		4			2	2
Total	28	12	16	6	12	1	8	1	3	6	4

Their ordinary beverage was water, but they were allowed half a pint of Port wine each twice a week; as we came into a warmer climate it was considered prudent to sub-divide this quantity, when each man was served with a quarter of a pint four times a week.

Superadded to the provisions specified in the above list, the following articles of comfort were allotted for the use of the convicts, guard and passengers:

Mustard . . . . 150 lb.
Soap . . . . 456 lb.
Combs . . . . 27 large and 27 small
Razors 10
Hone 1
Strop 1
Portable Soup . . . . 206 lb.
Lemon Juice . . . . 81 gallons

And likewise in case of sickness the stores undermentioned:

Tea . . . . 30 lb.
Sugar . . . . 178 lb.
Chocolate . . . . 9 lb.
Tapioca . . . . 18 lb.
Scotch Barley . . . . 300 lb.
Ginger . . . . 12 ounces.
Black Pepper . . . . 3 lb.
Allspice . . . . 6 lb.
Red Port Wine . . . . 102 bottles.
Rice . . . . 28 lb.
Pearl Barley . . . . 28 lb.

Of medicines there was an abundant supply and the different articles were of the very best quality having been furnished from Apothecaries' Hall. Indeed as far as a solicitude for the health of this crew was concerned, I am persuaded that if a number of respectable families had embarked as colonist-adventurers, the outfit for the prevention and remedy of disease could not have been more complete and efficient. And to such persons, the compulsion to habits of cleanliness so promotive of health, which was exercised over the convicts, could not have been adequately enforced.

On coming on board each convict was supplied with a new suit of clothes, together with a change of linen.

From former experience I was fully acquainted with the necessity of a scrupulous and unremitting attention to cleanliness and ventilation: for which purpose the whole of their bedding was daily brought on deck to be aired. The prison which contained them was daily washed, and thoroughly cleansed, and though it was the seat of their confinement, they were allowed, under a sufficient guard to come on deck in parties consisting of a third of their number, where they continued in rotation about two hours at a time, from six in the morning until evening approached.

It may here be of some utility to observe that when from a higher temperature the action of the skin is more considerably excited, and a consequent increase of perspiration ensues, that the bowels always become torpid, and the process of digestion is more difficultly performed. If due attention and timely remedy be not administered to counteract these affections, diarrhoea or dysentery commonly supervene, and are often of obstinate continuance. To prevent such occurrences they were adequately purged, the skin was cooled, and the excreted matter of more copious perspiration was removed by frequent bathing. By such attentions very little sickness occurred during the voyage. Two fumigating lamps with vinegar were kept burning in the prison from morning until night,—they had likewise wind-sails and air-pipes night and day. In addition to these precautions, they were three times a week inspected jointly by the master and myself, at which muster each convict brought up his clothing for our examination.

As the moral survey of this depraved assemblage was also confided to my charge, a series of momentous reflections crowded into my mind. Of late much had been said of the tractable nature of the human heart: that its ferocity was to be subdued by kindness, and its wanderings reclaimed by mild and patient admonition. It was confidently asserted that there were moments when the sternest spirit relented, and when Vice, on reflection, shuddered at the deformity of her own image. These aphorisms imparted great consolation, and gave additional energy to my humble endeavours. Even to arrest the progress of immorality appeared an important success, and this seemed in a great degree practicable by vigilance and the force of example: but the grand object was to display to them the beauties and conveniences which the high road of truth and rectitude of conduct would present, contrasted with the infamy and contempt they now experienced, from having deviated into the secret paths and tortuous avenues of vice. In the commencement of my labours the zeal which excited my endeavours was ably supported by the hope of success. The materials of religious instruction were amply supplied. From Mr. Capper of the Secretary of State's Office, who had furnished me with an account of the dispositions and characters of these delinquents, together with every minute instruction that could contribute to the success of the voyage, I received numerous Bibles and Prayer Books, and by the disinterested kindness of a pious and intelligent friend, an additional stock of both these articles. Every sabbath day, I read to them the service performed in the Church of England with appropriate exhortations to repentance.

Although their crimes had consigned them to a distant land, I felt that the amelioration of their lives was as much the wish of the legislature of their country, as their separation from the main body was expedient to arrest the source of contamination. It was necessary to guard them against revolt and consequent escape, which they hourly meditated to defeat their legal destination; but it was never forgotten that they were men, nor the hope abandoned that they might by reclamation become good subjects and worthy members of a Christian community.

It may be naturally supposed that many of these degraded objects were grossly ignorant; some were certainly without the rudiments of education, but the majority had received a degree of instruction which ought to have conduced to a better model of life. I had fondly hoped to be able to state that it was the invariable tendency of education to exempt the heart from imbibing the deeper tints of depravity, or that this salutary preparation had rendered the stain more easy to be expunged: but from my observations during this voyage I was led to infer that if education in some instances had diminished the temptation to crime, it had also augmented the facilities to its commission. To develop the faculties and illuminate the intellect certainly adapts the mind to the more ready attainment of its desires, and I am fully persuaded, that unless the ground-work of instruction be a moral, which implies a religious basis, the superstructure of letters seems to be of little advantage.

As the adage Nemo repenté turpissimus [sic] is founded on multiplied experience, so I discovered that the greater part of this crew had been early initiated into the mysteries and practice of their profession, and the daily pursuit of this craft was not likely to be discontinued by abstract precepts, which were calculated to enforce habits of restraint, patient toil and comparative privation. However these persons might differ in the complexions of vice, there was one strong feature which pervaded the whole mass,—the pertinacious and unflinching assertion of falsehood, and a solemn denial of the truth, even after its existence had been demonstrated. Although they might combine by strength or stratagem for a common plunder, yet these partners would rob each other of their dividend of the booty, with as little ceremony as they had defrauded the original possessor. From enquiries in which I could not be mistaken, I found that most of them had had a premature commerce with the other sex: from such intimacy they became more thoroughly corrupted, and incited to the repeated commission of crime, for the maintenance of female favour, and for the supply of their extravagance.

The first difficulty I had to encounter was the want of reciprocal communication:—they comprehended sufficiently every thing I said to them, but in their discourse with each other, they spoke a language wholly unknown to me. This copious and figurative vocabulary I was compelled to acquire, and for my progress in this new tongue was principally indebted to a convict who had been a school-master, and who for his amusement kept a journal in this mysterious dialect. By this acquisition I was in a great measure enabled to ascertain their proceedings, and comprehend their plans during the times I visited the prison in which they were confined.

Of their own degraded condition they appeared to be wholly insensible, and they seemed to be exempt from that reflection which is the attribute of rational beings, and the hopeful source of amendment. This moral insensibility was manifested even towards their nearest relatives, and of this fact the following is a striking instance.

When the ship lay off Deal, a convict about 33 years of age, who appeared to be one of the most orderly and decent of his comrades was visited by his wife, who had travelled from London to take an affectionate leave of her unfortunate husband. As it would have been improper to admit her into the prison, the convict was allowed to come on deck. She had kindly brought with her some articles which she conceived might contribute to his comfort during the voyage. After a tender and distressing adieu, she departed: and had nearly reached the shore, when I perceived the boat return with the woman. She had discovered that in the parting embrace he had picked her pocket of the money which was to convey her to town; and during the last pressure of her hand, he had dexterously contrived to detach the wedding ring from her finger. It was ineffectually endeavoured to compel him to restore the property; he reiterated the most solemn protestations that he had not taken it: and could not be prevailed on to see his wife again, under the hypocritical pretence that his feelings were so lacerated by the parting scene, that he could not sustain a repetition of the conflict.

Their hypocrisy was inscrutable, and there were not wanting a few who performed to admiration the mimicry of repentance. I confess my own liability to imposition, as it originated in a kinder survey of the human character, and a greater confidence in its amelioration: and though my hopes diminished as I became acquainted with my crew, yet there was an instance during the voyage of correct conduct in a young man about

22 years of age, which afforded some consolation for the general failure. This youth had received a competent education; and without being a traitor to his community, he appeared to be weaned from their practices: although obliged to associate with the others, he never joined in their indecent merriment, nor did I ever hear an oath escape from him. He officiated as clerk during divine service, and regularly distributed the Prayer Books in the chapel. His leisure time was frequently occupied in perusing the Holy Scriptures, and he exerted a proper spirit of activity and diligence in keeping the prison clean. This continuance of exemplary conduct had determined me to report his case to the Governor. On our arrival at Port Jackson, the convicts according to custom, were assembled in the gaol-yard for inspection; where to my utter mortification, my hopeful penitent was detected in picking the pocket of an inhabitant, whom curiosity had induced to become a spectator of the ceremony.

Concerning the future, which it was my constant solicitude to impress on their minds they appeared to be wholly indifferent. Many did not believe in the doctrine, and others were so heedless of its consequences, that it served only as the subject of vulgar jest or impious derision. This apathy I can only attribute as has been before observed to want of reflection. When their recollection reverted to former scenes, it was the revival of instances of impure gratification, or of successful plunder, which were recounted with triumph by the authors, and always received the applause of the hearers: and the prospective view was gilded with hopes that the remainder of existence would realise the sensualities of the past. On the 3rd of September when we were off the Cape of Good Hope, a heavy squall came on during the time I was officiating in the prison. There was a general apprehension that the vessel could not long withstand its fury. This appeared to me to be the favourable opportunity to impress the minds of the convicts with a due sense of their awful situation; and, as well as I was able from my own apprehensions I endeavoured to exhort them to a consideration of the necessity of employing the short time that probably remained in prayer and repentance—but in vain: the violence of the tempest had inspired them with additional excitement, and my admonitions were drowned in a roar of blasphemy. They recollected that it was the time of Bartholomew fair, and began a song commemorating the scenes of its licentiousness; and compared the rolling and pitching of the vessel to the swings which are employed during that festival.

Notwithstanding the utmost vigilance was exerted to prevent their confederation for the purpose of seizing the ship, yet they made the attempt at a time when it was least expected. On the 8th of September they contrived to open the prison door communicating with the forehold; this was speedily detected, but not until several articles had been stolen. On the 28th of the same month, during a tremendous storm at night, which excited the greatest alarm amongst those who navigated the ship; they found means during the general distress, to cut a hole in the deck of the prison communicating with the hold, by which in a short time they might have rendered themselves masters of the arm-chest, had they not been timely discovered. When I went into the prison accompanied by the master and a sufficient guard, they pretended the most perfect ignorance of the transaction, said they had been asleep, and wondered how it could have been effected.

That the failure of producing any moral reformation among these desperate outcasts which I candidly confess, and record with infinite regret, may be in some degree attributed to my own inexperience, is not improbable: yet my labours were unremitted, and although my hopes declined my zeal continued fervent. Notwithstanding, I may be deemed a novice in the science of moral therapeutics, it is with considerable satisfaction that I am able to state that of the 146 convicts carried out from this country, not one died, and moreover, that the whole number was landed on the 16th October, at Port Jackson; all of them, without a single exception, in good health, and fully capable of executing any labour that the Governor might direct them to perform.

Appendix II

Bills of Exchange and Promissory Notes involving John Croaker discounted by the Bank of New South Wales, as revealed by the directors' minute books

Date	By	Name	on/to	Name	Amount (£ s d)
30 Sept. 1817	J. J. Moore	Reiby	to	Croaker	45. 0. 0.
28 Oct. 1817	R. Jenkins	Moore	to	Croaker	50. 0. 0.
3 Feb. 1818	E. Eagar	Croaker	on	Moore	60. 0. 0.
16 June 1818	Robert Campbell, jun.	Moore	to	Croaker	50. 0. 0.
21 July 1818	Thomas Wylde	Croaker	to	Moore	152. 7. 0.
28 July 1818	T. W. Middleton	Croaker	to	Hankinson	127. 10. 0.
18 Aug. 1818	J. J. Moore	Croaker	on	Middleton	102. 10. 0.
8 Sept. 1818	Charles Armytage	Croaker	to	Hazard	103. 5. 6.
8 Sept. 1818	John Croaker	Croaker	on	Moore	65. 12. 11
29 Sept. 1818	Thomas Winder	Croaker	to	Terry	31. 0. 0.
6 Oct. 1818	Robert Jenkins	Croaker	on	Moore	138. 0. 0.
5 Nov. 1818	Thomas Rose	Croaker	to	Hankinson	150. 0. 0.
24 Nov. 1818	Robert Jenkins	Moore	to	Croaker	50. 0. 0.
8 Dec. 1818	Thomas Underwood	Croaker	to	Hazard	97. 0. 0.
8 Dec. 1818	Thomas Underwood	Croaker	to	Hazard	80. 13. 0.
15 Dec. 1818	Samuel Terry	Croaker	to	Stewart	20. 0. 0.
22 Dec. 1818	Edward Eagar	Croaker	to	Garrigan	54. 10. 0.
5 Jan. 1819	James Hankinson	Croaker	to	Bevan	22. 16. 0.
25 Jan. 1819	Charles Armytage	Croaker	to	Lord	24. 9. 6.
25 Jan. 1819	Robert Campbell, jun.	Croaker	on	Moore	21. 1. 8.
25 Jan. 1819	Robert Campbell, jun.	Croaker	on	Smith	20. 17. 0.
2 Feb. 1819	Thomas Wylde	Croaker	on	Middleton	117. 0.0.
16 Feb. 1819	John Croaker	Campbell, jun.	on	Moore J. J.	50. 0. 0.
23 Feb. 1819	George Howe	Croaker	on	Moore	21. 5. 0.
3 March 1819	Robert Campbell, jun.	Moore	to	Croaker	20. 0. 0.
3 March 1819	John Laurie	Campbell, jun.	to	Croaker	27. 9. 0.
27 April 1819	R. B. Hazard	Croaker	on	Moore	21. 8. 4.

Date	By	Name	on/to	Name	Amount (£ s d)
25 May 1819	Robert Campbell, jun.	Greenway	to	Croaker	20. 0. 0.
8 June 1819	William Redfern	Croaker	on	Middleton	57. 0. 0.
15 June 1819	William Browne	Croaker	to	Cooper	20. 13. 0.
29 June 1819	James Wilshire	Croaker	on	Moore	21. 11. 8.
20 July 1819	Robert Cooper	Croaker	on	Middleton	100. 0. 0.
10 Aug. 1819	James Chisholm	Croaker	on	Middleton	150. 0. 0.
24 Aug. 1819	Robert Cooper	Croaker	on	Moore	21. 15. 0.
28 Oct. 1819	Thomas Palmer	Tompson	to	Croaker	51. 0. 0.
25 Dec. 1819	Robert Cooper	Croaker	on	Moore	21. 18. 4.
26 Sept. 1820	Simeon Lord	Carne	to	Croaker	45. 0. 0.

Notes

Chapter 1

[1] William Shakespeare, *King Henry VI*, Part 2, iv. 7.

[2] 'For a yeoman of Kent, with his yearly rent, There was never a widow could say him nay', *Ivanhoe*, chapter 40.

[3] P. H. Reaney (R. M. Wilson, ed.), *A Dictionary of English Surnames*, pp. 115, 117, and P. Hanks and F. Hodges, *A Dictionary of Surnames*, pp. 130, 131, from which refs in next two sentences are also taken.

[4] There was a John Wilkinson who married at Birchington in 1788 and another who was declared bankrupt at his windmill in Appledore in 1811 (*Kentish Gazette*, 9 July and 3 Sept. 1811), but there is no evidence to link either with the Croakers.

[5] Canterbury Cathedral Archives, U3/141/1/4, from which all refs to Croaker baptisms are taken.

[6] cf. E. Hasted, *The History and Topographical Survey of the County of Kent*, vol. II, p. 117: St. Dunstan's Street is 'broad and handsome'.

[7] *Universal British Directory* (1793–98), vol. 2, pp. 499–509.

[8] Ibid.

[9] W. Gostling, *A Walk in and about the City of Canterbury*, p. 13.

[10] *Dictionary of National Biography (DNB)*; M. Worgan, *The Church of St Dunstan's Canterbury*; F. W. Cross and J. R. Hall, *Rambles Round Old Canterbury*.

[11] Cross and Hall, op. cit., p. 86; L. Richmond and A. Turton, *The Brewing Industry*, p. 142.

[12] The brewery of Fenner and Flint, which was later (without Fenner) to take over Abbott's brewery, began in Sturry Street in 1780 (Richmond and Turton, *The Brewing Industry*; Centre for Kentish Studies, U1724, B1).

[13] Facts about Abbott's life and career are taken from friends' letters (discussed in chapter 3), printed in the pamphlet *Poisonous Beer* (London, 1816).

[14] *Kentish Chronicle*, 14 Aug. 1821, p. 4.

[15] It is possible that the collection of settlement certificates for St Dunstan's (Canterbury Cathedral Archives U3/141/13/3) is incomplete.

[16] Abbott's magistracy, and friendships, are evident from *Poisonous Beer* (see note 13 above). The concept of freemen is discussed in the opening paragraphs of chapter 2. Rates (i.e. taxes) for relief of the poor were levied from owners and/or occupiers of property in parishes from the late 16th to mid 19th centuries. In 1797, Abbott's contribution to the poor rate was £10 18s out of £28 4s (Canterbury Cathedral Archives, U3/141/12/5).

[17] We are grateful to Mr Paul Pollak, The King's School archivist, for much help and advice.

[18] Canterbury Cathedral Archives, U3/141/12/5, 6, from which remaining refs in this para. are taken. The public houses were the Unicorn and the Blue Anchor.

[19] The Canterbury charity schools are listed and discussed in the *First Report of the Commissioners Appointed [under] 'An Act for appointing Commissioners to enquire concerning Charities in England, for the Education of The Poor'* (1819), pp. 88–92. Canterbury Cathedral Archives (CC/S16/1) has rules for the Blue Coat (Girls) and Grey Coat (Boys) schools, with lists of admissions (1761–1843), but no Croaker children appear.

[20] W. Gostling, *A Walk . . .*, pp. 73, 74: 'In St. Dunstan's-street stands a long range of building, converted into school rooms for the education of the children of the poor, on the system of Dr. Bell. These premises were formerly the prison for the eastern division of the county of Kent, before it was removed to St. Augustine's'. The ref. to Andrew Bell (see *DNB*), whose system involved the teaching of younger children by the older ones (the 'Madras System'), implies a date just too late for John Croaker.

[21] See press reports, e.g. *Kentish Chronicle*, 17 Jan. 1815. In 1808 a Canterbury Free School for Boys was opened, of which one John Abbott was a major benefactor (see *Kentish Gazette*, 19 Feb. 1811), but again this was too late to benefit the Croakers.

[22] Francis Price, illegitimate son of Mary Croaker, was baptised in St Dunstan's on 16 Feb. 1823 (Canterbury Cathedral Archives, U3/141/1/4).

[23] S. Corpe and A. M. Oakley, *Canterbury Freemen 1800–1835*.

[24] This date is implicit in the testimony of John Garrett at Croaker's trial in 1815: 'as partner in a banking-house at Ramsgate, in which the prisoner lived previous to his going to Margate as clerk, he had known him about seven years, and he had universally born a very good character' (*Kentish Gazette*, 20 Oct. 1815).

[25] J. W. Gilbart, *A Practical Treatise on Banking*, vol. 1, p. 197, from which (and p. 198) all remaining refs in this para. are taken.

[26] Ibid., pp. 198, 199, and also for the next sentence.

[27] Ibid., pp. 197, 198, and also for the next sentence.

[28] An analysis of the apprenticeship indentures in Lloyds TSB Group Archives was published in *Stable Companion* (Lloyds Bank pensioners' magazine), no. 26 (Summer 1996), p. 6.

[29] This traditional English folk-song begins: 'When I was bound apprentice in famous Lincolnshire, full well I served my master for more than seven year'. In the chorus, the singer contradicts himself: ''Twas my delight [to poach] on a shining night in the season of the year'.

[30] Sir William Forbes, *Memoirs of a Banking-House*, p. 14.

[31] The only source even approaching a systematic list is IR 1 in the Public Record Office, comprising Apprenticeship Books maintained under 8 Anne c.5 (1710) to register stamp duty. But the duty was widely avoided (see PRO Records Information sheet).

[32] Papers of the mainstream Garrett family, which included such notables as Lt Gen Sir Robert Garrett (see *DNB*), are at Ramsgate Library (ref U888).

[33] The main secondary sources used in this, and following sentences, were: *An Alphabetical List of all the Country-Bankers residing in England, Scotland, and Wales* (London, 1797); *Universal British Directory 1793–1798*, vol. 2, p. 508; lists published in annual volumes of the *Bankers' Almanac and Year Book*.

[34] Lloyds TSB Group Archives, A53/60b/3, p. 16; Centre for Kentish Studies, U1724 B1–4. There is a useful summary of the history of Flint's brewery in an 1834 memo. by Benjamin Flint (CKS, U1724 B1) which describes the relationship with Fenner (cf. Richmond and Turton, *The Brewing Industry*).

[35] The best detailed analysis of the period is in L. S. Pressnell, *Country Banking in the Industrial Revolution*.

[36] This was the result of a privilege granted in 1708 to the Bank of England, which had been founded in 1694.

[37] *An Alphabetical List* (see note 33 above), from which all refs in rest of this para. are taken.

[38] Barclays Bank is the well known modern example of a business founded initially on brewing.

[39] See introduction to Kent Archives Office (i.e. Centre for Kentish Studies) catalogue of Cobb MSS., Part 1, and contents.

[40] A good recent study of bills of exchange is contained within I. S. Black, 'The London Agency System in English Banking, 1780–1825' in *London Journal*, no. 21/2 (1996), pp. 112–29.

[41] Centre for Kentish Studies, U1453 B3/14/5 (1815).

[42] The suspension, meant to be temporary, lasted until 1821.

[43] The principle of limited liability was not extended to English banks until 1858. In Scotland the three early chartered banks had enjoyed it from the beginning.

[44] Refs in this, and the next, sentence come mainly from L. H. Grindon, *Manchester Banks and Bankers* pp. 46, 133–5.

[45] By the 1826 Act, joint-stock banks could only be founded 65 or more miles from London. Only in 1833, under certain conditions, were joint-stock banks allowed to form within that radius.

[46] Centre for Kentish Studies, Q/RPl 319. No connection has been traced between this Blaxland and the family of that name who were later to become famous in Australian history.

[47] T. Joplin, *An Essay on the General Principles and Present Practice of Banking in England and Scotland*, p. 83.

[48] Lloyds TSB Group Archives, A53/60b/2, and A20b/1. In the case of the Canterbury Bank records, the earliest double-entry ledger is actually 1782 (A53/60b/1), but it relates to the days when the partners were hop factors rather than bankers.

[49] *First Report of the Commissioners* (see note 19 above), p. 88, mentions that children at Eastbridge Hospital were taught 'to write, read, and cast accounts', while at St Margaret's Blue Coat School (p. 92) boys were 'to be instructed in reading, writing, and accounts'. These benefits were by no means restricted to schools within Canterbury.

[50] *Kentish Gazette*, 11 June 1811. In later advertisements (1814), the school claims to teach 'Merchants Accompts'.

[51] e.g. P. Kelly, *The Elements of Book-Keeping*, advertised in *Kentish Chronicle*, 31 July 1801, and J. Morrison, *The Elements of Book-Keeping by Single as well as Double Entry*, advertised in *Kentish Gazette*, 29 Nov. 1811.

Chapter 2

[1] *Universal British Directory 1793–1798*, vol. 2, p. 501, contains a good summary of Canterbury's constitutional position.

[2] S. Corpe and A. M. Oakley, *Canterbury Freemen 1800–1835*, introduction.

3 J. M. Cowper, *The Roll of Freemen of the City of Canterbury*; Kent *Poll Books*, 1790, 1796; A. J. Willis, *Canterbury Marriage Licences 1781–1809*; will, Centre for Kentish Studies, PRC 17/103/527; *Kentish Chronicle*, 29 March 1803.
4 Will, loc. cit.
5 *Kentish Chronicle*, 24 April 1801.
6 These facts are implicit in his will, Public Record Office, PROB 11/1359.
7 *The Times*, 16 June 1819, has a note of his bankruptcy.
8 The daughters' baptisms are recorded in the registers of St Margaret's, Canterbury: Canterbury Cathedral Archives, U3/6/1/2, 3. The baptism of Philip Henry has not been traced.
9 Will, Public Record Office, loc. cit.
10 We are grateful to Carolyn Kemp of Canada for drawing our attention to the Harbledown vault. It is interesting that Harbledown is very close to St Dunstan's.
11 *Kentish Chronicle*, 24 April 1811.
12 The accounts of both men were held by The Canterbury Bank of Gipps, Simmons & Gipps (Loyds TSB Group Archives, A53/60b/3). Kemp borrowed often, but repaid quickly, to maintain his account at around £400. Sankey was normally in debt to the bank at around £800, but was clearly the master of his affairs, as the account was healthily in credit before his death.
13 Will, Centre for Kentish Studies, PRC 17/103/594.
14 Will, Centre for Kentish Studies, PRC 17/106/153.
15 Ibid. Philip Henry Kemp, a tide-waiter, married Mary, a daughter of Augustine Kemp. She is mentioned in her father's will, as her husband was by then (1819) deceased.
16 Centre for Kentish Studies, PRC 17/103/594. Philip Henry Kemp inherited the real estate.
17 As the locality of Wilgate Green in Leaveland held one William Kemp, died 1829, aged 71 (Throwley burial register), the possibility exists of a link between him and Henry Kemp in Canterbury. However, as no Kemps were witnesses at Susannah's Leaveland wedding, this seems most unlikely.
18 'G.E.C.', *The Complete Peerage*, vol. 12, pp. 115–18, from which refs in the next sentences are also taken. For a general description of Leaveland, and surrounding villages, see F. F. Giraud and C. E. Donne, *A Visitor's Guide to Faversham*, pp. 84, 93, 103, 106, 107.
19 Leaveland manor court book, Centre for Kentish Studies, U390 M26, from which all refs in this para. are taken, unless otherwise stated.
20 *Archaeologia Cantiana*, vol. 22 (1897), p. 92.
21 The facts here, and in the next paragraph, are derived from a pamphlet in Canterbury Cathedral Archives assembled at the time from press and periodicals (e.g. *Ladies Magazine*, nos. 13, 14, 16). Much of this information was collated by S. Clark and forms the article 'When his Sins Caught up with John Collington', in *Bygone Kent*, vol. 13, no. 10 (Oct. 1992), pp. 585–91.
22 Centre for Kentish Studies, U390 M26.
23 Lloyds TSB Group Archives, Cox & Co. regimental ledgers, A56e/107.
24 Will, Public Record Office, PROB 11/1451.
25 Willis, *Canterbury Marriage Licences 1781–1809*, p. 72.
26 Corpe and Oakley, *Canterbury Freemen 1750–1799*.
27 Centre for Kentish Studies, loc. cit.
28 Will, Centre for Kentish Studies, PRC 17/103/137.

[29] Willis, *Canterbury Marriage Licences*, pp. 97, 305.

[30] Frances Collington married later than Susannah Kidder Kemp (A. J. Willis, *Canterbury Marriage Licences 1810–1837*, p. 74). Occupations for the Amos family are derived from wills, e.g. Centre for Kentish Studies, PRC 17/105/370, and directories. Molash itself is described in Kelly's *Kent Directory* (1855) as 'obscurely situated among the hills, and but little frequented'.

[31] However, with the east side of what was effectively Leaveland village lying in the parish of Badlesmere, it is possible that the best acquaintances of the Collingtons lay in that parish. It is interesting that Badlesmere Court, for instance, was occupied by one John Kemp in the early 19th century (Throwley burial register, 1852), but again there is no evidence of a link with Henry Kemp of Canterbury.

[32] Public Record Office, PROB 11/1383. Will is dated 14 Oct. 1800, with codicil 29 Sept. 1801.

[33] The house was called Leaveland Court in the codicil to the will, but Leaveland Farm in a map of 1798, Centre for Kentish Studies, U1175 P54.

[34] Cowper, *The Role of Freemen of the City of Canterbury*, p. 51; Corpe and Oakley, *Canterbury Freemen*.

[35] Kent *Poll Book*, 1796.

[36] Kelly's *Kent Directory* (1903), under Sheldwich.

[37] Giraud and Donne, *A Visitor's Guide*, p. 107.

[38] *Report of the Commissioners for Inquiring Concerning Charities*, vol. 30 (1837), p. 477.

[39] For Parsons, see *DNB* and *Gentleman's Magazine*, vol. 82, Part 2, pp. 291, 292. He was at the free school in Oakham, Rutlandshire, until 1761, but most of his teaching was at Wye Grammar School (south-west of Canterbury), part of the ancient Wye College. The estate accounts of Lees Court have survived mainly in Northamptonshire Record Office (owing to the family's predilection for Rockingham Castle). Certain household account books have survived for Lees Court (e.g. WR 1193, for 1765–69), but there are no references to education.

[40] He had four acres of hop-ground at the date of his will (Centre for Kentish Studies, PRC 17/103/527).

[41] Giraud and Donne, *A Visitor's Guide*, pp. 40, 41. The favourite bank for the Kemp trust fund, given the existing Kemp and Sankey connections, must be Gipps, Simmons & Gipps, but the ledgers are missing for the crucial years. It has already been suggested, in chapter 1, that Croaker was unlikely to have been apprenticed there.

[42] Kent *Poll Book*, 1790, has a Henry Kemp and a Richard Kemp as owner-occupiers in Ramsgate.

[43] Canterbury Cathedral Archives, U3/185/1/2.

[44] According to Convict Indents in New South Wales, Croaker was 5 ft $6\frac{1}{2}$ ins, with a fair, ruddy complexion, brown eyes, and brown hair.

[45] *Bankers' Almanac and Year Book* (all editions), appendix of amalgamations.

[46] Public Record Office, HO 47/55, p. 4. This is also the source for Sackett being sole principal.

[47] K. J. Lampard, Cobb & Son, Bankers of Margate c.1785 to c.1840, pp. 273, 274, quoting *The New Margate, Ramsgate and Broadstairs Guide*, 5th ed. (Margate, 1809), p. 68.

[48] We are grateful to Mr Alan Kay of Birchington and Mrs Patricia Cole of The Kent Family History Society for assistance with the Sacketts' background. In June 1813 seven Sackett brothers were active (Mr Kay). Centre for Kentish Studies has a map of the Sackett estate, U1511 P25, 26.

49 Lloyds TSB Group Archives, A20b/46 (accounts of Commissioners of Margate Pier and Harbour Company).

50 Centre for Kentish Studies, Cobb MSS., U1453 B2/1/1, p. 268.

51 Sources, as note 48. Henry Sackett's will, Public Record Office, PROB 11/1565, seems to indicate that John Henry Sackett was his only son.

52 Will, Public Record Office, PROB 11/1833.

53 *Kentish Gazette*, 20 Oct. 1815.

54 Kent's *London Directory*, 1814–1816.

55 *Kentish Gazette*, loc. cit.

56 All the known names connected with Sackett's Bank (e.g. Kidman, Hunter, Griffith) had an interest in the liquor trade.

57 Lloyds TSB Group Archives, A20b/2, 6, 51.

58 Ibid., A20b/46.

59 Ibid., A20b/2, p. 147.

60 Ibid., A20b/51, p. 75.

61 *The Times*, 26 Dec. 1812, p. 2d, from which all refs in this para. are taken.

62 Public Record Office, KB16 25/4, p. 4.

63 Ibid., HO 47/55, p. 1.

64 *Kentish Gazette*, 28 June 1814, p. 4. Addressed to 'Bankers, Merchants, &c. &c.', the advertiser claimed to be 'conversant in Accompts and Book-keeping, together with the general routine of Counting-House Business'.

65 Ibid., 20 Oct. 1815.

66 Both baptised in St John-in-Thanet (i.e. Margate). As the name Mary Ann honours Susannah's sister, the Wilkinson element probably honours a male family connection on Croaker's side.

Chapter 3

1 The main source throughout this chapter is a 16-page anonymous pamphlet, to be discussed below, entitled *Poisonous Beer*, in Canterbury Cathedral Archives, ref. CA40-ABB.

2 Ibid., p. 15.

3 Ibid., p. 11, makes it clear that another writer was a Mr Marryatt, but his significance has not been traced.

4 Ibid., p. 6. Sir William Curtis referred to Blake as 'this vile wretch' (p. 5).

5 Ibid., p. 6, from which refs in next two sentences are also taken. Early proceedings in this matter have not been traced in the records of the Treasury itself.

6 See *Dictionary of National Biography (DNB)*.

7 Public Record Office, CUST 48/63, p. 461, from which refs in next two sentences are also taken.

8 *Poisonous Beer*, pp. 8–15, and T. C. Hansard, *The Parliamentary Debates*, vol. 33, pp. 863–82 *passim*, from which remaining refs in this para. are also taken.

9 See *DNB*. There are interesting coincidences between names among Croaker's family and friends (i.e. Pennell and Lawrence) and the names of Croaker's third son, Thomas Lawrence Pennel, born in Australia, but nothing more than coincidence can be postulated.

10 *The Times*, 3 April 1816, p. 3.

11 There are differences between reported interjections, and also in the text: e.g. in the eyes of the Dean of Canterbury, ale-drinkers are described as a *caput lupinum* (wolf's head) in the pamphlet, and *ferae naturae* (wild animals) in Hansard.

12 See note 1 above.

[13] Public Record Office, PROB 11/1709.

[14] Centre for Kentish Studies, Q/RPl; Canterbury Cathedral Archives, U3/141/12/7. Abbott's assessment fell from £10 0s 5d to £4 14s 5d in 1814, but rose again to £7 10s soon afterwards, a sum taken over by Flint & Kingsford in April 1821. It is also indicative that Abbott's will made a bequest to every labourer in the brewhouse, so in February 1817 he was certainly in business.

[15] Abbott had considerable investments, from which his sons benefited, and his four daughters received £500 apiece.

[16] John Abbott junior was assessed separately at £1 5s in 1814, when his father's assessment fell, as indicated in note 14 above.

[17] See P. Mathias, *The Brewing Industry in England 1700–1830*, pp. 420–2, and especially sources quoted in his note 1, p. 421.

[18] Centre for Kentish Studies, Cobb MSS., U1453 B2/40/1. Under the same reference is a letter from John Abbott to Cobbs dated 8 Sept. 1785 which, although not specifically about brewing, could mark the very beginning of Abbott's foray into that business.

[19] Demand from the Navy was strong enough to encourage Cobbs to open a branch of their Margate brewery at Deal (G. E. Clarke, *Historic Margate*, p. 53).

[20] For the effect of this on another local brewery, see T. Gourvish, *Norfolk Beers from English Barley*, pp. 20–2. The author points out (p. 20) that the duty on hops and malt was on average 30 and 320 per cent higher respectively in 1804–16 than before 1801.

[21] A. J. Willis, *Canterbury Marriage Licences 1810–1837*; S. Corpe and A. M. Oakley, *Canterbury Freemen 1800–1835*; Canterbury Cathedral Archives, U3/141/12/9 (rating assessments for St Dunstan's).

[22] *The Times*, 5 Aug. 1834, p. 3e.

[23] *British Parliamentary Papers* (1818), vol. 3, p. 295, from which refs in the next four sentences are also taken.

[24] Many of these cases are the subject of petitions, etc., in Public Record Office, CUST 30/29, 30 and other Report Books under that catalogue heading.

[25] John Croaker senior was regularly assessed at 9 shillings for the poor rate, rising to 10 shillings in 1820 (Canterbury Cathedral Archives, U3/141/12/7), which must mean that he had a property independent of John Abbott. In his will of 1817 the latter makes his bequest of 10 guineas to Croaker conditional on his 'living with me at the time of my decease', but that clearly must be taken loosely: the cottage was within Abbott's freehold and very near the brewery itself.

[26] Canterbury Cathedral Archives, U3/141/4/3, 4.

[27] *The New Canterbury Guide* (Canterbury, n.d.), p. 8.

[28] *Kentish Chronicle*, 14 Aug. 1821.

[29] Centre for Kentish Studies, PRC 16/510.

[30] Canterbury Cathedral Archives, loc. cit., and U3/141/12/8. May Inge was the owner of the cottage until 1832.

[31] *Kentish Chronicle*, 20 Oct. 1814.

[32] The position is complicated by John Abbott junior who was assessed on his own, in 1810, for the 11 properties normally attributed to his father (Canterbury Cathedral Archives, U3/141/12/6). The extent of his *de facto* involvement in the brewery is unknown.

[33] *Poisonous Beer*, p. 7.

34 A slight flaw in this argument is that Abbott knew he had vitriol and 'prepared powders' in the brewery (ibid.). But this merely increases the probability of Croaker going wildly astray, because a dishonourable Abbott would have been more likely to implicate his associates.

35 All refs in this para. are taken from the trial proceedings, as reported in *Kentish Gazette*, 20 Oct. 1815.

36 Ibid.

37 All refs for the narrative of Croaker's flight, in this and the next para., are taken from the affidavit of John Baker, Public Record Office, HO 47/55, 3rd doc.

38 Called Minet and Fector at their London office. Their strong relationship with Calais derived from the fact that Isaac Minet (1660–1745) was the fourth son of a Calais provision merchant (*Archaeologia Cantiana*, vol. 81 (1966), pp. 39–43). From July 1814 the firm traded at Dover as J. Minet, Fector & Co. (printed announcement in Centre for Kentish Studies, Cobb MSS., U1453 B3/14/16), but is known only as Fector and Minet in the Croaker trial reports.

39 Public Record Office, HO 47/55, 1st doc.

40 *Kentish Gazette*, 31 Jan. 1815.

41 The newspaper (28 Jan. 1815) is held in the *Bibliothèque nationale de France*, at Paris.

42 One explanation for this error is that the money was actually being reckoned in *livres tournois*, which at that time was being replaced by the French franc. The ratio is roughly correct.

43 Another interesting point is why the Paris press bothered with the story at all, as it was not the normal kind of report which they carried. Their newspapers at that time were small in format, and mainly concerned with matters of state; foreign stories were generally much meatier.

44 See, for instance, advertisements in *Kentish Gazette*, 6 Sept. 1814, by packet boat owners. The service had been suspended during the French Wars. Margate also had trading links with Flushing.

Chapter 4

1 Public Record Office, HO 47/55, 3rd doc., from which all refs in this and next two paras are taken, unless otherwise stated. This doc. is the deposition of one John Baker, and this chapter will argue that his version of events was the right one.

2 This is the first evidence that Croaker himself was a property-owner, and the extent of it cannot be traced. As for his wife's real estate, this was revealed in the later appeal as 'a property' (Public Record Office, HO 47/55, 4th doc.), and was evidently a residual part of the estate of her late father and then brother.

3 *Kentish Gazette*, 31 Jan. 1815.

4 Ibid., 2 May 1815, in the report of the habeas corpus hearing: the writ had been obtained 'by the friends of the prisoner'.

5 Centre for Kentish Studies, Cobb MSS., U1453 B3/15/1104.

6 We are grateful for information from Mr Alan Kay.

7 In *Kentish Gazette*, 12 July 1811, Kidman advertised his wares, and announced his intention to relinquish the wine trade at the end of that season. However, ibid., 20 May 1814, carried an advertisement for the sale of his newly-erected business premises in Hawley Square, while ibid., 20 June 1815, carried a similar advertisement in which Kidman is stated to be only then retiring.

8 Public Record Office, KB 16 25/4.

9 Public Record Office, KB 21/50, p. 533; KB 36/389, p. 38. These original depositions (referred to in KB 36/389) have not survived, but that of John Baker was presumably the same as his later one, dated 10 Jan. 1816 (HO 47/55, 3rd doc.). The identity and relevance of Robert Baker are unclear. KB 36/389 makes no reference to a deposition by William Keys of Dover, mariner, but in fact that doc. (dated 7 April 1815) has survived (HO 47/55, 2nd doc.). It was apparently not presented until the time of Croaker's appeal, when it would have reinforced the deposition of John Baker.

10 These facts are known from the press report of the hearing, in *Kentish Chronicle*, 2 May 1815. A different, and slightly less full version, appears in *Kentish Gazette* of the same date. All remaining refs in this para., and the next one, are taken from these sources.

11 *DNB.*

12 *The Times*, 4 March 1845; *Law Magazine*, vol. 1 (1845), p. 278.

13 *Kentish Chronicle*, 20 Oct. 1815.

14 Ibid., 26 May 1815, from which refs in next three sentences are also taken.

15 The auction notice of Sackett's estate, in *Kentish Gazette*, 11 Aug. 1815, makes it clear that the banking-house contained, on the same floor as the bank itself, one sitting room and two small bedrooms. The rest of the house was let to a Miss Robinson.

16 It might be significant that Kentish newspapers, in October 1811, carried an advertisement from an anonymous young lady wishing to engage herself as an under-teacher in a respectable ladies' boarding school. At that time the Croakers had just moved from Ramsgate to Margate.

17 A. J. Willis, *Canterbury Marriage Licences 1810–1837.*

18 Public Record Office, HO 47/55, 4th doc.; the will of Augustine Kemp, dated 1819 (Centre for Kentish Studies, PRC17/106/153) mentions Mary, widow of Philip Henry Kemp, late of St James, Clerkenwell, tide-waiter. Philip was certainly dead by 1816 (otherwise Susannah would not have inherited), but the placing of his widow there at that date is conjectural.

19 All refs for the trial, unless otherwise indicated, are taken from the long recital of events in the *Kentish Gazette*, 20 Oct. 1815.

20 See *DNB* entry.

21 The firm of Messrs Rayner has not been traced. It is possible that the spelling is a misprint for Rainier (therefore Rainier, Ballard & Morgan, stock and bill brokers in the City of London). This conjecture is strengthened by the incidence of the name Rainier in Sandwich, East Kent, but weakened by the apparent fact that Sackett was lending them money.

22 Post Office, *London Directory* (1815).

23 These bills were promissory notes issued at intervals by Government, rather than the Bank of England. They were interest-bearing but could circulate at their face value like banknotes at periods well before their maturity.

24 The effect of the Suspension of Cash Payments by the Bank of England (see chapter 1) was that all forms of paper money, although they continued to circulate, were disadvantaged in comparison to specie. However, the real difference between the Exchequer bills and the bills of exchange, in this instance, was minimal.

25 *Kentish Chronicle*, 20 Oct. 1815.

26 These bills are discussed in J. S. Mill, *Principles of Political Economy*, vol. 2, p. 42. He notes that they are sometimes called 'with a tinge of disapprobation, *fictitious* bills'.

27 All refs for the conduct of the trial continue to be taken from the *Kentish Gazette*, 20 Oct. 1815.

28 The italics are used in the newspaper report.

29 Public Record Office, HO 47/55, 5th doc.

30 Ibid., 1st doc.

31 London street directories.

32 Public Record Office, HO 47/55, 4th doc.; this petition (which was addressed to Sivewright) referred at length to Susannah's distress at the loss of her property, which threatened 'misery and want' to herself and her children.

33 Public Record Office, HO 13/28, p. 8.

34 Public Record Office, HO 47/55, 10th doc.

35 An advertisement in *Kentish Gazette*, 15 Dec. 1815 mentioned, as just published, a booklet entitled *The Trial of John Croarer [sic] for Felony*, by a short-hand writer. It was printed and sold by G. Witherden at Margate, and sold also at the libraries in Canterbury, Margate, Ramsgate, Deal, and Dover. The mis-spelling of Croaker was presumably in the newspaper and not in the booklet.

36 An appeal was published in *Notes and Queries*, vol. 242, No. 2 (June 1997), p. 242.

37 *Kentish Gazette*, 8 Aug. 1815.

38 Ibid., 11 Aug 1815 (announcement of auction). The sale contracts have not been traced.

39 Centre for Kentish Studies, Cobb MSS., U1453 B3/14/5.

40 Ibid.

41 *Kentish Gazette*, 20 Oct. 1815.

42 Ibid.

43 39 Geo. III, c.85. This brief Act (just one clause) was passed specifically to clarify the point as to whether or not embezzlement was a felonious offence. It was. The penalty on conviction was transportation 'for any term not exceeding fourteen years, in the discretion of the court'. It was therefore quite legal for Kenrick to have sentenced Croaker to 7 years, although 14 (as it was amended) was apparently the norm.

44 *Statutes at Large*, vol. 38 (1794). The first general act in this subject was 7 Geo. IV, c.46 ('The Country Bankers' Act, 1826'), but even this was not interested in the relationship between bankers and their clerks.

45 Lloyds TSB Group Archives, A20b/6 (16 Oct. 1815).

Chapter 5

1 J. Walker, *The Universal Gazetteer*.

2 W. Branch-Johnson, *The English Prison Hulks*, pp. 1–35.

3 J. H. Vaux, *The Memoirs of James Hardy Vaux*; N. McLachlan, ed., p. 198.

4 *British Parliamentary Papers 1810–1811* (199) III, 567, and (217) III, 691; cf. Branch-Johnson, *The English Prison Hulks*, pp. 36–44, and *The Times*, 23 June 1815.

5 Vaux, *Memoirs*, p. 199.

6 Public Record Office, HO 47/55.

7 Most of the above facts are from the narrative of the voyage by John Haslam, R.N., ship's surgeon, which will be discussed in detail below.

[8] AJCP/PRO CO 201/82. For a discussion of this matter, with statistics, see M. Phillips, *A Colonial Autocracy*, pp. 112, 113.

[9] Vaux, *Memoirs*, p. 198.

[10] Public Record Office, HO 47/55.

[11] It is still possible that the concession to allow Susannah and the children to travel was arrived at with the authority of the Prince Regent.

[12] M. Phillips, *A Colonial Autocracy*, p. 114. The adult fare was about £35–£40. Infants travelled free, and children at a discount of about 50 per cent.

[13] AJCP/PRO CO 201/81, 82.

[14] The fare for one adult to travel inside the mail coach was about 24 shillings.

[15] It is not, for instance, referred to in C. Bateson, *The Convict Ships*, an authoritative secondary source.

[16] The original text of Haslam's narrative is held in the State Library of NSW and is reproduced here by kind permission of the library council. The original has been faithfully transcribed, so as to make available a new primary printed source. In consequence, there are inevitable anomalies of grammar and expression when compared to modern usage.

[17] For which, see Bateson, *The Convict Ships, passim,* and plate opp. p. 36. This book is especially useful for its commentary on the slowly rising status of ships' surgeons, and their eventual role as superintendents of the voyage.

[18] See also W. Munk, *The Roll of the Royal College of Physicians of London*, vol. 3, pp. 282, 283.

[19] *Merchant Taylors' School Register 1561–1934*, vol. 1 (unpag.).

[20] Haslam last appears in the 1823–24 *Navy List* so he soon became disillusioned with his job.

[21] The clothes list also included 2 pairs of yarn stockings, 1 neck handkerchief, 1 pair of shoes, and a woollen cap. More clothing, including a yellow kersey jacket, was available to each convict before disembarkation (AJCP/PRO CO 201/82).

[22] An alternative weekly diet for a mess of five men was published as an appendix to W. C. Wentworth, *A Statistical, Historical, and Political Description of the Colony of New South Wales*, p. 466. This had fewer commodities, in significantly smaller quantities, but it is noticeable that plums, albeit only to the extent of 2 lbs a week, were on the menu. These would have been a stronger protection against scurvy than Croaker's raisins.

[23] AO Fiche 636, Principal Superintendent of Convicts: Bound Indents, 1814–1818, 4/4005, pp. 201–12. The skilled tradesmen aboard included a cabinet maker and upholsterer, engraver and silversmith, goldsmith and jeweller, shipwright, and gunmaker.

[24] 'Flash' was the name given to a form of underworld slang of which certain phrases, for example 'try it on' and 'tog'd out to the nines', and even 'chum', are still readily understandable today. The first dictionary of flash was compiled in 1812 by James Hardy Vaux, and was published as an appendix to his memoirs. See also *Australian Dictionary of Biography.*

[25] During his second transportation Vaux represented his clerical abilities to the ship's master, and had a comfortable voyage maintaining the victualling accounts and the ship's log (see *Memoirs*, p. 202).

[26] If this incident was as serious as Haslam suggested, it is difficult to see why the convicts were not charged with mutiny once the ship docked at Port Jackson. On 29 Oct. 1816 Macquarie agreed to a request by Haslam that he be allowed to leave

the colony as early as possible, and at public expense (£95). The agreement terminated with the comment: 'Mr. Haslam is directed to send in his Journal [of the voyage] for the Governor's perusal'. Presumably this contained a less direct reference to mutinous conduct than Haslam allowed himself later in his book.

[27] Bateson, *The Convict Ships*, pp. 340, 341.

[28] For all of whom see *Australian Dictionary of Biography*.

[29] De Quirosville (pseudonym), 'Times Gone By', in *Sydney Gazette*, 18 April 1829, p. 2d.

[30] Wentworth, *A Statistical . . . Description*, p. 164.

[31] W. Vamplew (ed.), *Australians: Historical Statistics* (Sydney, 1987), pp. 25, 104.

[32] M. J. E. Steven, 'Public Credit and Private Confidence' in J. Broadbent and J. Hughes (eds), *The Age of Macquarie*, pp. 9, 10.

[33] J. P. McGuanne, 'A Hundred Years Ago', in *Journal and Proceedings of the Royal Australian Historical Society*, vol. 5, part 2 (1920); F. Driscoll, 'Macquarie's Administration of the Convict System' in ibid., vol. 26, part 6 (1942).

[34] Wentworth, *A Statistical . . . Description*, p. 223.

[35] Phillips, *A Colonial Autocracy*, pp. 64–5; M. Barnard, *Macquarie's World*, pp. 120, 121.

[36] [J. MacArthur], *New South Wales; its Present State and Future Prospects*, p. 60. The new restrictions were embodied in 2 & 3 Will. IV, c.62, s.2 (1832).

[37] This estimate is based on the ticket of leave serial numbers entered on the Bound Indents (see note 23 above).

[38] Colonial Secretary's Papers, 1788–1825, reel 6005, pp. 203–5.

[39] Ibid., reel 6046, pp. 111, 112, which is a letter from Wylde to Macquarie seeking a continuation of the concession.

[40] Croaker gave his address as George Street when he applied for employment with the Bank of New South Wales (see next chapter).

[41] Wentworth, *A Statistical . . . Description*, pp. 6, 7; J. Broadbent, 'Macquarie's Domain' in Broadbent and Hughes (eds), *The Age of Macquarie*, pp. 6, 7.

[42] Broadbent, 'Macquarie's Domain', p. 6.

[43] Wentworth, *A Statistical . . . Description*, p. 8.

[44] McGuanne, 'A Hundred Years Ago', p. 75.

[45] Ibid., p. 76.

[46] Wentworth, *A Statistical . . . Description*, p. 29.

[47] We are grateful to Margaret Steven for explaining the meaning of this elusive term.

[48] D. Macmillan, 'The Rise of the British–Australian Shipping Trade, 1810–1827' in A. Birch and D. Macmillan (eds), *Wealth and Progress*.

[49] Colonial Secretary's Papers, 1788–1825, reel 6023, p. 99.

[50] Ibid., reel 6046, pp. 111, 112 (letter from Wylde to Macquarie, 17 April 1817).

[51] Ibid, reel 6005, p. 328 (letter of W. Hutchinson, Superintendent of Convicts).

[52] 'Judge Advocate's Office', in *Concise Guide to the State Archives of NSW* (Sydney, n.d.), p. 1.

[53] Colonial Secretary's Papers, 1788–1825, reel 6046, pp. 117–19.

Chapter 6

[1] The main published sources for this bank are: R. F. Holder, *Bank of New South Wales. A History. Volume One: 1817–1893*, and S. J. Butlin, *Foundations of the Australian Monetary System 1788–1851*, pp. 110–41. For Wylde, see *ADB*; Holder, *Bank of New South Wales*; Butlin, *Foundations*. Much of the information which follows is from the Bank of New South Wales Directors' Minute Book No. 1.

² cf. Holder, *Bank of New South Wales*, pp. 11, 25. Macvitie was one of three merchants to set up in Sydney at this time who had arrived from places where banks had recently been established. Macvitie is of particular interest, not only for his later banking role, but because he came from Dumfries in Scotland (*ADB*, vol. 2), where a bank had been established in 1766. There is no evidence that he trained there in any capacity, but he would have been familiar with both private and joint-stock banking practice—perhaps a unique advantage in New South Wales.

³ The bank's earliest records (ledger 1817–20; stock book 1818–19; and cash book 1820–21) are in double entry. See also R. W. Gibson, 'Early Double Entry Records in Australia' in *Accounting History Newsletter*, no. 13 (Summer 1986), pp. 5, 6; R. H. Goddard, 'An Historical Survey' in *Chartered Accountant in Australia*, vol. 7 (1938), p. 694; R. H. Parker, 'Bookkeeping Barter and Current Cash Equivalents in Early New South Wales', p. 149. The surviving records of accounting in the colony, before 1817, are essentially tallies of such things as debts owed and stock held. Each business transaction was recorded by one book entry: that is, by single-entry accounting, although sometimes the modern terms 'debit' and 'credit' were also used. The basic characteristic of double-entry book-keeping was the recording of each transaction by two matching entries of equal amount, one a debit entry, the other a credit entry, so that for each transaction (singly and in aggregate), the sum of the debit entries would always be in balance with the sum of the credit entries. Another feature of the system was that entries were 'posted' from one form of record to another, with cross-referencing between pages.

⁴ 'J. H. Potts' in *The Etruscan*, vol. 6, no. 1 (June 1956) pp. 14–17; 'Joseph Hyde Potts (1793–1865)', Economic Department of the Bank of NSW, 7 Sept. 1961; Holder, *Bank of New South Wales*, pp. 34, 88.

⁵ For a discussion of the significance of this passage, see also R. Craig and S. Jenkins, 'Conjectures on Colonial Accounting History in Australia', pp. 214–38.

⁶ See advertisements in the *Sydney Gazette* of 28 Aug. 3c, 11 Sept. 3c and 9 Oct. 4a, 1803. William Broughton, deputy commissary in 1812, who described himself as an 'accountant' (*Historical Records of Australia*, part 1, vol. 7, pp. 532, 536).

⁷ Butlin, *Foundations*, pp. 119, 120; Holder, *Bank of New South Wales*, p. 15.

⁸ Bigge's examination of Wylde, in *Historical Records of Australia*, part 4, vol. 1, pp. 787–8.

⁹ Holder, *Bank of New South Wales*, p. 34.

¹⁰ Bank of NSW, Minute Book No. 1, p. 97, from which following ref is also taken. For Croaker's role as 'the Wales's first bookkeeper', see also T. Sykes, *Two Centuries of Panic*, p. 10. Sykes makes the point that: 'A known embezzler is the subject of deep suspicion in a bank. Invariably, however, the greatest larcenies are committed not by those we distrust, but by those we trust'. He was referring to the cashier, Francis Williams, discussed below.

¹¹ *ADB*, vol. 1.

¹² Both had proved themselves unreliable. Although Campbell worked in Sydney as a merchant's clerk (1806–11) and was 'an importer and retailer of general goods with extensive interests in the colonial fisheries' (1811–17), he was in financial difficulties in 1817. The annual salary of £150 might have motivated him to apply for the post. Campbell was uncomfortable as head accountant and resigned in January 1818. He was described as 'convivial, charming, a bon viveur, with a sentimental and romantic temperament, and with dash and personality'. E. S. Hall, a 'Free

Gentleman Settler', engaged in some trading activities, but was most prominent for his religious and social work. There can be little confidence in his accounting acumen, and his duties did not necessitate a knowledge of double-entry book-keeping. He resigned in March 1818. See Holder, *Bank of New South Wales*, pp. 34–5; Craig and Jenkins, 'Conjectures', p. 231; *ADB*, vol. 1, pp. 500–2.

¹³ G. W. D. Allen (ed.), *Early Georgian: Extracts from the Journal of George Allen (1800–1877)*.

¹⁴ Bank of New South Wales, Directors' Minute Book No. 2, from which all refs in this and following para. are taken, unless otherwise indicated.

¹⁵ Petition for mitigation of sentence, AONSW, Fiche 3207 4/1862, pp. 50–50c.

¹⁶ T. G. Parsons, 'Colonial Commissaries' in R. T. Appleyard and C. B. Schedvin (eds), *Australian Financiers*, pp. 11–14.

¹⁷ M. Scorgie, 'The Bank of New South Wales Ledger: Double Entry System or Not?', unpublished working paper, La Trobe University, 13 Aug 1997.

¹⁸ Craig and Jenkins, 'Conjectures', pp. 217–19.

¹⁹ See note 6 above.

²⁰ Jenkins asked to be released from his position as auditor (which might better be termed arbitrator), so 'that some person of Superior ability may be appointed in his stead' (Court of Civil Jurisdiction, AO 5/2279).

²¹ cf. R. W. Gibson, 'Two Centuries of Australian Accountants' in *The Accounting Historian's Notebook* (Spring 1988), p. 18; and R. H. Parker, 'Bookkeeping Barter and Current Cash Equivalents in Early New South Wales', pp. 139–51.

²² L. Goldberg, 'Some Early Australian Accounting Records', in A. C. Littleton and B. S. Yamey (eds), *Studies in the History of Accounting*. An abridged version of this paper appears in *The Australian Accountant* (October 1952).

²³ Lord's counting house is referred to by N. Cay, in *A Likely Lad. The Story of Simeon Lord*, pp. 83, 122. Robert Campbell junior is said to have worked in his uncle's counting house (*ADB*, vol. 1; M. J. E. Steven, 'Enterprise' in G. J. Abbott and N. B. Nairn (eds), *Economic Growth of Australia, 1799–1821*, p. 125). For wider discussion on counting houses, see G. J. Previts and T. K. Sheldahl, 'Accounting and "Counting Houses": An Analysis and Commentary', pp. 52–8.

²⁴ Steven, 'Enterprise'.

²⁵ Butlin, *Foundations*, p. 114; Holder, *Bank of New South Wales*, p. 15.

²⁶ Information from Jan Power, Archivist to Bank of Ireland, who has kindly searched the transactions of the Court of Directors. It is possible that this is another Campbell altogether, but in that case J. T. Campbell never worked there.

²⁷ *Historical Records of Australia*, part 1, vol. 9, p. 220.

²⁸ *ADB*, vol. 1, p. 199; cf. Holder, *Bank of New South Wales*, pp. 7, 21.

²⁹ E. H. D. Arndt, *Banking and Currency Development in South Africa (1652–1927)*.

³⁰ The initial term of 11 years allowed in 1694 to the Bank of England was the nearest equivalent.

³¹ Butlin, *Foundations*, pp. 113, 114; Holder, *Bank of New South Wales*, p. 12.

³² Banks were at first excluded from The Limited Liability Act, 1855, and many shareholders were happy with this situation, as the risk was deemed mitigated by provisions in each bank's deed of settlement. Moreover, if shareholders' risk was unlimited, it was argued that depositors had greater security. It took the failure of the City of Glasgow Bank in 1878 to persuade shareholders to take greater care of their own interests.

[33] Lloyds TSB Group Archives, A53/60a/1, which is the source for all refs below to the Canterbury Bank.

[34] *Historical Records of Australia*, part 1, vol. 9, pp. 228–33, which is the source for all refs below to the charter.

[35] The issue of banknotes of less than one pound had been banned in England from 1775. Country tradesmen often issued tokens, to be exchanged against their own goods, to make up the shortfall, and between 1811 and 1816 even the Bank of England issued tokens for 3s and 1s 6d.

[36] A. H. Gibson, *Bank Rate. The Banker's Vade Mecum*, p. 56.

[37] Lloyds TSB Group Archives, A53/60b/3, p. 16.

[38] Ibid., A53/60b/2. This book was the bank's current account ledger, and an analysis of the first page (listing debit or credit balances in June 1789), shows that of the 34 accounts named, no fewer than 24 were overdrawn, for sums between about £4 and as much as £1854. The bank was only solvent because one partner, George Gipps, had over £10 500 in credit, in his own account.

[39] Butlin, *Foundations*, pp. 30–3; Holder, *Bank of New South Wales*, p. 12.

Chapter 7

[1] cf. W. C. Wentworth, *A Statistical, Historical, and Political Description of the Colony of New South Wales*, p. 194. Even in the 1840s commercial morality in New South Wales was giving a foreigner cause for concern. According to Andrew Cheyne, a young Scots entrepreneur, the merchants of Sydney were 'far from being respectable or honourable, and little they cared what they did as long as they got their own interests served'. (D. Shineberg (ed.), *The Trading Voyages of Andrew Cheyne 1841–1844*, p. 64).

[2] Macquarie made Dr William Redfern a magistrate in November 1819, but Earl Bathurst was to reverse the appointment (*ADB*, under Redfern). Regarding convicts in general, Macquarie's view was 'That Emancipation when united with rectitude and long-tried good conduct should lead a man back to that rank in society which he had forfeited, and do away, inasfar as the case will permit, all retrospect of former bad conduct' (*Journal and Proceedings of the Royal Australian Historical Society*, vol. 14 (1928), p. 74, quoting *Historical Records of New South Wales*, vol. 7, p. 357).

[3] John Thomas Bigge (1780–1843) was authorised by a royal commission of 5 Jan. 1819 to enquire into the effectiveness of transportation as a deterrent. His brief extended to examining the whole way of life peculiar to New South Wales, which seemed somewhat at odds with British tradition. He reached Sydney that year, on 26 Sept. His reports of 1822 and 1823 (but not the appendices of evidence) were published by the House of Commons. (See *ADB* entry for Bigge as first point of reference.) The quotation here (from p. 194 in his *Report into the State of the Colony of New South Wales*) was made, and italicised for impact, by [J. MacArthur] in *New South Wales; its Present State and Future Prospects*, p. 24.

[4] Wentworth, *A Statistical . . . Description*, p. 203.

[5] Technically, promissory notes were 'made' rather than 'drawn', but the latter term was used by the Bank of New South Wales and is adopted in this chapter. The phrase 'value received', invariable in bills of exchange, was added to promissory notes to impart *gravitas*, and may not exclude the use of the note as a money-lending instrument, rather than evidence of a commercial transaction.

6. Bank of New South Wales, Directors' Minute Book No. 1, from which (and No. 2) all entries relating to the discounting of bills and notes are taken.
7. Clause 33 of the bank's charter indicates that this was the directors' favoured term.
8. For W. H. Moore, see *ADB*, vol. 2, which explains that he was anti-emancipist. That such a man could nevertheless have been helpful to Croaker should also have swayed the directors' minds. It also speaks well for Croaker's reputation among his colleagues, of whom Moore was one. A slightly complicating factor at this time, however, is that Macquarie had violently fallen out with Moore, and the bank's directors would have taken that into account.
9. Bank of New South Wales, Directors' Minute Book No. 1, p. 80. For the bank's policy in superseding promissory notes, see *Bigge Report*, p. 67. For a discussion on the abuse of promissory notes by merchants, and Macquarie's reaction, see T. Sykes, *Two Centuries of Panic*, pp. 2–5.
10. An example of a six-party promissory note is given in the unpublished Appendices to the *Bigge Reports* (Public Record Office, CO 201/126, pp. 59ff.).
11. The bank's ledger reveals that another £196 went out of John Wylde's account, in Croaker's favour, during 1818.
12. *ADB*, vol. 2.
13. Colonial Secretary's Papers, 1788–1825, reel 6046, pp. 167–70, from which all remaining refs in this para. and the next are taken, unless otherwise stated.
14. M. Phillips, *A Colonial Autocracy*, p. 63.
15. 'The term "emancipist" was applied to any individual who had been, but no longer was a convict. It mattered not how he had gained his freedom, whether by the expiration of the sentence he was serving, or by a pardon—absolute or conditional—granted by the Governor' (*Journal and Proceedings of the Royal Australian Historical Society*, vol. 14 (1928), p. 73).
16. There was always a risk of sequestration of his assets, if he was deemed to have contravened the terms of his ticket of leave.
17. There was nothing radical about this, and when the bill cited above (note 10) was the subject of legal proceedings the pursuing of the endorser(s) was mentioned as conforming to the 'statute'. The first Act of Parliament effectively to legislate in this area, and to treat promissory notes *pari passu* with bills of exchange, was 3 & 4 Anne, c.8 (1704).
18. Bank of New South Wales, Directors' Minute Book, No. 2, pp. 72, 37.
19. *Bigge Report*, pp. 66, 67.
20. For instance, the promissory note for £25 which he drew in favour of George Williams on 2 March 1818 (Supreme Court of Civil Jurisdiction, Judgement Rolls (1818), 133/1).
21. *Bigge Report*, pp. 62, 99. The inner rings were known as 'dumps', worth 1s 3d; the outer rings were called 'holeys', worth 5 shillings. The intrinsic value of the silver was worth less than these combined sums.
22. Supreme Court of Civil Jurisdiction, from which (133/1–7, along with Bank of New South Wales, Directors' Minute Books Nos 1 and 2), all refs in this para. and the next are taken, unless otherwise stated.
23. *ADB*, vol. 1.
24. We are grateful to Margaret Steven for insight into court practice. Although the rate of interest charged by the bank was 10 per cent, it could rise to 40 per cent in certain agreements between individuals.

25 A less formal directive from Judge Field to the provost marshal, on 30 Nov., was apparently unsuccessful. The writs issued for distraint were the normal *fieri facias* ('that you cause to be made') instruments, as found in all actions for debt or damages in the King's courts.

26 Supreme Court of Civil Jurisdiction, (1819), 151/1–4, from which all refs in this para. are taken.

27 Ibid., 157/1, 2, 4, 6 , 8.

28 Ibid., 239/1–3.

29 See *ADB*, vol. 1.

30 Public Record Office, from which all refs in this para. are taken. The *Sydney Gazette*, 18 Sept. 1819, carried a notice from Eagar requesting 'that all Persons indebted to him will forthwith arrange their Accounts up to the 30th June last'. This was a true measure of financial despair.

31 *ADB*, vol. 1.

32 Supreme Court of Civil Jurisdiction, (1822), 482/2, 3.

Chapter 8

1 F. Clune, *Serenade to Sydney: Some Historical Landmarks*, p. 194.

2 Social activity at Ultimo House is described in S. Fitzgerald and H. Golder, *Pyrmont and Ultimo Under Siege*, p. 20. For the area generally, with its 'elegant residences dispersed with discrimination in the pleasantest of situations', see W. and O. Harvard, 'A Frenchman Sees Sydney in 1819', in *Journal of the Royal Australian Historical Society*, vol. 24, part 1 (1938), pp. 33–4.

3 Principal Superintendent of Convicts: Bound Indents, 1814–1818, AO Fiche 201–12.

4 Archives Office of NSW, Sydney, SZ 779, Information no. 41, pp. 89–98. Roach was convicted and executed.

5 The property was advertised in the *Sydney Gazette*, for sale or lease, on 6 July 1816, 26 Feb. 1820, and 24 May 1822, as well as the date which was out of sequence, 14 Aug. 1819.

6 The Lawrence element in the name will be discussed below. Pennel appears to be an affectation, possibly introduced to suggest to the worldly-wise a family link with J. W. Croker in England (see *DNB*), who married a Miss Rosamond Pennell in 1806. If that was indeed the case, any link cannot now be substantiated. It is interesting that the Sydney district of Ultimo, which now covers the site of Perroquet Hill, includes a Mary Ann Street and a Thomas Street. It is conceivable that the two youngest Croaker children, at this date, are commemorated by these names, but other streets in the area are dedicated to other first names.

7 *Bigge Report Appendix*, Bonwick Transcripts, Box 20, p. 3527.

8 *Report of the Commissioner of Inquiry on the State of Agriculture and Trade in the Colony of New South Wales [Bigge Report*, vol. 3] (1823), p. 72.

9 Ibid., pp. 42, 102. Mrs Greenway taught 9 girls, and it might be significant that her entry (see note 7) directly followed that of Susannah Croaker. For the Greenways' large family, and the architect's character, see his entry in *ADB*, vol. 1.

10 Supreme Court of Civil Jurisdiction, Judgement Rolls (Campbell v. Croaker), 1818, 133/4.

11 The best contemporary accounts of farming practice are in W. C. Wentworth, *A Statistical, Historical, and Political Description of the Colony of New South Wales*, and J. Atkinson, *An Account of the State of Agriculture and Grazing in New South Wales*.

See also B. H. Fletcher, *Landed Enterprise and Penal Society*, pp. 132, 133 and *passim*.

[12] Public Record Office, CO 201/123. They gave evidence in August and September 1820.

[13] Wentworth, *A Statistical . . . Description*, p. 202. For his long and damning diatribe against dealers, see pp. 193–203.

[14] Public Record Office, CO 201/123, ff.153/4, which also covers all unreferenced sentences in next para.

[15] It will be shown below that Daniel Cooper was a large landowner in the Sydney district. The only prominent 'Cowper' was the Revd William Cowper, who can be excused any involvement. All the Bigge papers being quoted are very rough in character, and appear to be the actual notes taken at the time of the interviews, when the clerk had no way of verifying the spelling of a name he heard mentioned.

[16] Wentworth, *A Statistical . . . Description*, p. 194.

[17] Atkinson, *An Account . . .*, pp. 33, 34.

[18] Public Record Office, CO 201/123, f.184. The full list is contained in ff. 182–4.

[19] For Levey, with whom Croaker had desultory business dealings, see *ADB*, vol. 2. He was an emancipist and merchant, who arrived in the colony in January 1815. He 'was soon dealing in real estate'.

[20] *Sydney Gazette*, 27 June 1818.

[21] *Bigge Report* Appendix, Bonwick Transcripts, Box 12, p. 274.

[22] Principal Superintendent of Convicts: Bound Indents, loc. cit.

[23] Wentworth, *A Statistical . . . Description*, p. 96.

[24] *Bigge Report* Appendix, Bonwick Transcripts, Box 10, p. 4270.

[25] Wentworth, *A Statistical . . . Description*, p. 420; [J. MacArthur], *New South Wales; its Present State and Future Prospects*, p. 62.

[26] Wentworth, loc. cit.

[27] J. Atkinson, *An Account . . .*, p. 43. In 1817 the colony had 18462 acres under wheat, 11714 acres under maize, but only 856 under barley (Wentworth, *A Statistical . . . Description*, p. 158).

[28] Public Record Office, CO 201/123, pp. 89, 123.

[29] Ibid.; *Bigge Report*, vol. 3, p. 13.

[30] Wentworth, *A Statistical . . . Description*, pp. 419, 420.

[31] Atkinson, *An Account . . .*, p. 40.

[32] Land Titles Office, Sydney, 'Old Register', Book C, no. 130.

[33] Ibid., no. 131.

[34] Although Middleton's brewing interests are more appropriately discussed in the next chapter, it can be noted here that he had 'concluded rather an extensive brewery' in 1824 (*Sydney Gazette*, 29 July 1824), and some two years earlier had, as a brewer, petitioned Macquarie about licences.

[35] Daniel Cooper owned the Manchester Arms hotel, about 50 yards away. Eagar advertised (for himself or another party) 3 Upper Pitt Street for sale in *Sydney Gazette*, 12 June 1819.

[36] C. H. Bertie, 'Old Pitt Street', pp. 69–96.

[37] *Sydney Gazette*, 15 May 1819.

[38] Ibid., 4 Nov. 1820 (advertisement for sale of public house called the Chelsea Pensioner).

[39] In Aug. 1820 Croakers' maid, Mary Coppinger, was robbed at the George Street address (see chapter 9).

[40] *Sydney Gazette*, 15 March 1822.

[41] Bertie, 'Old Pitt Street', mentions that 'one Lawrence' bequeathed the brewery site to Mrs. Murphy. This could have been Nathaniel Lawrence, who died in 1826. When Middleton advertised his new Pitt Street brewery for sale (*Sydney Gazette*, 10 June 1824), the proprietor was Daniel Cooper.

[42] Mitchell Library, Sydney: Wentworth Papers: Petitions for Wine and Spirit Licences 1819–20, pp. 149, 150, A764.

[43] J. Booker, *Essex and the Industrial Revolution* (Chelmsford, 1974), pp. 72, 73. An alternative word to malthouse is maltings, but the implication is business on a larger scale.

[44] *Bigge Report* Appendix, Bonwick Transcripts, Box 10, p. 4270.

[45] *Sydney Gazette*, 27 Sept. 1817.

[46] Land Titles Office, Sydney, 'Old Register', Book 7, no. 210.

[47] Ibid.

[48] The other litigant was 'Riley' who forced Devoy into an auction of 6 horned cattle (*Sydney Gazette*, 21 March 1818).

[49] Land Titles Office, loc. cit., no. 360. Eagar paid £44 2s for the Pitt Street property and £7 for Mary Redman's Farm.

[50] Devoy petitioned Macquarie in 1820 for a grant of real estate, stating that he had held lands formerly 'by lease and purchase as a farmer but by unforseen misfortunes is deprived of longer living than by daily labour' (Colonial Secretary's Papers, 1788–1825, Fiche 3017, 4/1823, p. 420).

[51] *Sydney Gazette*, 7 April 1821.

[52] The property was not then named as Hartigan Farm, but the description fits. Presumably, by that time the association with Hartigan was wearing rather thin.

[53] *ADB*, vol. 2, from which all refs in this para. are taken, unless otherwise stated.

[54] Public Record Office., CO 201/123, f.192.

[55] Bank of New South Wales, Directors' Minute Book No. 1. On 8 June 1819 Redfern had the bank discount a bill of exchange which Croaker had drawn on Middleton for £57. This was effectively an assignment from Croaker to Redfern of Middleton's money, less the amount which the bank deducted for discounting the bill. As Eagar had paid £44 for the farm in 1817 (no doubt a rock-bottom price), the figure of some £50 is not unreasonable as a purchase price.

Chapter 9

[1] *Report of the Commissioner of Inquiry on the State of Agriculture and Trade in the Colony of New South Wales* [*Bigge Report*, vol. 3] (1823), p. 62.

[2] *Sydney Gazette*, 8 April 1820.

[3] *Report of Commissioner of Inquiry on the Judicial Establishments of New South Wales and Van Diemen's Land* [*Bigge Report*, vol.2] (1823), p. 73.

[4] Ibid., p. 74.

[5] Ibid.

[6] AONSW, Fiche 6051, 4/1748, pp. 88–91.

[7] *Sydney Gazette*, 26 Aug. 1820, 25 Jan. and 1 Feb. 1822.

[8] *Bigge Report Appendix*, Bonwick Transcripts, Box 27, p. 6305.

[9] Mary's name was also cast as Copenger. On 9 Aug. 1820 a box containing more than £9, and 'sundry articles of wearing apparel' was stolen from her bedroom. A week later the property was discovered, by which time Coppinger was the servant of Captain Brooks. Witnesses testified to the guilt of Mayo, along with Jeremiah

Simmons and James Tyler. Croaker was called upon to testify that Simmons was unknown to him, although he (Croaker) had paid him 12s some three weeks earlier for shoes which Mayo was supposed to have ordered (Court of Criminal Jurisdiction, SZ 792, Information no. 19, pp. 272–84; *Sydney Gazette*, 25 Nov. 1820; Colonial Secretary's Papers, reel 6023, X820, p. 21).

10   cf. J. Ritchie, *The Wentworths*, who points out (p. 140) that the governor 'had set a thief to catch a thief'.

11   *ADB*, vol. 2. The same memoir notes 'Macquarie's high respect for Wentworth's probity'.

12   K. M. Dermody, *D'Arcy Wentworth 1762–1827*, pp. 292–4; see also, J. M. Freeland, *The Australian Pub* (Melbourne, 1966), p. 42.

13   Ritchie, *The Wentworths*, p. 16; *Old Bailey Proceedings* (12 Dec. 1797), pp. 15–20. The connection is discussed more fully in chapter 1.

14   Lawrence's memorial to the judge advocate, Mitchell Library, A764, p. 149; *Sydney Gazette*, 4 March 1820.

15   Colonial Secretary's Papers, 1788–1825, reel 6050, cargo of ship *Midas*. Shortly afterwards, Lawrence opened a new brewery in Market Street.

16   Mitchell Library, Wentworth Papers.

17   *Sydney Gazette*, 4 Nov. 1820.

18   *Bigge Report*, vol. 3, p. 86.

19   Ibid., quoting *Sydney Gazette*, 3 Feb. 1821.

20   *Bigge Report*, vol. 3, pp. 86, 87.

21   Ibid., p. 86.

22   AONSW, fiche 6056, 4/1763, pp. 149–50. The petition, which is undated but filed among papers of 1822, recites that the brewers had previously been allowed a number of retail houses, but these 'at the last Licence Day, were entirely abolished to the great injury of your Memorialists'.

23   Supreme Court of Civil Jurisdiction, Judgement Rolls, 1820, 302/1, 2, 303/3–5, from which all refs in this para. are taken, unless otherwise stated.

24   Ibid., 1821, 372/2. For the amount of the loan (stated in court as £60), see note 37 below.

25   Campbelltown Local Studies Library, map 13, parish of Manangle [*sic*], surveyed 13 March 1811, indicates that he held a 20-acre farm at that date. According to the Colonial Secretary's Papers, he was issued with stock from the Government herds on 24 July 1813, and received two cows from the same source in 1816. By 1814 (see next note) he was farming 40 acres.

26   Land Titles Office, Sydney, 'Old Register', Book 6, no. 1310.

27   On 16 Jan. 1816 McEwen was on a list of people to receive grants that year (Colonial Secretary's Papers).

28   *Sydney Gazette*, 28 Sept. and 28 Oct. 1816, refers to auctions of McEwen's goods to satisfy Redman and Cullen respectively.

29   The quotation is from W. C. Wentworth, *A Statistical . . . Description*, p. 194. Wentworth's analogy was to the peasants of Russia.

30   Land Titles Office, Sydney, 'Old Register', Book 6, no. 169.

31   Ibid., no. 15.

32   The uncertainty over McEwen's title perhaps stemmed from doubts as to his status. He was mentioned in *Sydney Gazette*, 16 Nov. 1816, as required to produce a certified copy of a document establishing he was not still a convict.

33   Land Titles Office, loc. cit., no. 16.

34 Colonial Secretary's Papers, reel 2561, p. 19. It cannot be ruled out that McEwen received wholly new grants in 1819 (which is what the register states, if taken at face value), but there was no reason for this generosity by Macquarie. The inclusion of other minor landholders at Airds in grants at the same date (another recipient being John King, mentioned above), suggests that the registration of the original grants for the whole district was in disarray, and that the grants were regularised together in 1819.

35 Public Record Office, CO 201/123, f.152 (evidence of P. Hart to Commissioner Bigge). Ironically, in 1820 Airds suffered from 'incessant and weighty rain', with disastrous consequences (Colonial Secretary's Papers, reel 6007, pp. 475, 476).

36 Land Titles Office, 'Old Register', Book 8, No. 206. It is interesting that the assignment recited the recent grant from Macquarie to McEwen, thus avoiding all ambiguity this time as to McEwen's entitlement to the land.

37 It is probable that Croaker lent him only some £30, as the warrant of attorney (Supreme Court of Civil Jurisdiction, Judgement Rolls, 1820, 372/8) was for £30 and 8 pence with interest. The sum of £60, although expressly said to have been borrowed, would simply represent the normal practice of doubling the debt in the courtroom. The fact that the debt soon rose to £100 suggests that McEwen made no attempt to defend himself, and interest was therefore added to the nominal debt (£60) rather than the actual.

38 Supreme Court of Civil Jurisdiction, Judgement Rolls, 1822, 493/2–21, from which all refs in the Bloodsworth case are taken. It is interesting that neither note was discounted by the Bank of New South Wales, suggesting that the directors no longer saw Croaker as a safe risk.

39 *Sydney Gazette*, 17 Feb. 1821.

40 Supreme Court of Civil Jurisdiction, loc. cit., 499/1–7. Hart waited exactly a year for his money. The debt was £53 11s 11d, with 8 per cent interest, rounded up to £100 in litigation, in the normal way.

41 Bank of New South Wales, Directors' Minute Book, No. 2, p. 176; *Sydney Gazette*, 10 Feb. 1821.

42 Public Record Office, CO 201/94. It is ironical that part of this (undated) petition sought the right to distil spirits in the colony. Croaker also signed a memorial welcoming back Macquarie from a trip to Van Diemen's Land.

43 Supreme Court of Civil Jurisdiction, Judgement Rolls, 1821, 372/2, 3, 6.

44 Ibid., loc. cit., 1822, 493/2–21.

45 Ibid., 493/1, 20.

46 Ibid., 482/1–3.

47 Ibid., loc. cit., 1820, 372/1–27, from which all refs in this para. are taken.

48 Ibid., loc. cit., 1822, 499/2.

49 Ibid., 493/13.

50 AONSW, fiche 3207, 4/1862, pp. 50–50c, from which all refs in this para. are taken unless otherwise stated.

51 For careers of Croaker's sponsors, see *ADB*, vols 1 and 2.

52 In the 1822 census Mary 'Copenger' was listed as a servant employed by Captain Piper. However, she had worked for a Captain Brooks after leaving Croaker's service.

53 AONSW, reel 800, p. 62.

54 *Sydney Gazette*, at stated dates.

55 Mitchell Library, Sydney, Wentworth Papers, A765, pp. 143, 147, 197.

56 *Sydney Gazette*, 10 June 1824.

57 Ibid., 29 July 1824.

58 Ibid., 12 April 1822.

59 Supreme Court of Civil Jurisdiction, Judgement Rolls, 1822, 493/17.

60 Ibid., 566/1–17, 568/1–4, from which all refs. in this para. are taken.

61 Colonial Secretary's Papers, 1788–1825, reel 6055, 4/1761, p. 182.

62 Market Street was Croaker's address when tendering for the lease. Buxton (for whom Croaker provided a character reference) had been assigned by the government, probably as a replacement for Mayo (AONSW, fiche 3123, 4/1864, p. 53).

63 Colonial Secretary's Papers, 1788–1825, loc. cit. Tenders were opened on 24 Sept. 1822 for a lease from 1 October. Hankinson (who had the advantage of being solvent) tendered £135, which was accepted on 4 October.

64 N. M. Tuck (compiler), NSW: Ship Musters (Departures) 1816–25, MCG 3468.

Chapter 10

1 *Lloyd's Register of Shipping for the Year 1823*, Underwriters' Edition, Society for the Registry of Shipping (London, 1823).

2 *Sydney Gazette*, 9 and 16 Jan. 1823.

3 *Lloyd's Register of Shipping*.

4 This and the following quotation are from an incomplete letter in the Wollstonecraft General and Family Correspondence (July 1821), Mitchell Library, Sydney, manuscript 315/85, p. 41.

5 A portrait of Reibey appears on the reverse side of the Australian $20 note. Reibey was returning to Sydney after visiting her birthplace in Blackburn, Lancashire. Her experience of the *Mariner*, reported in this paragraph, is from N. Irvine, *Mary Reibey —Molly Incognita*, p. 83, chapter 10; N. Irvine (ed.), *Dear Cousin: The Reibey Letters*, pp. 33–9; and Mary Reibey, Journal 1820–1821, CY reel 324, Mitchell Library, Sydney.

6 Although her passage was purchased in February 1821, she had been aboard the *Mariner* subsequently on several occasions, only to record 'nothing doing'. On 14 June 1821 another passenger informed her that the ship could not proceed 'for want of means'. When the *Mariner* arrived in Portsmouth en route to Sydney, Reibey recorded that Captain Douglass was 'in difficulties in regard to provisions on the ship. Heard the owner was in gaol. The passengers were obliged to consent paying for the provisions'.

7 J. S. Cumpston, *Shipping Arrivals and Departures: Sydney, 1788–1825*.

8 Colonial Secretary's Papers, 1788–1825; Naval Officer's Quarterly Reports, 1821–1825, quarter ending 31 March 1823, reel 6023.

9 Rules forbade a ship's captain from dealing with any person in the settlement without the permission of the commandant. Captains were only allowed to depart after two days written notice, and no vessel could enter or leave the port between dusk and daylight. Any person landing spirits in the settlement was liable to be shot. (J. Windross & J. P. Ralston, *Historical Records of Newcastle 1797–1897*, pp. 24–5).

10 Church of England Baptisms, vol. 1, entry 6141 (1823), NSW Registry of Births, Deaths and Marriages.

11 N. M. Tuck (compiler), NSW: Ship Musters (Departures) 1816–25, MCG 3468, National Library of Australia, Canberra. See also AONSW 4/4472, reel 562, p. 78. The crew comprised Douglass (master), Cornish (mate), McDonald (boatswain), McKail (carpenter), Baptist (cook), Lafouse (cook's mate), Harding (seaman), Hill

(seaman), Whittam (seaman), Hawking (seaman), Owen (steward), Sims (included in crew manifest but described as a passenger), Richardson (servant), Wayman (seaman), and Rouse Belles (seaman).

[12] J. S. Cumpston, *Shipping Arrivals*, p. 141. The name of the *Angerstein's* master was sometimes written as Thompson.

[13] *Lloyd's List*, 17 Feb. 1824. It is likely that the *Angerstein* relayed the news.

[14] AONSW 4/1841, fiche 3126, memorial no. 179 (1825), p. 163.

[15] *Sydney Gazette*, 1 April 1824.

[16] C. K. Webster, *Britain and the Independence of Latin America, 1812–30*, vol. 1, p. 353; S. Collier, *Ideas and Politics of Chilean Independence, 1810–33*.

[17] On 25 Jan. 1822 the *Mariner* had been advertised in the *Sydney Gazette* as bound for Valparaiso and Lima, but the voyage did not eventuate.

[18] R. A. Humphreys, *Liberation in South America, 1810–1827*, p. 77; see also B. V. Mackenna, *The First Britons in Valparaiso, 1817–1827*.

[19] There are many accounts of storms in the area. Captain Anson, R.N., reported in 1741 that his ship had almost capsized after taking a wave on the starboard quarter which broke several shrouds and moved the ballast and stores (R. L. Woodward jr, *Robinson Crusoe's Island: A History of the Juan Fernandez Islands* (Chapel Hill, 1969), p. 69). Charles Darwin, who explored this part of the world in 1834–35, described storms of 'wanton fury' (R. D. Keynes (ed.), *Charles Darwin's* Beagle *Diary*, p. 273).

[20] F. V. Gormaz, *Algunos naufragios ocurridos en las costas chilenas desde su descubrimiento hasta nuestos dias*, pp. 146–58. June was a predictably stormy month, with 1823 no exception. Captain Wight (*Sydney Gazette*, 1 April 1824) reported a north-westerly gale at Valparaiso on 12 June when 16 vessels were driven on shore and totally lost.

[21] *Sydney Gazette*, 1 April 1824.

[22] Ibid.; *Lloyd's List*, 30 April 1824.

[23] Gormaz, *Algunos*; F. J. Cavada, *Naufragios ocurridos en las costas de Chiloé o en sus proximidades desde el año 1555 hasta hoy*. There is also no mention in R. & J. Marx, *New World Shipwrecks: 1492–1825*.

[24] C. Darwin, *Narrative of the Surveying Voyages of His Majesty's Ships* Adventure *and* Beagle, p. 387.

[25] C. Darwin, *Journal of Researches*, entry 22 Jan. 1835.

[26] R. D. Keynes, *Charles Darwin's* Beagle *Diary*, p. 284.

[27] I. Cameron, *Kingdom of the Sun God*, p. 25.

[28] D. Barros Arana, *Las Campanas de Chiloe (1820–1826)*, pp. 48, 55fn. Castro had the 'usual quadrangular arrangement of Spanish towns', with sheep grazing in the streets (Keynes, *Charles Darwin's* Beagle *Diary*, pp. 269–70).

[29] Darwin described them as 'simple, humble and polite' (J. Goldsmith, *Voyage in the* Beagle, p. 171). Elsewhere, he called them 'noble, industrious and docile', while acknowledging that others had described them as 'dishonest, idle and ill-disposed' (Darwin, *Narrative*, p. 379). Captain Blanckley, R.N., 'Account of the Island and Province of Chiloe', in *Journal of the Royal Geographical Society*, vol. 4 (1834), p. 357, considered them to be 'very cheerful, the happiest race I ever beheld'.

[30] Quintanilla, for example, ran out of paper on which to write orders. These were issued orally, or written in the margins of books, or on the soles of boots (Barros Arana, *Los Campanas*, p. 41).

[31] C. F. Duro, *Armada Espanola desde la union de los Reinos de Castilla y de Aragon*, vol. 9, p. 306; D. E. Worcester, *Sea Power and Chilean Independence*, pp. 82–7.

[32] Extract from letter, 2 March 1824, by South American correspondent of a British newspaper, printed in *Sydney Gazette*, Nov. 1824.

[33] *Sydney Gazette*, 1 April 1824.

[34] AONSW, 4/1841, fiche 3126, memorial no. 179 (1825), p. 163.

[35] Unless otherwise indicated, sources in this para. are Barros Arana, *Las Campanas*, pp. 50–1, and *Historia Jeneral de Chile*, vol. 14; J. Miller, *Memoirs of General Miller in the Service of the Republic of Peru*, vol. 2, pp. 78, 129.

[36] *Lloyd's Register 1823*, Underwriters' Edition; *Lloyd's List*, 13 May (No. 5802), 13 June (No. 5811), 8 July (No. 5818), 1823.

[37] Father Puig's brutal treatment at the hands of the inquisitors is described in *The Times*, 4 Dec. 1822.

[38] Generally, the patriot naval forces allowed free passage to non-Spanish ships not carrying cargoes for, or otherwise in the service of, the Spanish royalist forces. British ships, such as the *Medway*, were granted free passage by both the royalists and the patriots if they were not in the service of either side.

[39] The second voyage of the *Jeneral Valdes*, with orders 'to patrol the seas as far as Callao' began on 14 October. The ship was lost in the course of this sortie. It had taken on board 30 men from a captured transport, the *Mackenna*, and was escorting this ship and another prize, the *Colombia*, towards Chiloé when it was caught in a furious storm on 22 November. There are conflicting accounts of the exact circumstances, but all aboard were lost (Barros Arana, *Las Campanas*, pp. 50, 51, and *Historia Jeneral*, vol. 14, p. 276; G. F. Cruz (ed.), *Coleccion de Historidores y de Documentos relativos a la Independencia de Chile*; J. R. Ballesteros, *Revista de la Guerra de la Independencia de Chile*, vol. 3; Duro, *Armada Espanola*, appendix: 'Relacion extractada de Naufragios').

[40] R. Proctor, *Narrative of a Journey across the Cordillera of the Andes, and of a Residence in Lima*, p. 109.

[41] A strong circumstantial case can be made that those accounts were conveyed by Captain Richards, master of the *Jane*. The first account of the loss of the *Mariner* appeared in *Lloyd's List* of 17 Feb., 1824. By coincidence, the same issue of *Lloyd's List* also reported the arrival, at Ramsgate, two days earlier, of the ship *Jane* (Richards) from Valparaiso.

[42] *Sydney Gazette*, 1 April 1824; Cumpston, *Shipping Arrivals*.

[43] The Quilca area was well known to Quintanilla who sent Ballesteros to nearby Arica as his emissary at the end of 1821. Ballesteros proceeded to Arequipa and Cuzco before returning to Chiloé at the end of 1822 (Barros Arana, *Las Campanas*, p. 42).

[44] Proctor, *Narrative*, p. 151; *Lloyd's List*, 3 Oct. (no. 5843) and 12 Dec. (no. 5863) 1823; *Lloyd's List*, 9 March (no. 5888) 1824.

[45] Public Record Office, ADM 37/6634.

[46] J. N. T. Howat, *South American Packets*, pp. 49–58.

[47] Cameron, *Kingdom of the Sun God*, pp. 155–7, describes the disastrous attempt by General San Martin to cross the Cordillera of the Andes in January 1817. Many soldiers perished and of 10 600 mules, only 4300 survived.

[48] Proctor, *Narrative*, p. 64.

[49] Public Record Office, ADM 37/6537.

[50] There is weak circumstantial evidence that Carthagena is implicated in the explanation of Croaker's fate. A more detailed account of the loss of the *Mariner* appeared in *Lloyd's List* and *The Times* at the end of April 1824. Interestingly, in the

two days before those reports, two ships arrived at Gravesend from Carthagena: *Sylph* (Mason) and *Aurora* (Brown). The *Sylph* was reported to have arrived at Carthagena on 7 Dec. 1823. It would therefore have been at Carthagena at a convenient time to suit this theory (*Lloyd's List*, 30 April (no. 5903) 1824; *Lloyd's List*, 3 Feb. (no. 5878) 1824).

[51] The following references are taken from *Recollections of a Ramble from Sydney to Southampton* (London, 1851), pp. 162–205; cf. Ruth J. Campbell (ed.), 'Crossing the Isthmus, an anonymous 1846 account', in *Americas*, vol. 28 (May 1976), pp. 14–16.

Epilogue

[1] Supreme Court of New South Wales, Probate Index (1800–1901), vol. A–C, MCM 696, Series 1, no. 250.

[2] AONSW 4/1841, fiche 3126, memorial no. 179 (1825), p. 163.

[3] Middleton, then proprietor of the Nelson Brewery in Sydney, was a witness. Lawrence, Croaker's other colleague in the Upper Pitt Street consortium, had drunk himself to death a few months earlier.

[4] Colonial Secretary's Papers, 1788–1825, reel 6061, 4/1778, p. 90. In the 1822 census of New South Wales, Love (under his alias Lovegrove) was recorded as a brewer in Pitt Street.

[5] Ibid., reel 6063, 4/1786, pp. 80, 80a, 80b.

[6] In May 1824 Love obtained a licence to marry Phoebe Anderson of Liverpool, but she married John Clegg at Parramatta in 1825. It is, of course, possible that *she* broke off the earlier engagement.

[7] *Sydney Gazette*, 9 May 1827.

[8] *Australian*, 5 Dec. 1827; *Sydney Gazette*, 30 Nov. 1827.

[9] *Sydney Gazette*, 21 March 1829.

[10] Ibid.; *Sydney Morning Herald*, 22 Jan. 1842, 1 Jan. 1845, etc. For a time, Susannah's address was distinctly sugary: 'Mrs. Love, Harmony House, Concord, near Kissing Point' (S. Coupe, *Concord—A Centenary History*, pp. 184, 5).

[11] Letter kindly made available by Judy Lindsay, a Croaker descendant.

[12] V. L. Cremer, *Yass Post Office History*, pp. 3, 4; W. A. Bayley, *Yass Municipal Centenary History*, p. 18.

[13] E. F. Penzig, *Frank Gardiner the Bushranger*, pp. 52, 54; C. White, *History of Australian Bushranging*, vol. 1, p. 295.

[14] R. Maroney, *Jerrybang*, pp. 38, 51.

Bibliography

Unpublished

Australia

(Many Public Record Office sources were accessed via microform copies produced for the Australian Joint Copying Project (AJCP) in the National Library of Australia.)

Archives Office of New South Wales (AONSW): microfiche collections.

N. G. Butlin, 'What a Way to Run an Empire, Fiscally!', Working Paper no. 55, Department of Economic History, ANU (1985).

Campbelltown Local Studies Library: maps.

Colonial Secretary's Papers, 1788–1825: microfiche and microfilm collection, National Library of Australia.

'Joseph Hyde Potts (1793–1865)', paper, Economic Department, Bank of New South Wales (1961).

Land Titles Office, Sydney: Land Grants Registers.

Mitchell Library, Sydney: Wentworth Papers; Mary Reibey, Journal.

M. Scorgie, 'The Bank of New South Wales Ledger: Double Entry System or Not?', working paper, La Trobe University (13 August 1997).

Supreme Court of New South Wales: Civil Jurisdiction, Judgement Rolls; Probate Index.

N. M. Tuck (compiler), NSW: Ship Musters (Departures) 1816–25 (National Library of Australia).

Westpac Banking Corporation: Bank of New South Wales, Directors' Minute Books Nos 1 and 2.

British Isles

Bank of Ireland: records of Court of Directors.

Canterbury Cathedral Archives: parish records of St Dunstan's, Canterbury (U3/141), St Margaret's, Canterbury (U3/6), and Leaveland (U3/185).

Centre for Kentish Studies, Maidstone: Cobbs' brewery and banking records (U1453); Flint's brewery records (U1724); wills (PRC 17); Leaveland parish records (U390); Leaveland map (U1175); map of Sackett estate (U1511); land tax records (Q/RPl); probate records (PRC 16, 17).

International Genealogical Index: records of births and marriages.

Lloyds TSB Group Archives: Cobb & Co. records (A20); Cox & Co. regimental ledgers (A56e); Hammond & Co. records (A53/60).

Northamptonshire Record Office: Rockingham Castle papers (WR 1193).

Public Record Office: apprenticeship books (IR 1); wills (PROB 11); Home Office records (HO 13, 47); King's Bench records (KB16, 21, 36); Colonial Office papers (CO 201); Customs & Excise records (CUST 30, 48).

Ramsgate Library: Garrett family papers (U 888).

Chile

Archivo Nacional, Santiago: catalogue, maritime documents and manuscripts.

Archivo Biblioteca Chiloé, Isla de Chiloé: maritime documents relating to Chiloé.

Biblioteca Nacional, Santiago: maritime documents and manuscripts.

France

Bibliothèque Nationale: newspaper files.

Spain

Archivo General de las Indias, Seville: shipping records.

Biblioteca Central del Cuartel de la Armada: shipping records.

Biblioteca Nacional, Madrid: catalogues, periodicals, miscellaneous manuscripts.

Biblioteca Naval, Madrid: records of shipwrecks.

Published

Books, Reports and Pamphlets

G. J. Abbott & N. B. Nairn (eds), *Economic Growth of Australia, 1899–1921* (Melbourne, 1969).

G. W. D. Allen (ed.), *Early Georgian: Extracts from the Journal of George Allen (1800–1877)* (Sydney, 1958).

Anon., *An Alphabetical List of all the Country-Bankers residing in England, Scotland, and Wales* (London, 1797).

Anon., *The New Canterbury Guide* (Canterbury, n.d.).

Anon., *The New Margate, Ramsgate and Broadstairs Guide*, 5th ed. (Margate, 1809).

Anon., *Poisonous Beer* (London, 1816) (pamphlet in Canterbury Cathedral Archives, ref. CA40-ABB).

Anon., *Recollections of a Ramble from Sydney to Southampton* (London, 1851).

Anon., *The Trial of John Croarer [sic] for Felony* (Margate, 1815).

R. T. Appleyard & C. B. Schedvin (eds), *Australian Financiers, Biographical Essays* (Melbourne, 1988).

Archaeologia Cantiana, vols 22 and 81.

E. H. D. Arndt, *Banking and Currency Development in South Africa (1652–1927)* (Cape Town, 1922).

J. Atkinson, *An Account of the State of Agriculture and Grazing in New South Wales* (London, 1826; reprinted Sydney University Press, 1975).

Australian Dictionary of Biography, vols 1, 2.

J. R. Ballesteros, *Revista de la Guerra de la Independencia de Chile*, vol. 3 (Santiago, 1901–4).

Bankers' Almanac and Year Book.

M. Barnard, *Macquarie's World* (Melbourne, 1949).

D. Barros Arana, *Las Campanas de Chiloé (1820–1826)* (Santiago, 1856).

D. Barros Arana, *Historia Jeneral de Chile*, vol. 14 (Santiago, 1897).

C. Bateson, *The Convict Ships* (Glasgow, 1969).

W. A. Bayley, *Yass Municipal Centenary History* (Yass, 1973).

Bigge Report: see *Report of the Commissioner of Inquiry into the State*, etc.

A. Birch & D. Macmillan (eds.), *Wealth & Progress* (Sydney, 1967).

Captain Blanckley, R.N., 'Account of the Island and Province of Chiloé', in *Journal of the Royal Geographical Society*, vol. 4 (1834).

J. Booker, *Essex and the Industrial Revolution* (Chelmsford, 1974).

W. Branch-Johnson, *The English Prison Hulks* (London, 1957).

British Parliamentary Papers, vol. 3.

J. Broadbent, 'Macquarie's Domain' in J. Broadbent & J. Hughes (eds), *The Age of Macquarie* (Melbourne, 1992).

S. J. Butlin, *Foundations of the Australian Monetary System 1788–1851* (Melbourne, 1958).

I. Cameron, *Kingdom of the Sun God: A History of the Andes and their People* (London, 1990).

F. J. Cavada, *Naufragios ocurridos en las costas de Chiloé o en sus proxi-midades desde el año 1555 hasts hoy* (Temuco, 1927).

N. Cay, *A Likely Lad. The Story of Simeon Lord* (Quirindi, NSW, 1989).

G. E. Clarke, *Historic Margate* (Margate, 1957).

F. Clune, *Serenade to Sydney: Some Historical Landmarks* (Sydney, 1967).

S. Collier, *Ideas and Politics of Chilean Independence, 1810–33* (Cambridge, 1967).

S. Corpe & A. M. Oakley, *Canterbury Freemen 1750–1799* (Canterbury, 1984).

——, *Canterbury Freemen 1800–1835* (Canterbury, 1984).

S. Coupe, *Concord—A Centenary History* (Concord, 1983).

J. M. Cowper, *The Roll of Freemen of the City of Canterbury* (Canterbury, 1903).

V. L. Cremer, *Yass Post Office History* (Sydney, 1984).

F. W. Cross & J. R. Hall, *Rambles Round Old Canterbury* (London and Canterbury, 1882).

G. F. Cruz (ed.), *Coleccion de Historidores y de Documentos relativos a la Independencia de Chile* (Santiago, 1900–).

J. S. Cumpston, *Shipping Arrivals and Departures: Sydney, 1788–1825* (Canberra, 1964).

C. Darwin, *Narrative of the Surveying Voyages of His Majesty's Ships* Ad-venture *and* Beagle, *between the Years 1826 and 1836, describing their Examination of the Southern Shores of South America and the* Beagle's *Circumnavigation of the Globe*, vols I, II (London, 1839).

——, *Journal of Researches into the Natural History and Geology of Countries Visited* (London, 1890).

——, *A Naturalist's Voyage: Journal of Researches into the Natural History and Geology of the Countries Visited during the Voyage of H.M.S. 'Beagle' round the World under the Command of Capt. FitzRoy* (London, 1890).

Dictionary of National Biography.

C. F. Duro, *Armada Espanola desde la union de los Reinos de Castilla y de Aragon*, vol. 9 (Madrid, n.d.).

J. R. Edwards, *A History of Financial Accounting* (London, 1989).

First Report of the Commissioners Appointed [under] 'An Act for appointing Commissioners to enquire concerning Charities in England, for the Edu-cation of the Poor' (1819).

S. Fitzgerald & H. Golder, *Pyrmont and Ultimo Under Siege* (Sydney, 1994).

B. H. Fletcher, *Landed Enterprise and Penal Society* (Sydney, 1976).

Sir William Forbes, *Memoirs of a Banking-House* (London and Edinburgh, 1860).

J. M. Freeland, *The Australian Pub* (Melbourne, 1966).

'G.E.C.' [Cockayne], *The Complete Peerage*, vol. 12 (London, 1953).

A. H. Gibson, *Bank Rate. The Banker's Vade Mecum* (London, Leeds and Halifax, 1908.

J. W. Gilbart, *A Practical Treatise on Banking*, vol. 1 (London, 1865; first published 1849).

F. F. Giraud & C. E. Donne, *A Visitor's Guide to Faversham* (Faversham 1876).

L. Goldberg, 'Some Early Australian Accounting Records' in A. C. Littleton & B. S. Yamey (eds), *Studies in the History of Accounting* (London, 1956).

J. Goldsmith, *Voyage in the* Beagle (London, 1978).

F. V. Gormaz, *Algunos naufragios ocurridos en las costas chilenas desde descrubrimiento hasta nuestos dias* (Santiago, 1901).

W. Gostling, *A Walk in and about the City of Canterbury with many Observations* (Canterbury, 1825).

T. Gourvish, *Norfolk Beers from English Barley. A History of Steward & Patteson 1793–1963* (Norwich, 1987).

L. H. Grindon, *Manchester Banks and Bankers* (Manchester, 1877).

P. Hanks & F. Hodges, *A Dictionary of Surnames* (Oxford, 1988).

T. C. Hansard, *The Parliamentary Debates*, vol. 33 (London, 1816).

J. Haslam, *A Narrative of a Voyage to New South Wales in the Year 1816 in the Ship Mariner* (London, 1819).

E. Hasted, *The History and Topographical Survey of the County of Kent*, vol. II (Canterbury, 1800).

Historical Records of Australia.

R. F. Holder, *Bank of New South Wales. A History. Volume One: 1817–1893* (Sydney, 1970).

J. N. T. Howat, *South American Packets* (York, 1984).

R. A. Humphreys, *Liberation in South America, 1810–1827: The Career of James Paroissien* (London, 1952).

N. Irvine, *Mary Reibey—Molly Incognita: A Biography of Mary Reibey 1777–1825, and her World* (Sydney, 1982).

——, *Dear Cousin: The Reibey Letters* (Sydney, 1992).

T. Joplin, *An Essay on the General Principles and Present Practice of Banking in England and Scotland*, 6th ed. (London, 1827).

Kelly's *Kent Directory* (1855), (1903).

Kent *Poll Book* (1790), (1796).

Kent's *London Directory* (1814–16).

R. D. Keynes (ed.), *Charles Darwin's* Beagle *Diary* (Cambridge, 1988).

A. C. Littleton & B. S. Yamey (eds), *Studies in the History of Accounting* (London, 1956).

Lloyds Register of Shipping for the Year 1823, Underwriter's edition (London, 1823).

[J. MacArthur], New South Wales; its Present State and Future Prospects (London, 1837).

T. McCormick, R. Irving, E. Imashev, J. Nelson & G. Bull (eds), First Views of Australia, 1788–1825: A History of Early Sydney (Sydney, 1987).

B. V. Mackenna, The First Britons in Valparaiso, 1817–1827 (Valparaiso, 1884).

N. McLachlan (ed.), The Memoirs of James Hardy Vaux (London, 1964).

R. Maroney, Jerrybang: the Maroneys of Bulla Creek (NSW, 1975).

R. & J. Marx, New World Shipwrecks: 1492–1825 (Dallas, 1994).

P. Mathias, The Brewing Industry in England 1700–1830 (Cambridge, 1959).

Merchant Taylors' School Register 1561–1934, vol. 1 (London, 1936).

J. S. Mill, Principles of Political Economy, 2nd ed., vol. 2 (1849).

J. Miller, Memoirs of General Miller in the Service of the Republic of Peru, vol. 2 (London, 1829).

W. Munk, The Roll of the Royal College of Physicians of London, vol. 3 (London, 1878).

R. H. Parker (ed.), Accounting in Australia: Historical Essays (New York, 1990).

T. G. Parsons, 'Colonial Commissaries' in R. T. Appleyard & C. B. Schedvin (eds), Australian Financiers (Melbourne, 1988).

E. F. Penzig, Frank Gardiner the Bushranger: A Definitive History (Katoomba, 1987).

M. Phillips, A Colonial Autocracy. New South Wales under Governor Macquarie, 1810–1821 (Sydney, 1971).

Post Office London Directory (1815).

L. S. Pressnell, Country Banking in the Industrial Revolution (Oxford, 1956).

R. Proctor, Narrative of a Journey across the Cordillera of the Andes, and of a Residence in Lima (London, 1825).

P. H. Reaney (R. M. Wilson, ed.), A Dictionary of English Surnames (London and New York, 1991).

Report of the Commissioner of Enquiry into the State of the Colony of New South Wales (1822) (Bigge Report, vol. 1); Report of the Commissioner of Enquiry on the Judicial Establishments of New South Wales and Van Diemen's Land (1823) (Bigge Report, vol. 2); Report of the Commissioner of Inquiry on the State of Agriculture and Trade in the Colony of New South Wales (1823) (Bigge Report, vol. 3); Appendix to Bigge Report; these sources consulted in various formats: British Parliamentary Papers; original records in Public Record Office, London; Bonwick Transcripts,

Australia (for *Appendix*); and *Australiana Facsimile Editions No. 70* (Adelaide, 1966).

Report of the Commissioners for Inquiring Concerning Charities, vol. 30 (1837).

L. Richmond & A. Turton, *The Brewing Industry. A Guide to Historical Records* (Manchester, 1990).

J. Ritchie, *Punishment and Profit* (Melbourne, 1970).

——, *Lachlan Macquarie: A Biography* (Melbourne, 1986).

——, *The Wentworths: Father and Son* (Melbourne, 1997).

M. R. Sainty & K. A. Johnson (eds), *Census of New South Wales 1828* (Library of Australian History, 1985).

D. Shineberg (ed.), *The Trading Voyages of Andrew Cheyne, 1841–1844* (Canberra, 1971).

Statutes at Large, vol. 38 (1794).

M. J. E. Steven, 'Enterprise' in G. J. Abbott & N. B. Nairn (eds), *Economic Growth of Australia, 1799–1821* (Melbourne, 1969).

——, 'Public Credit and Private Confidence' in J. Broadbent & J. Hughes (eds), *The Age of Macquarie* (Melbourne, 1992).

T. Sykes, *Two Centuries of Panic* (Sydney, 1988).

Universal British Directory (1793–98).

W. Vamplew (ed.), *Australians: Historical Statistics* (Sydney, 1987).

J. H. Vaux, *Memoirs of James Hardy Vaux, A Swindler and Thief; Now Transported for the Second Time, and for Life* (London, 1829; first published 1819).

J. Walker, *The Universal Gazetteer*, 6th. ed. (London, 1815).

C. K. Webster, *Britain and the Independence of Latin America, 1812–30*, vol. 1 (Oxford, 1938).

W. C. Wentworth, *A Statistical, Historical, and Political Description of the Colony of New South Wales* (London, 1819).

C. White, *History of Australian Bushranging*, vol. 1 (Melbourne & Sydney, 1970).

A. J. Willis, *Canterbury Marriage Licences 1781–1809* (Folkestone, 1969).

——, *Canterbury Marriage Licences 1810–1837* (Chichester, 1971).

J. Windross & J. P. Ralston, *Historical Records of Newcastle 1797–1897* (Newcastle, 1897).

R. L. Woodward jr, *Robinson Crusoe's Island, A History of the Juan Fernandez Islands* (Chapel Hill, 1969).

D. E. Worcester, *Sea Power and Chilean Independence* (Florida, 1962).

M. Worgan, *The Church of St Dunstan's Canterbury. A General Guide to the Church* (Canterbury, n.d.).

Journal Articles

H. Bertie, 'Old Pitt Steet', *Journal of the Royal Australian Historical Society*, vol. 6 (1920).

I. S. Black, 'The London Agency System in English Banking, 1780–1825', *London Journal*, no. 21/2 (1996).

Ruth J. Campbell (ed.), 'Crossing the Isthmus, an anonymous 1846 account', *Americas*, vol. 28 (May 1976).

S. Clark, 'When his Sins Caught up with John Collington', *Bygone Kent*, vol. 13, no. 10 (October 1992).

R. Craig & S. Jenkins, 'Conjectures on Colonial Accounting History in Australia', *Abacus*, vol. 32, no. 2 (1996).

F. Driscoll, 'Macquarie's Administration of the Convict System', *Journal and Proceedings of the Royal Australian Historical Society*, vol. 26, part 6 (1942).

R. W. Gibson, 'Early Double Entry Records in Australia', *Accounting History Newsletter*, no. 13 (Summer 1986).

——, 'Two Centuries of Australian Accountants', *The Accounting Historian's Notebook* (Spring 1988).

R. H. Goddard, 'An Historical Survey', *Chartered Accountant in Australia*, vol. 7 (1938).

W. & O. Harvard, 'A Frenchman Sees Sydney', *Journal of the Royal Australian Historical Society*, vol. 24, part 1 (1938).

J. P. McGuanne, 'A Hundred Years Ago', *Journal and Proceedings of the Royal Australian Historical Society*, vol. 5, part 2 (1920).

R. H. Parker, 'Bookkeeping Barter and Current Cash Equivalents in Early New South Wales', *Abacus*, vol. 18, no. 2 (1982).

T. G. Parsons, 'Governor Macquarie and the Assignment of Skilled Convicts in New South Wales', *Journal of the Royal Australian Historical Society*, vol. 58, part 2 (1972).

'J. H. Potts', *Etruscan*, vol. 6, no. 1 (1956).

G. J. Previts & T. K. Sheldahl, 'Accounting and "Counting Houses": An Analysis and Commentary', *Abacus*, vol. 13, no. 1 (1977).

Newspapers, Magazines and Periodicals
Australian (1827)
Gentleman's Magazine
Kentish Chronicle
Kentish Gazette
Le Journal de Paris, 28 Jan. 1815
Law Magazine, vol. 1 (1845)
Lloyd's List, 1822–24

Old Bailey Proceedings (12 Dec. 1797).
Stable Companion
Sydney Gazette, 1803–1826 (including De Quirosville [pseudonym], 'Times Gone By', 18 April 1829).
Sydney Morning Herald
The Times

Theses

K. M. Dermody, D'Arcy Wentworth 1762–1827. A Second Chance, PhD, Australian National University, 1990.
K. J. Lampard, Cobb & Son, Bankers of Margate c.1785 to c.1840, PhD, University of Kent, 1986.

Index

Abbott, John, 1, 4, 13, 16, 17, 21, 24, 30, 35–45 *passim*, 50, 52, 62, 67, 114, 164 n.16, 165 n.21
Abbott, John, junior, 39, 170 n.16
Abbott, T., 86
Acapulco, Mexico, 148
accountants, 4, 82–6
accounting, *see* book-keeping
Adolphus, John, 53
agency arrangements, *see* banking
Airds, NSW, 117–19, 126–8; Hartigan Farm, 109, 117–19, 127, 128; Hyde Park Farm, 126; *see also* Bunburry Curran
ale, *see* beer
Amos, Daniel, 28
Ancud, *see* San Carlos
Anderson, Phoebe, 188 n.6
Andrewes, Gerrard, 37, 38
Angerstein (ship), 138
Appledore, Kent, 164 n.4
Arequipa, Peru, 144–6
Argentina, *see* Buenos Aires; Mendoza
Arica, Peru, 187 n.43
army: 46th Regiment, 79
Armytage, Charles, 162
Arndell, Thomas, 104
Ashford, Kent, 18, 25, 26
Atkinson, James, 111, 114
Atlas (ship), 126
Aurora (ship), 188 n.50
Austin & Co., 18
Australia: *see* New South Wales; *see also* Bank of Australia

Badlesmere, Kent, 25, 26, 30; Court, 168 n.31
Baker, Denne, Kingsford, Wigsell and Kingsford, 17
Baker, John, 17, 37, 38, 45, 46, 51, 59, 60, 62, 63, 66

Baker, Robert, 51
Ballesteros, Colonel Don José Rodriguez, 143
Bank of Australia, 81
Bank of England, 17, 19, 20, 87, 90, 166 n.36
Bank of Ireland, 87
Bank of New South Wales, 2, 3, 88, 105, 107, 114, 118, 128, 130; book-keeping, 83–5, 87, 88, 103, 136; charter and powers, 86–93; discounting, 95–100, 103, 162; foundation, 81–6
Bank of Scotland, 87
'Bankers Act', 62
banking: agency arrangements, 19, 34, 51, 53, 55, 62; current (running) accounts, 91, 98, 100; deposits, 90; drafts, 92; in England, 17, 18, 87, 88, 92; in Kent, 1, 3, 14–21 *passim*; 31–5, 61, 88–92; in New South Wales, 2–4, 81–100 *passim*; interest rates, 90, 106; joint-stock banks, 3, 17, 20, 87, 88, 92, 166 n.45, 176 n.2; limited liability, 19, 87, 166 n.43; loans, 89, 90, 99; 'Out and In' controls, 89; overdrafts, 91; posting-up ledgers, 20; recruitment, 3, 15, 16; 'runs', 18, 19, 31, 45, 61; *see also* banknotes; bills of exchange; Exchequer bills; letter of credit; Margate; promissory notes; store receipts; Treasury bills; and names of individual banks
banknotes, 19, 47, 49, 88–92, 101
Baptist (cook), 185 n.11
barley, 4, 113–16, 124, 130
barter, 100
Bathurst, Earl, 96, 178
Bathurst, NSW, 152
Bay of Islands, NZ, 138, 144
Bayley, Rev. W. F., 49